Praise for *Vast as t*

Beautifully written with a poetic feel, this study of the human condition as seen through selected poetic texts of the Hebrew Bible is a rich feast for any reader. Samuel Hildebrandt tackles difficult human issues such as loneliness, despair, trauma, imagined hope, the disintegration of known reality, and musings on time, death, and the good life. These are all viewed through the lenses of a rich appreciation of the power of Hebrew poetry and a deep engagement with the findings of modern psychological method—the findings of each individual chapter wrapped up in the metaphor of the sea of life with its characteristic tosses and turns.

> —**Katharine J. Dell,** professor of Old Testament literature and theology, University of Cambridge

Vast as the Sea provides a navigational chart for the ocean of human emotional well-being, carefully mapped out with the aid of Hebrew poetry and taking frequent bearings from contemporary psychology. Samuel Hildebrandt does not shy away from the challenges that this task presents. He explores anxiety amidst chaos and combat, plotting a course to calmer waters; loneliness as a place that can lead to creativity; hope in the wake of trauma and despair; the plight of theology amidst shattered assumptions; the tyranny of time; and the quest for wisdom amidst seeming meaninglessness. This beautifully written book should be of interest to all who wish to explore what the Bible has to teach about mental health and well-being.

> —**Christopher C. H. Cook,** emeritus professor, Institute for Medical Humanities, Durham University, United Kingdom

Samuel Hildebrandt begins *Vast as the Sea* with a mesmerizing word picture of the sea and its moods, painting a backdrop for his thoughts on what it means to be totally human, both in pleasant times and, most especially, in difficult times. He focuses on the connections between Hebrew poetry and human experience, and draws a clear path between aspects of poetry such as the shape of the text, the role of imagination, and the power of poetry for expressing emotions. This path leads through reflection on human psychology and the effects of trauma and then comes full circle as Hildebrandt demonstrates the power of words and of poetry to address the difficult things—the anxiety, loneliness, and despair that often come with the human experience. Hildebrandt chooses his words with artistic care, and his understanding that the biblical poetry offers "a language for acknowledging and articulating the unspeakable" is invaluable, as finding words to express the vastness of trauma can be the primary step in recovery. This trip to the seaside is not to be missed. The combination of well-explained biblical text, big life questions, and beautiful words is both compelling and productive.

—**Elizabeth Hayes,** affiliate professor of Old Testament,
Fuller Theological Seminary

Here is a book that sets forth the intimate, honest, agonizing, yet somehow life-giving relationship between the human condition and human words, even biblical poetic words. While avoiding mechanical analysis or finalized interpretations, and illustrating adept engagement with psychology and trauma, Samuel Hildebrandt turns Hebrew poetic texts such as Jeremiah, Job, and Ecclesiastes into soul friends in the struggle to face anxiety, instability, loneliness, despair, finitude, and other painful vicissitudes of our own humanity. In Hildebrandt's able hands, the difficult poetry of these biblical texts is a gift to anyone seeking language to wrestle with the hard realities of human life—and so is this book.

—**Brad E. Kelle,** professor of Old Testament and Hebrew,
Point Loma Nazarene University

This wonderful book examines the difficult question of the human condition (*conditio humana*) through texts like Psalms, Jeremiah, Job, Qohelet, and others. As Hildebrandt's poetic analyses show, each of these voices has its own evaluation of what it means to be human. But all of them have a common ground: the belief in the God of life and his empathy for the human condition.

—**Professor Bernd Janowski,** Evangelisch-theologische
Fakultät der Universität Tübingen

This beautifully written text offers an interpretation of Hebrew poetry that speaks to the experiences of many of us living during these stressful and anxiety-filled days. I would not hesitate to recommend this book for use in a parish or a classroom. It is accessible and clearly demonstrates how the imagery and language of Hebrew poetry connect with the psychological struggles of being human today. Hildebrandt is a skilled writer who has given to both the church and the academy a creative view of Hebrew poetic imagery that will help readers discover its value and relevance.

—**The Rev. Dr. Maryann Amor,** adjunct lecturer in Hebrew Bible,
St. Stephen's College, University of Alberta, and rector,
Anglican Parish of Christ Church, Grande Prairie,
Alberta, Canada

As a mental health therapist, I am all too familiar with the challenge of articulating the tensions and contradictions of human experience. Samuel Hildebrandt is not afraid to enter the deep end of the chaos, despair, and disappointment familiar to the ancient and modern person alike. *Vast as the Sea* gives us words—honest, compassionate, and hopeful words—that normalize and authenticate what it means to be human. It is a gift to me and to my clients.

—**Karen Gibson,** marriage and family therapist, Saskatoon, Canada

Plumbing the language of loneliness and alienation in the Old Testament's major prophets and wisdom literature, Hildebrandt brings to voice its questions of meaning and human existence, looking also to various psychotherapeutic models for healing of mental affliction. The book offers a creative approach to biblical theology.

—**Kathryn Greene-McCreight, PhD,** Episcopal priest and author
of *Darkness Is My Only Companion: A Christian Response
to Mental Illness* and *Galatians: A Commentary*

Hildebrandt's gentle, poetic book is a beautiful and scholarly contribution to an increasingly prominent area of biblical studies. He unpacks and explores the Psalms' language and what lies beyond language to speak of mental health, well-being, and the journey that all human beings are on in an uncertain world.

—**Rev. Prebendary Dr. Isabelle Hamley,** secretary for theology
and theological adviser to the House of Bishops,
Church of England

In *Vast as the Sea*, Samuel Hildebrandt takes his readers on an insightful and accessible journey through biblical poetry to unveil the texts' expressions of often negatively associated aspects of the human condition. In carefully formulated prose, he shows how biblical texts such as Psalms, Job, Jeremiah, and Ecclesiastes provide a language for loneliness, worry, despair, and hope to their ancient readers as well as their contemporary counterparts. A timely book on a timeless topic.

—**Dr. Karolien Vermeulen,** affiliate postdoctoral research fellow,
Institute of Jewish Studies, University of Antwerp

Hebrew poetry as a lifeguard in the turbulent, roaring waters of human existence—this is what Hildebrandt makes us see. He shows us a delicacy for those appreciating the Bible, consolation and help for all seeking orientation, and new strength in their various struggles on earth with anxieties, loneliness, and despair but also hope, imagination, and creative language.

—**Georg Fischer, SJ,** professor emeritus, University of Innsbruck, and author of commentaries on Genesis 1–11, Exodus, and Jeremiah

Samuel Hildebrandt's *Vast as the Sea* is a remarkable union of expert biblical scholarship and careful pastoral insights conveyed in striking and beautiful composition. It takes the rich expressions of emotion in Scripture and makes them intelligible to the wide array of human experiences. The academic will find much to appreciate. The pastor will find, at many points, observations to assist in caring for the church.

—**Andrew Kelley,** teaching pastor, Hope Chapel, Hermosa Beach, California, and author of *Thaumaturgic Prowess: Autonomous and Dependent Miracle-Working in Mark's Gospel and the Second Temple Period*

In this stunning short book, Samuel Hildebrandt dives into the oceanic depths of Hebrew poetry. He plumbs the biblical poets' depiction of the human condition—from the raw realities of anxiety, loneliness, and despair to the perennial possibilities of hope and comfort. Elegant, lyrical, and engaging, the book draws out ancient poetic wisdom for the complexities of human life, which confront us afresh each day.

—**Suzanna Millar,** chancellor's fellow in Hebrew Bible/Old Testament, New College, University of Edinburgh

Vast *as the* Sea

Vast *as the* Sea

*Hebrew Poetry and
the Human Condition*

Samuel Hildebrandt

Fortress Press
Minneapolis

Library of Congress Cataloging-in-Publication Data

Names: Hildebrandt, Samuel, author.
Title: Vast as the sea : Hebrew poetry and the human condition / Samuel Hildebrandt.
Description: Minneapolis : Fortress Press, [2023] | Includes bibliographical references
    and index.
Identifiers: LCCN 2023021504 (print) | LCCN 2023021505 (ebook) |
    ISBN 9781506485492 (print) | ISBN 9781506485508 (ebook)
Subjects: LCSH: Bible. Old Testament--Criticism, interpretation, etc. | Hebrew poetry,
    Biblical. | Human ecology--Religious aspects--Christianity.
Classification: LCC BS1430.52 .H55 2023 (print) | LCC BS1430.52 (ebook) |
    DDC 220.4/4--dc23/eng/20230808
LC record available at https://lccn.loc.gov/2023021504
LC ebook record available at https://lccn.loc.gov/2023021505

Cover design: John Lucas
Cover image: Bird flying over the sea during daytime, photo by Sasha Matic on Unsplash

Print ISBN: 978-1-5064-8549-2
eBook ISBN: 978-1-5064-8550-8

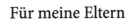

Für meine Eltern

Contents

Preface

"Of making many books there is no end." Having reached the point in history when we publish more than we can read, it is easy enough to agree with these words from Ecclesiastes's epilogue. But neither this concession nor our libraries and hard drives need to be read as a plea to make fewer books or stop writing altogether. The Hebrew poet who penned this line bemoans in the next that "much study is a weariness of the flesh," not that humans write too much. Thinking and writing are exhausting, they truly are. But as with anything worthwhile, this is to be expected and no reason to run from the desk. So instead of surrender or sneer, we might stop and ask *why* there is no end. We might ask why Ecclesiastes was written, why the library of humanity keeps on growing, why the weariness of time and effort has not long turned the final page of the bookish business.

This question opens a personal and yet pragmatic reflection on the human condition—on the nature, notion, and needs of being human. Such reflection can be made from several angles, and rightly so. Times change, people as well, and the complexities of life leave any monologue about the human condition fragile at best. Ecclesiastes's poet and the rest of the Hebrew writers provide an early snapshot of the long and layered conversation that needs to be had on this topic. Each voice has its own evaluation of what it means to be human yet there is some common ground. With the *imago dei* as its starting point, Gordon McConville's *Being Human in God's World* (2016) follows the Bible's articulation of the creator–creature relationship. Bernd Janowski's masterful *Anthropologie des Alten Testaments* (2019) highlights other constants, such as the phases of life and the experience of space and time. My reflection on the Hebrew poetic books finds some harmonies as well, yet *Vast as the Sea* is not a biblical theology or an encyclopedia. Instead, I hope to show that the Hebrew poets would answer the question about the endless making of books and the question of what makes a human being with one and the same sentiment: there is no end to the writing of books because there are people who cannot help but write them, people who think and talk and converse because that is what people do, have always done, and will always do.

The existence of the Bible as much as all the other books that Ecclesiastes has in view witnesses to a relentless need for expression and speech. Our daily output of words and pages, the inescapable pull of each comment and conversation, the inner voice and the racket of public discourse all assign language a central part in the exercise of being human. The plan to read the Hebrew poetic books, which themselves participate in this exercise, through this lens is pragmatic and perhaps a bit obvious. Yet, as I said above, it is also very personal. *Vast as the Sea* marks a milestone on a weary but worthwhile journey of listening to these ancient voices, yet it also bubbles with the weight and wonder of my own adventures with words. The frustrating search for the right English word in a translation. The surprising moments when a conversation suddenly becomes a real encounter. The speechless marvel when my colleagues or my children put something into words that I had never even thought before. The painful silences. Those conversations you never forget. The things we cannot say. Language has its limits, which often show their stern face when being human reaches its limits. But language also makes life possible. On rare occasions, it creates worlds we thought humans could not inhabit or articulate. This book is about speech as much as it is about being speechless. For better and for worse, the human condition knows both all too well.

For all their creativity and literary legacy, the Hebrew poets who penned the Psalms, Job, and Proverbs are shrouded in anonymity. As much as their words mean to me, I am thankful for all the wonderful human beings whose names I do know, who have listened, laughed, and learned with me while I was searching for the words for this book. I am grateful, first of all, for Darcy, with whom I enjoy the longest conversation of my life and without whom I had so little to say about so many things. Sophie, keep writing and I will read every word of yours. Ezekiel, there is no end to your golden ideas and golden words. I am so thankful for working at Nazarene Theological College, a place packed with thoughtful humans who know how to speak and who granted me a sabbatical without which this vast project would have never reached the shore. The team at Fortress Press shares in this compliment: thanks to Emily R. King (now at Notre Dame Press) and Yvonne D. Hawkins for their enthusiasm and for giving this book a horizon I could not see myself. A special note of thanks goes to Dustin for giving me new words when I needed them the most; to Rob Wilms and Robert Parkinson, both so remarkably careful and caring in what they say; to Gwen and Randy for taking me on as a resident author; to Steve for driving us to Cardiff and all the other conversations; to Justs and Ben for all the best words; to Sam for every play on words. Thank you, Mom, for every coffee break on this long road. Micha, Daniel, Sonja und meine lieben Eltern, wo findet man die Worte, euch für jeden Anruf und Austausch zu danken? There are many, many other people who need to be mentioned here. You know who you are, I hope! Your words and your open ears have often made my days brighter and in many unspeakable ways, they have made me who I am. If the words that I have put down can be a friend to you, all the weary hours of writing will mean something and we will know, once again, why we should never stop making books.

Samuel Hildebrandt
Manchester, March 2023

List of Abbreviations

AB	Anchor Bible
AIL	Ancient Israel and Its Literature
AJPH	*American Journal of Public Health*
AnBib	Analecta Biblica
ANES	*Ancient Near Eastern Studies*
Ann Beh	*Annals of Behavioral Medicine*
ATR	*Anglican Theological Review*
BBR	*Bulletin for Biblical Research*
BCOT	Baker Commentary on the Old Testament
BETL	Bibliotheca Ephemeridum Theologicarum Lovaniensium
BibInt	*Biblical Interpretation: A Journal of Contemporary Approaches*
BibSem	The Biblical Seminar
BTB	*Biblical Theology Bulletin*
BTCB	Brazos Theological Commentary on the Bible
BThAT	Beiträge zur Theologie und Anthropologie des Alten Testaments
CC	Continental Commentaries
CBQ	*Catholic Biblical Quarterly*
CBW	*Conversations with the Biblical World*
Colloq	*Colloquium*
CovQ	*Covenant Quarterly*
CHANE	Culture and History of the Ancient Near East
CrStHB	Critical Studies in the Hebrew Bible
CT	*Christianity Today*

D Clin Neurosc	*Dialogues in Clinical Neuroscience*
DSD	*Dead Sea Discoveries*
DSM-V	Association, American Psychiatric Association. *Diagnostic and Statistical Manual of Mental Disorders.* 5th ed. Arlington, VA: American Psychiatric Association, 2013.
ESV	English Standard Version
FRLANT	Forschungen zur Religion und Literatur des Alten und Neuen Testaments
HBM	Hebrew Bible Monographs
HBR	Handbooks on the Bible and its Reception
HS	*Hebrew Studies*
HTR	*Harvard Theological Review*
HTS	*Teologiese Studies*
HUCA	*Hebrew Union College Annual*
IBC	Interpretation: A Bible Commentary for Teaching and Preaching
ICC	International Critical Commentary
IJPS	*International Journal of Philosophical Studies*
Int	*Interpretation*
Int J Geriatr Psy	*International Journal for Geriatric Psychology*
Int J Philos Stud	*International Journal of Philosophical Studies*
JAET	*Journal of Asian Evangelical Theology*
J Affect Disord	*Journal of Affective Disorders*
JAMA Netw Open	*Journal of the American Medical Association Network Open*
JBC	*Journal of Biblical Counseling*
JBL	*Journal of Biblical Literature*
JBQ	*Jewish Biblical Quarterly*
JESOT	*Journal for the Evangelical Study of the Old Testament*
JFSR	*Journal of Feminist Studies in Religion*

J Loss Trauma	*Journal of Loss and Trauma*
JNES	*Journal for Near Eastern Studies*
J Pastor Theol	*Journal of Pastoral Theology*
JPCC	*Journal of Pastoral Care & Counseling*
J Pers Soc Psychol	*Journal of Personality and Social Psychology*
JPS	Jewish Publication Society Translation
JPT	*Journal of Psychology & Theology*
JSMH	*Journal of Spirituality in Mental Health*
JSNTSup	Journal for the Study of the New Testament Supplement Series
JSOT	*Journal for the Study of the Old Testament*
JSOTSup	Journal for the Study of the Old Testament Supplement Series
JSSM	Journal of Semitic Studies Monograph
J Trauma Stress	*Journal of Traumatic Stress*
JTS	*Journal of Theological Studies*
JYM	*Journal of Youth Ministry*
KJV	King James Version
LHBOTS	Library of Hebrew Bible/Old Testament Studies
LSTS	Library of Second Temple Studies
MHRC	*Mental Health, Religion & Culture*
NICOT	New International Commentary on the Old Testament
NIV	New International Version
NKJV	New King James Version
NJPS	New Jewish Publication Society Translation
NLT	New Living Translation
NRSV	New Revised Standard Version
NSBT	New Studies in Biblical Theology
ORA	Orientalische Religionen in der Antike
OTE	*Old Testament Essays*
OTL	Old Testament Library
OTM	Oxford Theological Monographs
Pastoral Psychol	*Pastoral Psychology*

PT	*Psychology Today*
RBS	Resources for Biblical Studies
RelStud	*Religious Studies*
RIMA	Royal Inscriptions of Mesopotamia, Assyrian Period
RRJ	*Review of Rabbinic Judaism*
SANT	Studia Aarhusiana Neotestamentica
SBT	Studies in Biblical Theology
SciRep	*Scientific Reports*
SHBC	Smyth & Helwys Bible Commentary
SJOT	*Scandinavian Journal of the Old Testament*
SJT	*Scottish Journal of Theology*
SKI.NF	Studien zu Kirche und Israel. Neue Folge.
SOTSMS	Society of Old Testament Study Monograph Series
SymS	Symposium Series
SysRev	*Systematic Reviews*
TS	*Theological Studies*
TZ	*Theologische Zeitschrift*
UBL	Ugaritisch-Biblische Literatur
VT	*Vetus Testamentum*
VTSup	Vetus Testamentum Supplements
WBC	Word Biblical Commentary
ZAW	*Zeitschrift für die alttestamentliche Wissenschaft*
ZMR	*Zeitschrift für Missionswissenschaft und Religionswissenschaft*

INTRODUCTION

There is no Frigate like a Book
To take us Lands away
Nor any Coursers like a Page
Of prancing Poetry —
This Traverse may the poorest take
Without oppress of Toll —
How frugal is the Chariot
That bears the Human soul.[1]

Emily Dickinson

There lies the sea, wide and calm, gentle and vast. A blanket of blue that stretches to a simple line where heaven and earth touch. Here, all strands run together and all life takes a breath, here in the cradle of the world. The sea has been telling its story for longer than time can tell and it is a story of unspeakable momentum, strength, and grace. Every tide a chapter, every wave a paragraph, every shoreline a sentence. But the script of swell and surge cannot be sight-read, nor can its meaning be distilled from this surface of signs and wonders. The eye may capture the endless horizon all at once, the ear take hold of surf and gulls, the chest imprison the piercing cold, yet never will the sea be held in the palm of one's hand. Its current runs too deep, its reach stretches too far. A veil of silence lies across the sparkling expanse and there are no words for plumbing the bottomless beauty of the ocean, no speech adequate for the terrifying darkness, the brooding storm. There it lies, with majesty beyond words, with clamor unspeakable.

The sea has been many things to humanity and, for better or for worse, human life has not been able to stop heeding the siren sound of

---

1 "There is no Frigate like a Book" in *Emily Dickinson: Selected Poems* (London: Phoenix, 2010), 83.

its waves. The relationship between people and ocean has many faces yet never will the two meet at the beach as equals. The sea does not flow at the same pace as human life, does not know the limits of sleep, sickness, and death. Perhaps it is precisely this difference that brings the human heart so close to the shore. There is no competition and no comparison, just the common ground of depth and surface, ebb and flow, perspective and boundary. The open sea is a mirror for all who have carried their own tides and torrents to its shoreline in search of an open ear. This turn to the surf speaks of a profound solidarity between humanity and the world at large, but it also washes ashore the human search for words that can express the experience of living. To gaze at the horizon on a sunny day is easy enough. But whenever the waves rise too high, there are few places on earth that grant a more accurate language for the human condition than the unspeakable depth of the sea with its sharp winds, broken shells, and foaming swell.

> *What can I say about you, with what can I compare you,*
>   *O Daughter Jerusalem?*
> *To whom can I liken you that I may comfort you,*
>   *O Maiden Zion?*
> *For vast as the sea is your collapse.*
>   *Who can heal you?*

These ancient lines from Lamentations 2:13 were crafted by an anonymous Hebrew poet who looked for words in the aftermath of Jerusalem's destruction in 587 BCE—and who fell short of finding them. The trauma of defeat and violence, the confusion about one's place in the world, and the uncertainty about God and the future, such turmoil, such a complex catastrophe will evade all comparison and embarrass all analysis and description. And yet something needs to be said. Confronted with too many questions that cannot be answered, the poet turns to the sea and learns from it a language for the shattered city. Parsing Jerusalem's collapse with the phrase "vast as the sea" neither downplays the disaster nor attempts to cure it. In the place of assurances, promises, explanations, and encouragements stands a personal poem that extends an honest hand to the helpless, that finds a language for acknowledging and, somehow, articulating the unspeakable. Because even if there are no words, something needs to be said.

Human Condition, Human Communication

Witnessing beautiful sunsets and horrendous wars alike, the experience of being human is a search for words. The first chapters of the human story and the first years of every new living being manifest the unprompted urge to assign words to objects, to articulate to others what can be seen, touched, heard, and felt. Human beings are bent on communication unlike any other occupant of this planet. Deciphering, translating, and recording, the *homo communicatio* busily casts net after net into the world to capture every facet of reality in a system of sounds, signs, and syllables. Non-human animals trump this effort in some areas, such as distance, frequency, and speaking under water. But no songbird builds a library and no cat learns zebra.

Whereas the scientific interest in this human trait often revolves around genetics, religious traditions around the globe have venerated language as a creative power, as a sign of human unity, and as a divine gift. Gods who speak the world into existence appear in the Babylonian *Enuma Elish*, in Hindu scriptures, and in the Bible's first chapter. Likewise, the Tower of Babel stands alongside other accounts of humanity's early years when people spoke in one tongue. Speech is at the heart of the Bible's anthropology. There are more words, more divine speech on the sixth day in Genesis 1 than in the previous five days. Birds and beasts are blessed like humanity, but only those who are made "in the image of God" are addressed directly ("and God said to them," v. 28). But unlike Norse, Greek, or Navajo literature, the biblical creation account does not depict language as a gift that is bestowed upon the earthlings from on high. From Adam's love poem to the destructive dialogues in Genesis 3, from Lamech's violent words to Noah's curse of his son, humans are masters of their own words, and with that agency, they are makers of their worlds. Every ancient text and modern theory has to be heard on its own, but as a whole they speak with one voice about the foundational place of language in the story of humanity.

From the first clay tablets and parchments to the torrents of books and blogposts, the past millennia have written this story with an impressive prowess of communicative and technological progress. But while the river of time flows onward and new words give voice to the bends in its course, there remains much hidden ground and many lonely islands that these waters cannot touch. Many of the essential aspects of the human condition will trouble recourse to the dictionary; many events in life will be too turbulent and diffuse to express with the language that one has learned. Here lies the problem: to be human is to speak but many human experiences cannot be put into words. The unfathomable ocean of life washes ashore experiences that humans would rather hurl back into the waters. Anxious thoughts, loneliness, and despair erode the foundations of living. Breakers of tragedy and swells of confusion, doubt, and struggle wear away even the most sturdy barriers that are built around the human heart. There are many calm days with no obstacle in sight; there is laughter and companionship, hope and healing. But speaking about the human condition must be bilingual. It must plant its feet at the shoreline to see both ebb and flow. It must visit broken dams and dry riverbeds.

It is difficult to explain why such language is so rare and why the monotone message of sunshine and success gets more air time. Perhaps the waters are clouded by sprinkles of raw optimism and denial or by blobs of shame and embarrassment. Perhaps they are diluted by the steady dribble of the advertising industry or the warm rush of political triumphalism and theologies of prosperity and fulfilment. Drinking from these foundations too deeply can dull the senses, numb and narrow the palate, and build up no reserves for the days that run dry. The difficult aspects of the human condition are not rinsed off the plate because they are small or unimportant or because they afflict only weak people. They are everyone's diet, yet the experience of despair, depression, and shattered hope is so hard to put into words that it does not often feature in conversation. The limits of life reveal the limits of language. Looking at the city that sits so lonely on her hill, at the people in their pain and broken world, the Hebrew poet of Lamentations 2 comes to the edge of the pool of human words—"What can I say about you?"—but knows that something needs to be said, nevertheless. The composition that has emerged is an attempt at saying something, at speaking past the limitations of language and life.

> We live on a little island of the articulable, which we tend to mistake for reality itself. We can and do make small and tedious lives as we sail through the cosmos on our uncannily lovely little planet, and this is

surely remarkable. But we do so much else besides. For example, we make language. A language is a grand collaboration, a collective art form which we begin to master as babes and sucklings, and which we preserve, modify, cull, enlarge as we pass through our lives.[2]

There is more to life than humans can say. The more words one can find, the more of life can be articulated, the larger the island can grow. Humans have always known that language is creative, that it can make worlds. But the stories of old also see language as a vehicle and sign of unity. It is impossible to see the world for what it is from a little island, let alone step on someone else's land and share their outlook at storm and sunrise. Inasmuch as the human condition is bound up with speaking, the turmoil of living calls for an adventurous quest for new words, for enlarging the limited vocabulary that would confine those who suffer to their articulable, alien, and unliveable reality.

The writer of Lamentations paves the way on this quest with words that break away from the familiar phrases and that airs an imagination that is itself vast as the sea. With their ear close to the catastrophic pulse of their day and their eye constantly above the horizon, the Hebrew poets know their small islands all too well but have no intention of staying in their comforting enclosure. They create words for the loneliness that cannot be uttered, for the anxieties that are too nebulous to be put into words, for the tyranny of time that ticks away in the background. Their language broadens the river of the human experience. At the same time, it builds bridges between those who wander at the rough edge of this stream and those who stand further inland and are yet just a wave or a whirlwind away from the unspeakable truth that they, too, are human.

The Language of Hebrew Poetry

Furnished with Hebrew, Greek, and Aramaic materials and accommodating several canonical layouts under its roof, the Bible is like a house with many doors and rooms that took several centuries to be built. Not all who enter here become occupants; not all visit every floor.

---

2 Marilynne Robinson, "Imagination and Community," in *When I Was a Child I Read Books* (London: Virago, 2012), 21.

Only Christian readers enjoy the revolving door between the Hebrew scriptures and the later extension of gospels and letters. Those who have a second home in their synagogue or church will walk the halls and look out the windows with different eyes than those who appreciate the Bible as a classic or as literature.[3] The foundation stone of this house reads 587 BCE, which marks the year of the traumatic destruction that Lamentations 2:13 strives to put into words and that all books of the Old Testament keep in view. The exit from God's garden, Abraham's life among the nations, Isaiah's explanations for exile, the laments of the Psalms, the memories of Chronicles, and all other chapters and stories digest in their own ways the fall of Jerusalem, the shattering of God's people, and the demolition of the temple.[4] That this crisis has given rise to such massive literary works like Genesis, Jeremiah, and Job is a testimony to the human need for language. The catastrophe had to be explained; God's ways had to be interrogated; the hopes of the future had to be written down. Something had to be said. The narratives about tribes and kings can provide explanation; the genealogies and laws can negotiate identity. The raw turmoil of human existence and the struggle of faith, however, are addressed nowhere with more abandon than in the poetic portions of the Bible.

In contrast to the New Testament where poetry is confined to short liturgical pieces and rewritten Hebrew poems (e.g., Phil 2:4–11; Luke 1–2; Rev 18–19), such language is at the heart of Old Testament literature. Though part of almost every book, its presence has at times been

---

3   For a reflection on the different modes of reading the Bible, see R. W. L. Moberly, *The Bible in a Disenchanted Age: The Enduring Possibility of Christian Faith* (Grand Rapids, MI: Baker Academic, 2018). An insightful dialogue between Jewish, Catholic, and Protestant approaches to the Hebrew scriptures/Old Testament can be found in Marc Zvi Brettler, Peter Enns, and Daniel J. Harrington, *The Bible and the Believer: How to Read the Bible Critically & Religiously* (Oxford: Oxford University Press, 2015).

4   A similar blueprint can be drawn up for the New Testament which was birthed under Roman occupation and in the shadow of the broken temple of 70 CE; cf. David M. Carr, *Holy Resilience: The Bible's Traumatic Origins* (New Haven, CT: Yale University Press, 2014); Adele Reinhartz, "The Destruction of the Jerusalem Temple as a Trauma for Nascent Christianity," in *Trauma and Traumatization in Individual and Collective Dimensions: Insights from Biblical Studies and Beyond*, ed. Eve-Marie Becker, Jan Dochhorn, and Else K. Holt, SANT 2 (Göttingen: Vandenhoeck & Ruprecht, 2014), 275–288.

blunted by printing the prophets, Psalms, and Job in the block-style of prose.[5] The line between poetry and prose is not rigid in Hebrew composition but the two can usually be distinguished by attention to content and function. Across Genesis 1–11, for instance, small poems conclude the preceding narratives (see, e.g., Gen 2:23–24; 9:25–28). On the book level, Genesis and Deuteronomy conclude with long poems by Jacob and Moses, the exodus account is matched with the "Song of the Sea" (Exod 14–15), 1–2 Samuel are framed by Hannah's and David's poems, and Job's short narrative of tragedy and restoration is expanded by thirty-eight chapters of poetic dialogues.

In each of these scenarios, prose and poetry speak about the same event but the latter lifts the perspective off the ground and reveals the cosmic reality behind the mundane affairs on earth. Poetry sings rather than speaks; it hovers above the literal realm of description. These transcendent qualities may explain why poetry is the preferred mode for divine speech in the ancient world,[6] but the lines and lyrics of the Bible are no divine prerogative. After all, the first human words in the story of scripture are cast in verse (Gen 2:23) and each of the countless poems that follow speaks for the human recourse to this mode of communication. Whatever its origins and orators, the recipients of such speech are promised the gift of Balaam, namely, to see with "eyes unveiled" (Num 24:4) and learn a language for speaking about God, the world, and themselves with lips unsealed.

Structure and Story
The poetic compositions of the Bible owe their revelatory power to a range of literary strands. In contrast to much English poetry, the Hebrew writers hardly ever use rhyme and they follow metrical patterns only

---

5 "Our notion of what is poetry (in our native tongue as well as in Hebrew, etc.) depends to a large extent on how the material is presented to us. In other words, if a passage is printed out as prose we automatically assume it to be prose;" W. G. E. Watson, *Classical Hebrew Poetry: A Guide to its Techniques* (Sheffield: Sheffield Academic Press, 2001), 45.

6 "Since poetry is our best human model of intricately rich communication, not only solemn, weighty, and forceful but also densely woven with complex internal connections, meanings, and implications, it makes sense that divine speech should be represented as poetry;" Robert Alter, *The Art of Biblical Poetry* (New York: Basic Books, 1985), 141.

loosely. They major instead in repetition and variation as they weave a tapestry in which every thread touches, entangles, and twists around the others. This dynamic is commonly labeled "parallelism," yet there is nothing static about their phrases. The poetic lines are not sealed off from one another but crisscross as they flow forward.[7] Structures emerge, small variations advance the message, patterns are established, deviations create emphasis.

> a What can I say about you, with what can I compare you,
> b   O Daughter Jerusalem?
> c To whom can I liken you that I may comfort you,
> d   O Maiden Zion?
> e For vast as the sea is your collapse.
> f   Who can heal you?

The three questions in lines a/c and the direct address in lines b/d may have all appearance of mere repetition yet the language shifts with subtle increments. In just one verse, the poet travels from saying anything at all to speaking in comparison, then moves from comparison to comfort, and finally—by picking up the thread in line f with a fourth question—from comfort to healing. None of the Hebrew verbs in lines a/c are identical and Jerusalem's situation becomes increasingly desperate as the spindle of questions releases its yarn. All threads tie together in line e, which breaks the endless questions and stops Jerusalem's descent from unprecedented suffering to unredeemable pain. An alien element in this verse, the statement about the sea in line e, acknowledges the city's unspeakable collapse rather than posing yet another unanswerable question. Something can be said, after all.

How each poetic verse and passage unfolds is impossible to predict, let alone be captured with labels like "synonymous" or "antithetical" parallelism. James Kugel was the first to move in the 1980s past

---

7 "Cross-references are built up and built in by means of equivalences across line and parts of lines, cross-references that are not ornamental but carry meaning.... They involve all linguistic and structural levels;" Beat Weber, "Toward a Theory of the Poetry of the Hebrew Bible: The Poetry of the Psalms as a Test Case," *BBR* 22 (2012): 165–166. As for Weber's last point, see Adele Berlin, *The Dynamics of Biblical Parallelism*, rev. and exp. (Grand Rapids, MI: Eerdmans, 2008).

categories of this sort to capture the cumulative progression of Hebrew poetry.[8] Robert Alter followed closely after Kugel but preferred to speak of "structures of intensification" and "narrativity."[9] More recently, biblical scholars have proposed "echoing and extending" to capture the play between correspondence and advance.[10] All of this terminology identifies poetry as a kind of storytelling that relies heavily on the reader. Each poem unfolds a complex narrative about self, world, and God. Each line and stanza bristles with lucid connections, complex transitions, and, at times, with a sprinkling of incongruity.

Compositions will pose questions, yet they might withhold answers. Hebrew poets are masters of parataxis, of putting two statements side-by-side without unpacking their relationship. Lamentations 2:13, for instance, neither spells out the journey from comparison to comfort, nor explains the contribution of the sober statement about the sea. Balance and symmetry must not be mistaken as a guarantor for a simple message. To the contrary, "poetry is open. The connection is mysterious, unexplained. Poetry articulates the mystery but leaves it there."[11] This particular quality makes poetic language such a meaningful medium for talking about the unspeakable, for creating connections and contrasts that can put human struggles into a new perspective, for expressing what may be hurt by direct words or trivialized by assured answers.

Image and Imagination
The indirection of poetic communication is enshrined in the structures of the text but is also at work in individual words. Along with

---

8   Cf. James L. Kugel, *The Idea of Biblical Poetry: Parallelism and its History* (New Haven, CT: Yale University Press, 1981), 8–9.

9   Alter, *Art of Biblical Poetry*, 11, 18–19.

10 Rolf A. Jacobson and Karl N. Jacobson, *Invitation to the Psalms: A Reader's Guide for Discovery and Engagement* (Grand Rapids, MI: Baker Academic, 2013), 12.

11 Patrick D. Miller, "The Theological Significance of Biblical Poetry," in *Language, Theology, and the Bible: Essays in Honour of James Barr*, ed. Samuel E. Balentine and John Barton (Oxford: Clarendon, 1994), 227. Such descriptions of poetry do not translate into a breakaway from biblical prose because ambiguity, gaps, and "the art of indirection" are defining features of narratives as well; cf. Meir Sternberg, *The Poetics of Biblical Narrative: Ideological Literature and the Drama of Reading* (Bloomington, IN: Indiana University Press, 1987), 43.

its openness and compactness, Hebrew poetry shares with many other languages a preference for brevity and terseness. This aspect is often muffled in translations—Lamentations 2:13, for instance, requires about forty words in English yet the Hebrew text counts only fifteen—but the compositions remain sparse enough to draw the reader into conversation. This is the case especially with comparisons and images. Equating Jerusalem's collapse with the vast sea may evoke a sense of magnitude and permanence, but it may also bring to the surface feelings of resignation and powerlessness, or whisper of a new life beyond the horizon. A game of association and selection, imagery relies on each individual reader to activate the aspects in the comparison that are most relevant to them. The sea will stir up happy memories and hope for better days for some people; for others, it will be alien and dark.[12] In the skillful hands of the Hebrew poets, comparisons and metaphors can express the unspeakable and give new words to speechless readers.

But these images do yet more. Whether someone thinks of themselves as a tree (Ps 1:3), an iron pillar (Jer 1:18), or a besieged city (Job 19:12) or whether one pictures God as a shield (Ps 7:10) or as dry rot (Hos 5:12) will shape one's attitudes and actions. "Metaphors *do* something to enable readers to perceive something differently."[13] The imagery that pervades the Psalms, prophets, and wisdom books reveals a poetic agenda that goes well beyond aesthetics and illustration. These words aim to broaden and reshape, or perhaps altogether abandon, the small islands of the articulable that their hearers inhabit. Drawing out assumptions, challenging narrow definitions, and creating new connections, the act of reading Hebrew poetry is by no means an innocent endeavor. No word is a "mere metaphor" and all figurative language can influence, for better or for worse, what humans think and do.[14]

---

12 These responses rely on a range of cognitive processes, such as mapping and transference, that operate on the complex blending of associations and experience. See, e.g., Gilles Fauconnier and Max Turner, *The Way We Think: Conceptual Blending and the Mind's Hidden Complexities* (New York: BasicBooks, 2002); Nicole L. Tilford, *Sensing World, Sensing Wisdom: The Cognitive Foundation of Biblical Metaphors*, AIL 31 (Atlanta, GA: SBL Press, 2017).

13 William P. Brown, *Seeing the Psalms: A Theology of Metaphor* (Louisville, KY: Westminster John Knox Press, 2002), 6 (emphasis original).

14 See, e.g., Renita J. Weems, "Gomer: Victim of Violence or Victim of Metaphor?" *Semeia* 47 (1989): 87–104; Sharon Moughtin-Mumby, *Sexual and*

Keenly aware of the gravity of graphic words, the Hebrew poets aim their comparisons at the areas that matter most. Central ideas about God, such as father, shepherd, and king, remain to this day a legacy of the psalmists and prophets and each has shaped faith, ethics, and politics for centuries. Likewise, regarding humans metaphorically as God's "children" or "images" can define one's views of self and society. Such comparisons activate some connotations, such as relationship and responsibility, and avoid others, such as physical resemblance. Encountering imagery in the Bible is challenging because the original communities in which these texts lived had different associations with shepherds and children than contemporary readers.[15] Yet perhaps it is precisely in this unfamiliar terrain that a language for the problems of life can take root and express experiences that cannot be articulated with the usual phrases and pictures.[16] Offering new words for being human and opening up new ways of seeing the world, the imagery of the Hebrew poets is as comforting as it is confrontational. Their pictures are ever ready to conjure up a different take on reality, ever kindling the imagination to look at the vast sea of sorrow with new eyes, ever hopeful that life may again "be like a watered garden, like a spring of water" (Isa 58:11).

Expressing Emotions
One of the main appeals of poetry is its way of speaking from the inside out. Whether on the lips of a single human being or with the tongue of a group, the reader is met by a speaking "I" or a lamenting "we" who shares what they see, seek, and suffer. This mode of direct address often

---

Marital Metaphors in Hosea, Jeremiah, Isaiah, and Ezekiel, OTM (Oxford: Oxford University Press, 2008).

15 For instance, the image in Psalm 63:7 ("in the shadow of your wings I will exult") may either be a symbol for God's bird-like protection, an application of imagery associated with sun gods (wings equal rays), or a reference to the winged cherubim who adorn the ark of the covenant. Cf. Craig C. Broyles, "The Psalms and Cult Symbolism: The Case of the Cherubim-Ark," in *Interpreting the Psalms: Issues and Approaches,* ed. David Firth and Philip S. Johnston (Downers Grove, IL: IVP Academic, 2005), 152–155.

16 "Living metaphors invariably create conceptual and emotional friction by which new meaning is created and the impossible becomes conceivable," Brown, *Seeing the Psalms,* 7.

takes the form of prayer, yet God also joins the conversation in many psalms (e.g., 2:4–9; 12:6; 46:10; 81:6–16; 91:14–16) and is the dominant speaker in prophetic poetry.

The blend of voices can at times be highly complex; speakers can shift suddenly, they can cite themselves and others, they can talk about someone or to someone. Since most poems are spoken with an anonymous voice, the identity of the speakers is not always easily determined and some lines can be heard on the lips of two or more participants.[17] The speaking voice of Lamentations 2:13, for instance, is not identified in the book and Jerusalem, who is addressed by this unnamed speaker, never responds. Other voices appear in the rest of Lamentations, summoning the readers to listen carefully, to take sides, to ask questions, and to imagine answers.[18] The drama of this polyphony enlivens the text and invites its listeners to add their voices to the choir of meaning-making.

Alongside its open structures, images, and voices, however, Hebrew poetry can also be shockingly direct. Inarticulate cries of fear and confusion ring from the page ("Ah!" "Alas!" "Oh!"); accusations of people and God break the silence ("Why do you sleep, O Lord?" Ps 44:23). Broken hearts and spirits ("we are weary, we find no rest;" Lam 5:5) mingle with calls of exuberant joy ("Rejoice and exult with all your heart!" Zeph 3:14). This breadth of emotive language is a key reason for the popularity of the Psalms, but it is also a trademark of the prophetic books, Job's dialogues, and the wisdom of Proverbs. "Poetry is, in fact, the preferred mode for the *expression of feeling and of thought.*"[19] While the characters in narratives allow for some identification, this

---

17 I have attended to these dynamics in my "Whose Voice Is Heard? Speaker Ambiguity in the Psalms," *CBQ* 82 (2020): 197–213; *Interpreting Quoted Speech in Prophetic Literature: A Study of Jeremiah 2.1–3.5,* VTSup 174 (Leiden: Brill, 2017). On the topic in general, see Rolf A. Jacobson, *"Many Are Saying:" The Function of Direct Discourse in the Hebrew Psalter,* JSOTSup 397 (London: T&T Clark, 2004).

18 See, e.g., Miriam J. Bier, *"Perhaps There Is Hope": Reading Lamentations as a Polyphony of Pain, Penitence, and Protest,* LHBOTS 603 (London: T&T Clark, 2015); Charles W. Miller, "Reading Voices: Personification, Dialogism, and the Reader of Lamentations 1," *BibInt* 9 (2004): 393–408.

19 Tod Linafelt, "Why Is There Poetry in the Book of Job?" *JBL* 140 (2021), 689 (emphasis original).

expressive quality lends to poetic compositions a more personal and intimate note. These direct exclamations reveal the ups and downs of life in sharp contours. They perform rather than present; they articulate rather than analyze.

Such emphatic shouts and heavy words are vital for expanding the small islands of the articulable. But to the extent that emotions, such as joy, fear, or envy, are hard to define in contemporary settings, it is all the more tricky with respect to a culture that is accessible only at a distance. There is little reason for assuming that the concept of emotion would have meant the same in ancient Israel as today.[20] To make matters yet harder, many of the Bible's emotive expressions, such as "melting hearts" (Ps 22:15), "drooping hands" (Jer 6:24), or "pain in the loins" (Isa 21:3–4), are stereotypical terms that allow no access to actual psychosomatic responses.[21] These observations trouble a straightforward reading of biblical poetry as a window into the past, let alone as a window into the soul and psyche of its authors. The cognitive and psychological dimensions of Hannah, Job, and Jeremiah will remain inaccessible, but the words, images, and expressions of their poems are a gift to anyone whose own language has reached its limits. Received through the ages as authentic expressions of happiness and hurt, these precious words have come across the ocean of time and can speak afresh about the human condition as it finds itself at the shores of the twenty-first century.

---

20 See, e.g., Françoise Mirguet, "What Is an 'Emotion' in the Hebrew Bible? An Experience that Exceeds Most Contemporary Concepts," *BibInt* 24 (2016): 442–465. The study of emotions in ancient texts has grown into a discipline in its own right; see, e.g., F. Scott Spencer, ed., *Mixed Feelings and Vexed Passions: Exploring Emotions in Biblical Literature*, RBS 90 (Atlanta, GA: SBL Press, 2017); Shih-Wei Hsu and Jaume Llop Raduá, eds., *The Expression of Emotions in Ancient Egypt and Mesopotamia*, CHANE 116 (Leiden: Brill, 2021).

21 "A major problem in the study of emotions in a 'dead' language such as Biblical Hebrew, though, is that most of the emotion scenarios (mostly attested in the poetic books) are cast in highly figurative language;" Paul A. Kruger, "Emotions in the Hebrew Bible: A Few Observations on Prospects and Challenges," *OTE* 28 (2015), 396. D. R. Hillers made a similar observation fifty years earlier in "A Convention in Hebrew Literature: The Reaction to Bad News," *ZAW* 77 (1965): 86–90.

Hebrew Poetry and Psychology

To speak about the experience of being human is no small feat. The difficult search for words is only part of a journey that is littered also with the challenge of vulnerability, the need for open ears, and the ambiguities of observation. The prevalent recourse to music, art, and literature can be interpreted as a natural reaction to these complications. Perhaps the only way to speak about one's own island and invite others onto its shores is to *not* speak about it, to avoid direct descriptions and details. There is more to life than humans can say and there will always remain some pockets of life than no human will ever put into words. The lines, images, and voices of Hebrew poetry will not yield the ultimate expression of human existence. But they can build a vessel that looks true enough to life to welcome aboard all landlocked, anchorless, and speechless travelers on their journey on the vast sea.

The question of human experience has, of course, not only cast its towline in the harbor of poetic literature. A scan of the horizon reveals a fleet of other disciplines that plough their path through the same waters. Non-identical twins at birth, philosophy and theology have shared from ancient days the common life of siblings, playing hand-in-hand but also trying to push each other off the swing from time to time.[22] For the big questions of meaning and existence, but also for specific phenomena, such as hope, time, and happiness, philosophical publications are a valuable conversation partner for reading Hebrew poetry. But there is another family relationship that promises to be yet more productive for speaking about anxieties, loneliness, and depression, namely, the discipline of psychology.

In part because of the growing impacts of pastoral psychology and trauma theory, the relationship between psychology and biblical studies has entered into an exciting new phase. In the first half of the twentieth century, it was quite common to treat the Bible like a patient on a couch. Scholars would diagnose King Saul with a "nervous disorder" and a "divided personality" or argue that the book of Job reflects its

---

22 See, e.g., Kevin Vanhoozer and Martin Warner, eds., *Transcending Boundaries in Philosophy and Theology: Reason, Meaning, and Experience* (Hampshire: Ashgate, 2007).

author's subconscious guilt about success.[23] A reflection of its time, the psychoanalytical approach shared the romantic disposition to conflate texts and authors and to trace back human behavior confidently to latent mental process. The excess of speculation and the imposition of modern terminology slowly eroded the academic project of Bible and psychology. With a critical eye on its own past, current scholarship focuses on the socio-historical and often traumatic contexts in which the Bible arose, the language of the Bible, and the effects that the Bible can have on its readers.[24]

That these three horizons of history, literature, and reception map neatly onto the interests of traditional exegesis suggests that psychology is neither an alien category nor a recent discovery in biblical studies. Modern paradigms and terminology will not always fit the ancient scriptures and the distance to their world must not be collapsed.[25] The Bible needs to be read in the light of its own cosmic worldview, its own ideas of personhood and communal life, and, at the center of it all, with its own commitment to God. At times, the language of the ancient world will be surprisingly close to human experiences today.[26] At other times, it will be shocking, confusing, and unconventional. Yet often it

---

23 See, e.g., H. C. Ackerman, "Saul: A Psychotherapeutic Analysis," *ATR* 3 (1920): 114–124; Robert L. Katz, "A Psychoanalytic Comment on Job 3:25," *HUCA* 29 (1958): 377–382. Such therapeutic readings of historical figures was not just common practice in biblical studies. See, e.g., Editha and Richard Sterba, *Beethoven and His Nephew: A Psychoanalytic Study of Their Relationship*, trans. William R. Trask (London: Dobson Books, 1957).

24 D. Andrew Kille summarizes these as the worlds "behind the text, of the text, and in front of the text;" "Psychology and the Bible: Three Worlds of the Text," *Pastoral Psycholl* 51 (2002): 125–134. See further J. Harold Ellens and Wayne G. Rollins, eds., *Psychology and the Bible: A New Way to Read the Scriptures*, 4 vols. (Westport, CT: Greenwood-Praeger, 2004).

25 A balanced approach is modelled by David J. Reimer, "Good Grief? A Psychological Reading of Lamentations," *ZAW* 114 (2002): 542–559, and Paul Joyce, "Lamentations and the Grief Process: A Psychological Reading," *BibInt* 1 (1993): 304–320, who read Lamentations 1–5 vis-á-vis the five stages of grief of Elisabeth Kübler-Ross's *On Death and Dying* (New York: Macmillan, 1969).

26 Bernd Janowski has identified body postures in poetic texts that reflect contemporary descriptions of depression; cf. "Das Erschöpfte Selbst: Zur Semantik der Depression in den Psalmen und im Ijobbuch," in *Das Hörende Herz*, BThAT 6 (Göttingen: Vandenhoeck & Ruprecht, 2018), 77–125. See further Michael L. Barré, "'Wandering About' as a Topos of Depression in Ancient Near Eastern Literature and in the Bible," *JNES* 60 (2001): 177–187; Randall

is exactly in these encounters with the text that the Hebrew poets can teach new words to lives that defy familiar and comfortable language.

Reading Jeremiah's woes about despair and shouting with Job in the darkness is never a substitute for professional mental health care, but neither do these literary expressions stand in competition with psychological services. To the extent that therapists, counsellors, and pastors may assign to literature and articulation a key role on the therapeutic journey, Hebrew poetry can contribute to disclosure, emotional literacy, and self-reflection. For everyone whose family or faith communities make no space for the difficult sides of being human, the words of the poets and prophets may reach out a liberating hand. They bring the gift of a language that is already theirs but that has gotten lost by a thin reading of the Bible.[27] These ancient compositions embrace their readers in their isolation, anxieties, and confusion and show them that these struggles, to varying degrees, are part of everyone's experience of being human. During the ebb and flow of life, these challenges may reach a constancy and intensity that requires medical support,[28] yet not all anxiety needs to be diagnosed as a form of mental illness, neither

---

M. Christenson, "Parallels between Depression and Lament," *JPCC* 61 (2007): 299–308.

27 John Swinton points out that many people have "become monolingual in their faith lives" and illustrates this problem with an anecdote about someone who had heard one of his sermons that "had given him a language to express his sadness, his pain, and his anger, and that this language came from within his faith tradition in a way that he had not noticed previously;" *Finding Jesus in the Storm: The Spiritual Lives of Christians with Mental Health Challenges* (Grand Rapids, MI: Eerdmans, 2020), 73–74. The loss of the Hebrew Scriptures in the life of the church and the benefits of relearning this vernacular are at the heart of Brent A. Strawn's *The Old Testament is Dying: A Diagnosis and Recommended Treatment*, Theological Explorations of the Church Catholic (Grand Rapids, MI: BakerAcademic, 2017).

28 The graded nature of mental health challenges is evident in the scaled assessment that is utilized by psychologists (see, e.g., the Goldberg Anxiety Scale or the UCLA Loneliness Scale). That depression or anxiety manifest themselves across a spectrum, however, need not lead to the conclusion that "everyone is a little mentally ill." As Kathryn Greene-McCreight observes, this perception is "demeaning to the experience of those who live with Major Mental Illnesses;" *Darkness Is My Only Companion: A Christian Response to Mental Illness*, rev. and exp. (Grand Rapids: Brazos Press, 2015), 184. See further Daniel J. Simundson, "Mental Health in the Bible," *Word & World* 9 (1989): 140–146; Christopher C. H. Cook, and Isabelle Hamley, eds., *The Bible and*

should despair be denounced as a sign of weak faith, nor loneliness as social failure.

The ocean of life is deep and many unpleasant experiences linger under its surface. Stoically keeping one's head above the waterline may suffice for staying atop these waters, at least for a while. But when the waves grow bigger and the shore seems farther away, the best swimmers will be those who have already braved the dark depths, who have seen the raw substance of their own lives. Leaving behind their safe islands, the Hebrew poets wade out to sea to lift up those who have gone under, who have tasted the salt and bitterness of the human condition. There they stand, at the shoreline between calm and chaos, at the beaches littered with shattered assumptions and shards of broken hope, ready to receive the weary swimmers. These lifeguards carry no soft towels nor promise safe passage. They know from experience that all refuge is temporary, that the flood will return, and that the swimming will again be demanding. But all who have sat with them can face the vast sea with the comfort of knowing that it is alright to struggle with being human, that there are words for that experience, that something can be said, after all.

Mental Health: Towards a Biblical Theology of Mental Health (Norfolk: SCM Press, 2020).

CHAPTER 1

Living in a Restless World
The Chaos and Calm of Psalm 46

Save me, O God,
*   for the waters have come up to my neck.*
I have sunk in deep mire,
*   without firm ground to stand.*
I have come into deepest waters,
*   the flood overwhelmed me.*
My cry weary,
*   my throat parched,*
*   my eyes dim.*
*   Waiting for God.*

Psalm 69:1–3

With every new sunrise and every step forward, the course of human life treads along the shoreline. Feet on solid ground, eyes set toward the horizon, this walk at the edge of the water whispers of perspective and peace. But for a species bound to the land, the line between soil and sea is more than a reflective path or a sunny promenade. The steady rush of the waves, the quick descent of the ocean's floor, and the incomprehensible vastness of the sea turn the shoreline into a precarious boundary. Here lies the limit of life, the end of the human enterprise. With more than 70 percent of the earth's surface under water, the human eye gazing out beyond the beach is met by an abysmal force that locks its look on life behind a barrier it cannot cross. The view across this line usually is blue and bright and the smooth surface of the sea carries its serenity into life on earth. But every so often, the whiff of certainty and calm disappears in a torrent of storm, darkness, and noise that overwhelms the senses and narrows all hope for a new day to that thin, thin line in the sand.

The beauty and the terror of the ocean has been a source for endless reflections about human life. Both sides can be heard, for instance, in Frances Ridley Havergal's poem "Under the Surface," which allows the sea's "foam and roar, restless heave and passionate dash" to be felt with the same intensity as the water's "soft green light" and "endless calm." In a similar way, John Betjeman's "Winter Seascape" can speak amid thunder, roar, and noise of "a huge consoling sea."[1] The lines from Psalm 69 present a much earlier sample of this artistic turn to the surf, yet here such language is used solely to articulate turbulence and trouble.

Amid all the aquatic admiration of the Bible,[2] the suffocating waves and disorienting depth of the sea appear as a consistent literary pool for speaking about the difficulties of life. The Hebrew poets are painfully aware that humans live on the edge between safe ground and drowning, between calm and chaos, between trust and uncertainty. Their compositions are creative and caring responses to the anxieties that this unstable territory breeds. Many of their contemporary readers may not be faced by the extremes of floods and torrential rains, yet the language of watery chaos remains a meaningful expression for the reality of tension and turmoil in everyday living.

The compact vision of Psalm 46 serves as an ideal platform for dipping a toe into the ancient realm of creation, chaos, and calm. For today's promenade at the shoreline, a gaze under the surface of this poem can yield the treasure of a language that acknowledges and articulates anxieties. Rather than blocking off or bypassing the essential fears and tumults of life, Psalm 46 and a range of other Hebrew poems cross the dreadful shoreline and wade out into the restless sea. Finding words amid the waves, they cast a literary lifeline to everyone who struggles to find their way back to the surface.

---

1 The full poem can be found in Havergal's *Under the Surface*, 3rd ed. (London: J. Nisbet, 1876), 11–12. Betjeman's lines come from his *Collected Poems* (London: John Murray, 2001).

2 Cf. Meric Srokosz and Rebecca S. Watson, *Blue Planet, Blue God: The Bible and the Sea* (London: SCM Press, 2017).

The Anxieties of Human Life

With the call "Do not be afraid!" echoing through its pages, the Bible is a showcase of life situations in which people respond with fear to something or, more often, to someone. The old text and every new day alike are filled with concrete outbreaks of danger. In such situations, a fearful reaction is as appropriate as it is healthy. A deeply embedded cognitive mechanism, fear triggers the brain's impulse to ensure survival. A tidal wave or a sudden current should be feared because this response will prompt an escape to safer ground. Whenever the threat is specific and identifiable, whenever it has a clear beginning and a definite resolution, human beings literally live by fear.[3] This good instinct, however, can become a problem when it exceeds its boundaries and morphs into anxious agitation.

Anxiety may be understood as "a more elaborate form of fear," although it is not always easy to determine where one ends and the other begins.[4] But this fuzziness itself hints at the basic character of anxiety. Unlike the concrete, real threat to which fear responds, the triggers of anxiety are vague and at least one step removed from the current situation.

> Anxiety is a tense unsettling anticipation of a threatening but formless event; a feeling of uneasy suspense. . . . In its purest form, anxiety is diffuse, objectless, unpleasant and persistent. Unlike fear, it is not so obviously determined. Usually it is unpredictable and uncontrollable. . . . Anxiety tends to be shapeless, grating along at a lower level of intensity; its onset and offset are difficult to time, and it lacks clear borders.[5]

This description draws out some of the most pertinent differences to fear and, right away, suggests a vital link between anxiety and articulation. Shapeless, timeless, and boundless, anxiety can overwhelm people

---

3 "It is virtually impossible *not* to attend to threats to our survival. Our brains operate automatically and irreversibly on a 'better safe than sorry' premise;" David A. Hogue, "Sometimes It Causes Me to Tremble: Fear, Faith, and the Human Brain," *Pastoral Psychol* 63 (2014), 661 (emphasis original).

4 Thierry Steimer, "The Biology of Fear- and Anxiety-Related Behaviors," *D Clin Neurosc* 4 (2002), 233. Diagnostic tools like the *Goldberg Anxiety Scale* highlight the complexity of the fear/anxiety relationship.

5 Stanley Rachmann, *Anxiety*, 4th ed. (London: Psychology Press, 2019), 3–5.

with unspecified concerns. A perceived threat that lingers vaguely in the unpredictable future can be difficult to put into words. For that reason, it is likely to grow yet further and occupy yet more thoughts, more time, more energy. Anxiety is a complex phenomenon but to the extent that it concerns human experiences of life and time, a substantial portion of the foggy path of anxious thoughts will be paved with words, especially since this path is trodden by so many people.

The public awareness of anxiety in recent decades suggests it has breached the shore with an unprecedented force. Mental health initiatives bear witness to the increased need to respond to this development and diagnosed anxiety disorders leave their mark on many individual lives, families, communities, and workspaces.[6] The personal suffering and the public impact of anxiety is severe, yet it would be just as misleading to paint every anxious thought with the broad brush of mental illness as it would be to elevate it as a novel phenomenon of the twenty-first century. Anxiety has a long history. It has "always been part of the human condition and will remain with us for the foreseeable future."[7] Ranging from the spiritual to the medical and from the financial to the psychological, every era has struggled with its own anxieties and has sought to identify its roots and reasons. But whether global wars, social unrest, and epidemics are singled out, or whether finitude and existential worry seem to provide an explanation, the contextual and biological factors of human life are too vast to allow for one single answer.[8] The anxieties of life are as complex as they are real. They

---

6   The 2022 statistics of the Anxiety and Depression Association of America show that 19 percent of the adult population in the United States lived with a diagnosed anxiety disorder in the past year; cf. "Anxiety Disorder: Facts & Statistics," https://adaa.org/understanding-anxiety/facts-statistics.

7   Isaac M. Marks, *Living with Fear: Understanding and Coping with Anxiety,* 2nd ed. (Maidenhead: McGraw-Hill, 2005), 3. For an insightful overview, see Allan V. Horwitz's *Anxiety: A Short History* (Baltimore, MD: Johns Hopkins University Press, 2013), which traces anxiety's "chameleonlike force" (p. 5) through the centuries.

8   Theologian Paul Tillich, for instance, sought to explain anxiety as "the state in which a being is aware of its possible non-being;" *The Courage to Be,* The Fontana Library: Theology and Philosophy (Glasgow: Fountain Books, 1977), 44. But as Horwitz reminds his readers, anxiety is more complex: "No less than in previous eras, current conceptions of anxiety and its disorders reflect

are as integral to the human experience as they are indescribable in their shape and strength.

This complexity and long-standing presence suggests that anxiety may be seen as a normal part of life and not solely as a diagnosis. In the words of psychologist Kirk Bingaman, "it is not a matter of *if* the particular individual will be feeling anxious, but *to what extent*."[9] Although it manifests itself differently for each individual and can at times require medical and psychological support, anxiety is a given for everyone who strives for security and stability in this restless world. Bingaman proposes that the current rise of anxiety stems from a loss of specific reference points, such as traditional narratives and family structures. Along with the increased speed of contemporary life, the over-abundance of information, choice, and agency can leave many citizens of industrial, digitalized countries adrift amid a confusing world.[10] Referring to Marc Augé's *Non-Places* (1995) and Kenneth Gergen's *The Saturated Self* (1991), Bingaman suspects that contemporary anxiety stems not so much from a loss of meaning, but rather from "the rapid acceleration and *excess* of meaning."[11] Wave upon wave of news, crisis, and possibility wash over the drenched figures who work out their existence as they anxiously wander along a hazy shoreline where everything matters, yet nothing is essential, where everything is possible, yet nothing offers a clear perspective through the fog.

Whereas contemporary analyses may be more concerned with the definitions, triggers, and economics of anxiety, previous generations appear to have kept their eye instead on the experience itself. Four millennia of poetic, philosophical, and spiritual compositions witness to an inspiring human effort of putting the unspeakable reality of anxiety

---

the social matrix in which they arise, are identified, and are treated;" *Anxiety: A Short History*, 18.

9   "A Pastoral Theological Approach to the New Anxiety," *Pastoral Psychol* 59 (2010), 660 (emphasis original).

10 "Today, especially in Western capitalist democracies, we also probably have more choice than ever in history.... Freedom of choice generates great anxiety;" Scott Stossel, *My Age of Anxiety: Fear, Hope, Dread and the Search for Peace of Mind* (London: Windmill Books, 2014), 302. Erich Fromm's *The Fear of Freedom* (London: Routledge, 1960) remains a classic articulation of this sentiment.

11 "New Anxiety," 666.

into words. The lines from Psalm 69 show that the biblical writers participated in this effort, yet these ancient words need to be read on their own terms. Fear, for instance, can describe a human involuntary reaction to danger (see, e.g. Gen 32:7; Exod 20:18; 1 Sam 7:7), but the biblical texts might also portray it as a rational attitude, as a decision.[12] The waters of Psalm 69 that "have come up to my neck" and the flood that "has overwhelmed me" are scenes neither of a swimming accident nor of an ecological disaster. But neither are they mere metaphors for feeling overwhelmed. These poetic expressions offer a language for the vague grip of anxiety that runs far deeper than the surface of the text, that has accepted anxiety as part of the human condition and has learned to articulate it alongside a firm belief in God. This language is embedded within the ancient drama of creation and chaos that Psalm 46 and other biblical poems perform in their pursuit of calm amid uncertainty, of stability amid the stormy waters.

An Unsettled View of the World

Most conversations about creation start where the Bible starts, namely, in Genesis 1. According to the solemn vision of this chapter, everything in the cosmos is orchestrated based on God's sight, speech, division, delegation, and blessing. With clinical precision, God carves out a living space for animals and humans amid the dark and shapeless environment in which the chapter begins. A hymn with seven verses, Genesis 1 constructs a holy and wholesome world that culminates in the creation of humanity and the sabbath. God's "rest" is not a recovery from creative toil but an expression of royal mastery. The lines between water and land are firmly established; sun and moon maintain life's

---

12 The "fear of the Lord," for instance, is something that can be taught and practiced (e.g., Deut 4:10; 14:23; 31:12; Ps 34:12); cf. Philip Michael Lasater, "'The Emotions' in Biblical Anthropology? A Genealogy and Case Study with ירא," HTR 110 (2017): 520–540; Mayer I. Gruber, "Fear, Anxiety and Reverence in Akkadian, Biblical Hebrew and Other North-West Semitic Languages," VT 15 (1990): 411–422. A biblical overview of reactions to fear, such as a raised heart frequency or a nervous stomach, can be found in Bernd Janowski, *Anthropologie des Alten Testaments: Grundfragen, Kontexte, Themenfelder* (Tübingen: Mohr Siebeck, 2019), 169.

rhythms; the fish and the birds, the animals and the humans are all in their right place in God's kingdom.

Genesis 1 is the default version of creation and its vision of sovereignty and stability starts the biblical story on a triumphant note. The deep waters in verse 2 are present but inactive; the sea monsters are mentioned only in passing in verse 21. There are no obstacles to God's work, no challenges, delays, or setbacks. The privileged position at the head of the Bible suggests that Genesis 1 sets the norm for God's work of world-making, yet the rest of the Old Testament begs to differ. Many poetic passages speak of significant opposition that, similar to the creation accounts of other ancient people,[13] arises in the person of the Sea, the watery serpent Leviathan, or some other aquatic beast. These texts share in Genesis's portrayal of divine kingship,[14] but their imaginative lines summon the vision of combat and victory that is absent from the Bible's first page.

> But God, my king from ancient days,
> worker of deliverance in the midst of the earth.
> You split with your might the sea,
> shattered the heads of the dragons on the waters,
> crushed the heads of Leviathan,
> gave him as food to the sharks of the sea.
> You cleaved open springs and brooks,
> dried up strong streams.
> Yours is the day, yours is the night,
> you set up light and sun.
> You fixed all boundaries of the earth,
> summer and winter you made.
>
> Psalm 74:12–17

From the defeat of Pharaoh to the hymns in the Psalms, the confident exclamation "The Lord reigns" stands at the heart of Israel's life.[15] The

---

13 Cf. Noga Ayali-Darshan, *The Storm-God and the Sea: The Origin, Versions, and Diffusion of a Myth throughout the Ancient Near East,* trans. Liat Keren, ORA 37 (Tübingen: Mohr Siebeck, 2020).

14 Mark S. Smith offers a sensitive dialogue between the Bible's versions of creation in *The Priestly Vision of Genesis 1* (Minneapolis, MN: Fortress Press, 2010).

15 See, e.g., Exod 15:18, Pss 96–99, Jer 10:7. Since the other four occurrences of "in the beginning" (בראשית) mark the start of a king's reign (Jer 26:1; 27:1; 28:1; 49:34), the opening of Genesis 1 expresses the same focus.

logic on which laments such as Psalms 74 or 89 rely is that God's kingship had been firmly established in the past but now has come under
threat. What these texts demand is the re-creation of that stable world
in which God's reign remains unchallenged and God's people dwell in
safety. The backbone of the Bible's liturgy and the heart of its prophetic
visions is the confession that God maintains the shoreline between existence and chaos, the order of summer and winter, of good and evil.

> *He set the earth on its foundations,*
> *   it will not be shaken ever again.*
> *The depths you covered as with a garment,*
> *   the waters stood up to the mountains—*
> *   From your rebuke, they fled!*
> *   From the sound of your thunder, they took flight!*
> *Up mountains they went, into valleys they sunk*
> *   to the place you established for them.*
> *A frontier you set up that they will not pass,*
> *   never again to cover the earth.*
>
> Psalm 104:5–9

> *Is it not I, says the Lord, whom you should fear?*
> *   Is it not me before whom you should tremble?*
> *For I set the sand as a boundary for the sea,*
> *   an abiding barrier it must not pass.*
> *It will swell and seethe, but cannot conquer.*
> *   Its waves will roar, but they must not pass.*
>
> Jeremiah 5:22

The Bible knows more than one way of speaking about creation and
these poetic passages complement the tranquil vision of Genesis 1 with
the reality of cosmic turbulence, with waters tossing and roaring. The
forces of chaos were conquered and curbed by God's creative power, yet
this was not the end of the story. The making and ordering of the world
is not a one-time event. In the worldview of the Hebrew poets, creation
is understood as God's ongoing, royal exercise of pushing chaos back
behind its prescribed limits, not once, not twice, but again and again.
"Until here you may come, but no further! Here your proud waves shall
stay" (Job 38:11).

Reading past the Bible's first chapter, the poetry of the Old Testament establishes a testimony of God's presence and activity in the world. Yet it also instills considerable tension into everyday life. The safe shoreline of existence is no given but needs to be drawn anew and anew in this unstable, restless world.[16] This cosmic reality defines the basic conditions for being human in this world. It bristles underneath the grand stage of political and military conflicts (e.g., Isa 30:26–33; Joel 3:14–16; Nah 1:2–11) as well as underneath God's deliverance from Egypt. Pharaoh is likened to a "dragon in the sea" (Ezek 32:2) and the portrayal of the exodus in Isaiah 51:9 and Psalms 77:16–20 and 106:9–12 likewise draws from the literary pool of creation and combat.[17] But the symbolic words about seas and waves are also used to articulate personal struggles.

> *The chords of death fastened around me,*
> *the torrents of destruction terrified me. . . .*
> *He reached down from on high and took me.*
> *He drew me out of many waters.*

Psalm 18:4, 16

> *Reach down your hand from on high,*
> *rescue me, deliver me from many waters,*
> *from the hand of a strange people,*
> *whose mouths speak empty words,*
> *whose right hand is but a lie.*

Psalm 144:7–8

---

16 "The confinement of chaos rather than its elimination is the essence of creation. . . . The world is not inherently safe; it is inherently unsafe," Jon D. Levenson, *Creation and the Persistence of Evil: The Jewish Drama of Divine Omnipotence* (Princeton, NJ: Princeton University Press, 1994), 17.

17 "The dragon is, as we see throughout the ancient world, chaos personified. The dragon is everything that is evil, everything that is disordered," Robert D. Miller II, "Dragon Myths and Biblical Theology," *TS* 80 (2019), 49. As creator, it is God's responsibility to push back all forms of chaos, including the Israelites should they shake the life-sustaining structures of the cosmos (see, e.g., Jer 4:22–26; 9:4–11; 12:1–4; Mic 3:1–12). For a particularly creative adaptation, see Kurtis Peters, "Jonah 1 and the Battle with the Sea: Myth and Irony," *SJOT* 32 (2018): 157–165.

The communities who first produced and received these texts experienced the world without a rigid divide between physical, concrete reality and supernatural reality.[18] Ancient Israelites knew that mountains are formed of stone and dirt, but they also approached the crumbling rocks as seats of gods (Ps 68:15–16). They knew that trees grow from saplings, but they also met angels under their branches (e.g., Gen 18:1; Exod 3:2; Judg 6:11). Likewise, the sea can be sailed and can be cultivated into channels, but its sheer force, its uncanny depth of beasts unknown, and its destructive flooding of human habitation are also signs of the cosmic struggle of chaos and death.

The ancient perception of the world is fluid, holding together the concrete and the symbolic as one and the same reality. At the exodus, the waters were terrified and "the depths trembled" as God thundered with arrows of lightning, paving a way through the sea, leading Israel "by the hand of Moses and Aaron." These final lines of Psalm 77 mention the down-to-earth reality of two brothers putting foot before foot in the same breath as the unutterable reality of divine combat. The sharp distinction that the modern mind draws between myth and history is foreign to Israel's ancient world and words. To narrate the human experience of God in the world means to speak the mythological language of creation and chaos that is highly symbolic and at home in poetry and song.[19] God's storm on high, the wind catching in Moses's beard, chaos of water and darkness, refugees in sandals: these supernatural and mundane realities are two sides of the same coin.

---

18 "We constantly run the risk of reading these pictures too concretely, or having avoided that risk, of treating them too abstractly. . . . Contexts are fluid, ranging from the realm of the historical to the magical–mythical;" Othmar Keel, *The Symbolism of the Biblical World: Ancient Near Eastern Iconography and the Book of Psalms,* trans. Timothy J. Hallett (Winona Lake, IN: Eisenbrauns, 1997), 9.

19 "In the ancient world, myth has to do with those deep, foundational realities and archetypal relations between heaven and earth. . . . Biblical authors would not have made a strong disjunction between what we might dismiss as 'mythic' and what is real;" Eric N. Ortlund, *Piercing Leviathan: God's Defeat of Evil in the Book of Job,* NSBT 56 (Downers Grove, IL: IVP Academic, 2021), 8–9. See further N. Wyatt, "The Mythic Mind Revisited: Myth and History, or Myth versus History, a Continuing Problem in Biblical Studies," *SJOT* 22 (2008): 161–175. For the mythic motifs in Psalms 74 and 77, see Dirk J. Human, ed., *Psalms and Mythology,* LHBOTS 462 (New York: T&T Clark, 2007).

The Language of Chaos and Combat in Psalm 46

From the flood narrative to Isaiah's visions of God's kingdom, from the laments of the Psalms to the whirlwind of Job 38, the biblical authors soak their compositions in the mythic reservoir of God, sea, and monsters. For readers who encounter these texts at a considerable distance, it can be challenging to see the drama play out in full, let alone appreciate the message it speaks beyond its day. The compact vision of Psalm 46 may offer a synopsis to aid this process. In just ten verses, the poem travels from creed to calamity, from chaos to combat, from crisis to calm. Tracing this outline with all its symbolic depths and poetic heights allows for a first-hand encounter with the biblical worldview. In turn, this exercise marks the first step for discovering how the language of this poem might acknowledge and articulate the anxieties of today's restless world.

Together with six other poems that are likewise attributed to the Korahite temple singers, Psalm 46 stands near the beginning of Book II of the Psalms (Pss 42–72). The literary shape of this collection suggests that the royal hymns in Psalms 45–48 respond to the laments in Psalms 42–44, offering a fresh perspective for the life that is cast down (Ps 42:6) and sunk into the dust (Ps 44:25).[20] This pastoral motivation is captured in Martin Luther's well-known hymn *A Mighty Fortress is our God*, yet Psalm 46 is no straightforward acclamation of protection. Mountains topple into the sea, nations rage, the earth melts! Though the main current of the poem is a celebration of divine help, a careful reading must not eclipse the threat that throbs in verses 1–3.

> *God is for us refuge and strength,*
> *helper in anxieties,*
> *through and through.*

> *Therefore, we will not fear*
> *when the earth quakes,*
> *when the mountains shake in the heart of the sea.*

> *Its waters roar and foam,*
> *the mountains shake at its arrogant swell.*

---

20 For the Korahite psalms, see David G. Firth, "Reading Psalm 46 in Its Canonical Context: An Initial Exploration in Harmonies Consonant and Dissonant," *BBR* 30 (2020): 22–40.

The poem opens with a triad of divine attributes: God is refuge, strength, and helper. This sequence of terms does not say the same thing with different words but piles accolade upon accolade, constructing and sharpening a case for God's ability to provide shelter.[21] The final element, God's "help" (עֶזְרָה), frequently appears in the context of military aid (e.g., Ps 35:2; Isa 20:6; Jer 37:7), suggesting that no human ally will help as God helps, no army will be able to match God's reliable presence. Highlighting the divine support and favor ("for us") with such magnitude lays a foundation for courage ("therefore, we will not fear") but it also prepares the way for a threat that is greater than any merely human opposition. The confession of God's strength is confronted in verse 2 by cosmic turmoil.[22] Not only are the positive attributes of refuge, strength, and help countered by verbs of unrest ("quake," "shake," "roar"), but the twofold mention of the shaking mountains opposes all claims to protection and the noise of raging torrents competes with the community's courageous slogan.

The parallel construction "when . . . when . . ." across verses 2–3 suggests that the collapse of the world is not some hypothetical thought experiment but a real threat that lingers behind the horizon of every new day. Even as the human voices of verse 1 are still heard and the confessions of divine strength still ring in the ear, the poetic tapestry of sound and scenery gives credence to the possibility of catastrophe. Mountains that break asunder are a terrifying sight for any reader at any time, yet for the first audience of Psalm 46, this loud scene speaks a yet more dramatic message. Because of their height and vertical expanse, mountains were quite naturally revered as divine dwelling places in the ancient world, as meeting points of heaven and earth (e.g., Ps 48:1–3;

---

21 "There is a progression of sorts in the descriptions of YHWH's power. . . . The term עֹז, 'strength,' extends מַחְסֶה, 'refuge,' in that the first term is defensive, while עֹז, 'strength,' is a general term, both offensive and defensive;" Marc Zvi Brettler, "Images of YHWH the Warrior in the Psalms," *Semeia* 61 (1993), 144.

22 Amos 1:1 and Zechariah 14:15 mention an earthquake that can be dated on the basis of geological data to around 750 BCE; cf. Ki-Min Bang, "A Missing Key to Understanding Psalm 46: Revisiting the *Chaoskampf*," *CBW* 37 (2017), 81–84. However, typical of the Psalms, the generic language of Psalm 46 resists any confident dating; cf. Robert D. Miller II, "The Zion Hymns as Instruments of Power," *ANES* 47 (2010): 218–240.

Mic 1:2–4).[23] But the Old Testament also portrays mountains as pillars that uphold the heavens (Job 26:11; Ps 18:7) and suspend the upper boundary line of the world. What Psalm 46 envisions is the narrowing of life space, the eclipse of the safe environment that exists below that boundary line above one's head, that keeps the waters from flooding through the heavenly windows (Gen 7:11; 8:2) to engulf the ordered realm in chaos and calamity.

It is not until the final word of verse 3 that Psalm 46 turns its attention to the culprit of this significant destruction. With a delayed introduction, the sea emerges on the cosmic stage and is immediately assigned the role of the foe. Poetically speaking, the repetition of the shaking mountains moves from independence to incitement. In verse 2 they seemed to have shaken on their own, yet in verse 3 the pillars of the earth are brought under the water's dominion. The nature of the roaring waves is only captured in part by translating the final word of verse 3 as "tumult" (NRSV) or "swelling" (NIV). As in Psalm 89:9, the sea is alive with arrogance, provocative in its pride,[24] sweeping against the cliffs as a force in its own right, opposing God as creator and king. As in Psalm 74 and Jeremiah 5, the proud waves push beyond their God-given boundary and Psalm 46 makes every effort for this threat to be heard and felt. The sound of the word pair "roar and foam" (yehĕmû yeḥmĕrû) makes the rolling waves come alive in the poem's imaginative vision and crashes the reality of calamity onto the shore of life.

By virtue of this poetic extravagance of personification, balance, and sound, the threat of the sea unfolds in such alarming detail that the initial confessions are matched, if not shaken or silenced. When the world is crushed by chaos, when the walls are closing in, there is less assurance and less air for the chorus who sings "we will not fear." In a

---

23 In the biblical world, "geography is simply a visible form of theology;" Jon D. Levenson, *Sinai & Zion: An Entry into the Jewish Bible*, New Voices in Biblical Studies (New York: Harper San Fransisco, 1985), 116.

24 As a divine attribute, גאוה (gaʾăwāt) has the connotation of "majesty" (e.g., Deut 33:26; Ps 68:34), but when used for hostile opposition, it has the sense of "pride" (e.g., Isa 13:11; Ps 31:18; Prov 14:3). "Likewise the mountains or cliffs are personalized: it is as if they shake with fright as the seas lift themselves up and throw themselves at them;" John Goldingay, *Psalms. Volume 2: Psalms 42–89*, BCOT (Grand Rapids, MI: Baker Academic, 2007), 68.

context of the cosmic crumbling, the limited living space, and rising waters, the short phrase "in anxieties" (בצרות) in verse 1 takes on a more specific nuance. Other terms related to צר (ṣar) can describe something that is "narrow, tight" or "cramped" (2 Kgs 6:1); they can refer to a situation of "restraint" (Job 7:11) or to a tightly wrapped "bundle" (Gen 42:35).[25] Reading this word field alongside the catastrophe that Psalm 46 envisions, the turmoil that the poem describes may be understood as a threat of suffocating force, as a menace that troubles breathing and narrows perspective.

The amount of detail that the opening verses of Psalm 46 and other Hebrew poems assign to the chaos of life speaks to a real need for finding words for human anxieties. As Psalm 46 continues its storyline, the tone shifts drastically yet still the use of symbolic language speaks to the same need.

> A river! Its streams gladden the city of God,
>   the holy dwelling of the Most High.
> God is in her midst—she shall not be shaken!
>   God will help her at break of day.
> Nations roar, kingdoms shake,
>   he sends forth his voice,
>   the earth melts.

Psalm 46:4–6

With the main protagonists introduced in verses 1–3, this next portion of the poem leaves no doubt as to how the conflict between a helping God and an arrogant sea resolves. The first words reframe the water imagery, highlighting the life-giving, even joyful nature of the natural element instead of its destructive power.[26] Following the bubbling flow of the stream, the focus shifts away from the unsettled cosmos to the firmly established city of God that is portrayed as a manifestation of

---

25 Based on these passages, one of the standard Hebrew lexicons lists along "need, distress" also "anxiety" as a possible translation of צר. Cf. Ludwig Koehler and Walter Baumgartner, *The Hebrew & Aramaic Lexicon of the Old Testament*, trans. M. E. J. Richardson (Leiden: Brill, 1994), 1053.

26 On the ambivalent character of seas and rivers, see Peter William Goodman, "Waters that Witness: How the Bible's Rivers Help Convey Its Message," *BTB* 53 (2023): 42–56.

divine presence and "help" (note the echo to v. 1: עזרה/יעזרה). Unlike the shaking mountains, this city "shall not be shaken" (מוט in vv. 2 and 5).

The word connections across verses 1–7 aim to assure the poem's readers that a stable world is possible, and they also model how chaos language can speak into concrete, earthly situations. Whereas in verses 1–3 mountains shake (מוט) and waters roar (המה), now nations roar (המה) and kingdoms shake (מוט). These parallels are not just aesthetic flourish but also a textbook example of how Hebrew poetry advances its storyline from abstract to concrete, from general to specific.[27] As in Psalm 65:7—"the roar of the waves, the tumult of the peoples"—the poet moves swiftly from water to warfare, yet this transition does not demythologize the presence of chaos. Rather, the nations are portrayed as one of the many concrete manifestations of the cosmic force that opposes God's world. They are chaotic, yet they are also flesh and blood, raging with their spears, bows, and chariots (v. 9).[28] This blurring of categories requires no resolution and neither must the raging armies be parsed as a metaphor for power. The worldview that informs this passage keeps the cosmic dimension alive and tells the story of human struggle in depth, portraying the threat at hand as a specific instance of the waters that shake the world.

This application of the language of storm and quake is accompanied by another abstract idea made concrete, namely, that of divine support. The material reality of army and city is met by Israel's God who "sends forth his voice," thundering in the typical fashion of an ancient storm deity who combats the chaotic forces to vindicate his reign.[29]

---

27 Barbara B. Kaiser refers to these parallel structures as a "cosmic slide" that moves "up and down between the concrete, everyday world and the realm of the divine;" *Reading Prophetic Poetry: Parallelism, Voice, and Design* (Eugene, OR: Pickwick, 2019), 30.

28 The "Enemy from the North" is a good illustration of this blend of this worldly and mythic language: "They seize bow and javelin, they are cruel and show no mercy; their sound is like the roaring sea, they ride on horses" (Jer 6:23); cf. David J. Reimer, "The 'Foe' and the 'North' in Jeremiah," *ZAW* 101 (1989): 223–232. See also Jeremiah 51:55: "The Lord is devastating Babylon, and stilling her great clamor. Their waves roar like mighty waters."

29 The phrase "giving voice" (נתן + קול) appears also in narratives of divine intervention (see e.g., Exod 9:23 or 1 Sam 12:18). For the use of storm imagery in the portrayal of God, see John Day, *Yahweh and the Gods and Goddesses of Canaan,* JSOTSup 265 (London: Sheffield Academic Press, 2002), which agrees

The voice of the Lord is above the waters,
*   the God of glory thunders,*
*   the Lord is above many waters. . . .*
The Lord sits enthroned over the flood,
*   the Lord is king forever!*

Psalm 29:3, 10

But the Lord is the true God,
*   he is the living God, king forever.*
From his wrath, the earth shakes,
*   nations cannot withstand his anger. . . .*
Maker of the earth with strength,
*   founder of the world with wisdom,*
*   he has stretched out the skies with insight.*
As he gives his voice,
*   there is a tumult of waters in the heavens,*
*   and the clouds rise from the ends of the earth.*

Jeremiah 10:10–12

The tremor of God's mighty roar and the descent of the creator into the created realm marks the climax of the ever-repeating narrative of the world. The poetic portrayal of boundary lines and battle speaks of a reality that is higher than words, that must be expressed as myth and symbolic language because mere descriptions cannot capture the cosmic truth that God is king, that the flood is pushed back, that life can go on. This dramatic interplay between creation and chaos is foundational—in the truest sense of the word—for the Bible's view of the world. It is God's good revelation,[30] both in its theological affirmation and in its language.

O Lord, God of hosts, who is mighty as you, O Lord?
*   Your faithfulness surrounds you.*
You rule the proud sea,
*   when its waves rise up, you quiet them.*

Psalm 89:8–9

---

that the nations in Psalm 46 are "an embodiment of the theme of Yahweh's conflict with the chaos waters;" 105.

30 "Myths can be narratives of revelation. They allow their human audience an opportunity to step into a deeper reality, one underlying its more mundane existence;" Smith, *Genesis 1*, 152.

Chaos Imagery and Articulating Anxieties

The compact vision of Psalm 46 moves with ease from chaos to combat, from raging waters to secure city. Clothing the earthly terrors in the garb of cosmic conflict, this poem is a superb example of the creativity with which Hebrew poetry applies the discourse of creation and chaos. This language can speak about political threats, stand as a symbol for hope, criticize social injustice, and express the anxieties of personal and communal struggles.

The story of the Bible is a "narrative of substitution" in which the same words are recycled to articulate ever-new moments of crisis and continuity.[31] This process extends beyond the Psalms and prophets and includes Jewish writing from the Second Temple Period as well as the New Testament, which speaks of Jesus trampling the waves and stilling the storm (Mark 4:37–41), and which portrays God's enemies as dragons (Rev 12–13).[32] To move from these texts to contemporary life is a leap, yet since the world has continued to be a restless place, these biblical poems can still be read as a meaningful expression of life.[33] The safe shoreline is still breached from time to time, the human condition is still marked by anxieties, and words are still needed to articulate the troubles and tensions of being human.

The idea that the Bible speaks to its readers when they struggle with fear, faith, and the future is not new. "Be strong and courageous" (Josh 1:9), "do not be anxious about anything" (Phil 4:6), "do not worry about tomorrow" (Matt 6:34)—calls like these permeate the scriptures and are routinely cited as encouragements, as is the opening statement of Psalm 46—"Therefore, we will not fear." The Bible is full of encouraging verses that are meaningful for many readers. But this is only one side of scripture's deep pool of words and not everybody will find these

---

31 Miller, "Dragon Myths," 56. "The OT tradition offers us a continual adaptation of myth over the course of a few hundred years in order to meet the changing needs of a dynamic faith community;" Alphonso Groenewald, "Mythology, Poetry and Theology," *HTS* 62 (2006): 920.

32 See, e.g., Andrew R. Angel, *Chaos and the Son of Man: The Hebrew Chaoskampf Tradition in the Period 515 BCE to 200 CE*, LSTS 60 (London: T&T Clark, 2006); Adela Yarbro Collins, *The Combat Myth in the Book of Revelation*, HBR 9 (Missoula, MI: Scholars Press, 1976).

33 Cf. Andy Angel, *Playing with Dragons: Living with Suffering and God* (Eugene, OR: Cascade Books, 2014).

waters warm and refreshing. Quoting these verses on their own can ask too much of suffering people as it suggests that there is a quick path to peace, an easy transition from hearing to heeding, from trembling to trusting, from chaos to calm.[34] Moreover, the persistence of anxious thoughts may be understood by the recipients and the speakers of such citation-comfort as a failure of faith.[35] But even a sensitive, contextual treatment of the Bible's call "do not be afraid" can skip too quickly past the actual experience of life's anxieties.

The impulse to point people who feel anxious to God and the Bible is understandable, but there is a good chance that this strategy will close the door for sufferers to give words to the vague threat that lingers over them. Searching the Bible for a language for articulating anxiety is troubled by the fact that Hebrew has no equivalent term for the English word "anxiety." In search of more precise terminology, David Firth has turned his attention to the Hebrew verb דאג (dāʾag). According to his analysis, "genuine faith and anxiety are not set against one another; rather, faith names anxiety within prayer that begins to face up to the situations that generate anxiety."[36] Instead of talking to those who suffer from anxiety about God, the Psalms portray anxiety talking to God

---

34 Edward T. Welch proposes a set of "biblical basics" that can alleviate anxious thoughts: "Remember that the Lord is near; Believe; Confess; Receive courage for today." Each of these basics comes with a list of passages and the invitation to meditate on them in order "to live fully today;" "Bible Basics for the Fearful and Anxious," *JBC* 34 (2020): 69–79. Along similar lines, B. G. White suggests that "our vocation as anxious believers is to see and appreciate the contradiction between our anxiety and the God who loves us. With the help of other techniques, and possibly medication, we battle anxiety simply by believing God;" "Fighting Anxiety with the Old Testament," *CT* (2020), 59.

35 Only a few authors will lay their finger directly into the wound: "Anxiety is basically a virulent form of self-centeredness, of looking towards ourselves, and not looking towards God.... Anxiety is one of the 'works of the flesh', although it is not specifically listed as such in the Bible;" Dick Whitehouse and Gwynn Devey, *Understanding Anxiety: Identifying the Causes and Discovering Freedom from Anxiety* (Aylesbury: Alpha, 1996), 107–108. But as Gregory Popcak has it, "To commit a sin, we have to *choose* to do what we know is wrong.... Emotions, including anxiety, can never be sinful;" "Anxious Hearts: A Faithful Look at a Frightening Emotion," *America* (Apr 2017), 22 (emphasis original).

36 "Anxiety: Some Perspectives from the Old Testament," in *The Bible and Mental Health: Towards a Biblical Theology of Mental Health*, ed. Christopher C. H. Cook and Isabelle Hamley (Norfolk: SCM Press, 2020), 99.

and elevate the need for communication, naming, and expression. In these first-person poems, "anxiety is not belittled, and neither are those experiencing it asked to ignore it."[37]

The dynamics of disclosure in Psalms 38, 94, and 139 are inspiring as they show that poetic language can bring anxiety from its dreadful depth to the surface and that the Bible envisions "no necessary contradiction between anxiety and faith"; rather, it promotes honest expressions of emotion and struggle.[38] Unfortunately, דאג is a rare word but this must not limit such language of anxiety to three texts. The Bible's poetry of chaos, combat, and calm can be utilized creatively as a script that continues the ever new application of waves and storm and that puts into words the anxieties that so often remain unspeakable.

Acknowledging Anxiety

A good place to start is to resist any quick solution and to simply and plainly consider the presence of chaos language in the Bible. Psalm 46 and its parallel passages confess that God is in control of the world but that the world is also beset with threat and trouble. Without diminishing all that Genesis 1 has to offer, the reality of chaos in texts like Psalms 46, 77, 89, and 104 might still today reflects the experience of human living better than the stable, predictable rhythms of the Bible's first chapter. The honest words about crumbling foundations and potential disasters can normalize anxious feelings about the world and justify them as a legitimate part of being human. The steady stream of turmoil that flows through the pages of scripture clashes with the belief that life should be without tides and torrents, that stability and safety are the norm. Seeing this chaotic current flow by with one's own eyes line by line and poem by poem reveals anxiety to be a universal companion of life.

The Bible's unabashed acceptance of chaos can allow its readers to embrace the floodwaters as a given. Such a posture is not to be confused with a pessimistic outlook on life, even less with a defeated or weak faith. To the contrary, the scenes of ongoing conflict show that anxieties and uncertainties should never be a cause for shame. Accepting the

---

37 Firth, "Anxiety," 103.
38 Firth, "Anxiety," 103.

shaky world for what it is instead is a sign of maturity and authenticity that knows of the waves of chaos even as it worships the creator. Pairing the confessions of God's power with the shaking mountains and giving voice to the raging waters along with God's thunder, Psalm 46 invites its readers to the complex, confounding, and comforting reality of being human.

The creative chaos of Hebrew poetry has been a meaningful description for countless generations who received it as an accurate reflection of reality. As readers come today to these ancient texts, however, their view of the world may stand in the way of hearing the waves toss with all their force. The confidence in scientific progress and the human command over the natural elements may quench the voice of these poems just as much as a faith posture that covers up the reality of anxiety under a blanket of Bible verses. Challenging both outlooks on life, the loud voice of chaos in the Bible is in itself chaotic in that it breaks down the facade of a tame and stable world and announces instead a universe in which tension is the norm. For the uncertain and overwhelmed context of postmodernity, such a view of the world may speak louder than any explanations and tales of mastery.

Life is still lived at the shoreline, walls and dams and beliefs are still shattered by the sudden upsurge of destruction, the water level still rises to the neck, and breath and life are still crushed by a world come undone. In a culture where some people experience a loss of meaning and, paradoxically, are also overloaded with meaning, the cosmological narrative of biblical poetry may be especially suited to become one's own story and language.[39] To see that this particular worldview lies at the heart of the biblical narrative can help remove the stigma of anxiety, put text and readers in conversation, and sketch the experience of living at the shoreline in accurate contours. Psalm 46 and its many parallel passages invite their readers to see the world anew and, in good faith, to embrace their shaky stance on its ever-shifting, restless ground.

---

39 "Human beings. . . cannot live with ambiguity and uncertainty alone. We need clearly defined points of reference, meaningful narratives in the form of value systems and belief frameworks;" Kirk A. Bingaman, "Caring for the Anxious: A Postmodern Approach," *JSMH* 10 (2007), 14.

Articulating Anxiety

Psalm 46 strives to open its reader's eyes to the reality of anxiety and it also labors to open their mouth to articulate the experience of anxiety. The imagery of this poem has enjoyed a long and lively history of interpretation, including, for instance, allegorical readings that saw the sea as demons or read the mountains as Christ who journeys across the sea toward the Gentiles.[40] These applications, once again, testify to the flexible and symbolic nature of the chaotic waters. There is no end to this current, no limits to the use of these words for the anxieties that humans face.[41] The language of Psalm 46 continues to speak, and contemporary readers may find in its lines the words and worldview for speaking about their own experience.

The need for such a language is directly related to one of the key challenges of anxiety, namely, its lack of a clearly defined object. To the extent that feelings of threat and restlessness cannot be specified, they can easily grow out of proportion. The basic anxieties that are part of the human condition can morph into a larger-than-life dread that casts a shadow even on the solid ground and the sunny days. This process, which psychologist Albert Ellis describes as "exaggerated thinking" and as "awfulizing and terribilizing," requires a counter-movement that restores perspective and establishes limits.[42] Toward this end, the image of the sea may become a profound literary resource for lending contour to this shapelessness, for adding color to the gray experience of anxiety. The quaking earth of verses 2–3, for instance, is a tangible expression of the loss of control and the fear of destruction. The shaking mountains can stand for the uncanny force of anxiety, the anticipation that the world will come undone, and the feeling of

---

40 Cf. Andrew T. Abernethy, "'Mountains Moved into the Sea:' The Western Reception of Psalm 46:1 and 3 [45:1 and 3 LXX] from the Septuagint to Luther," *JTS* 70 (2019): 523–545.

41 "It is in the nature of myth that it knows no boundaries, for the power of its symbolic and generally ideological content will tend to have carried weight wherever it went;" N. Wyatt, "The Mythic Mind," in *The Mythic Mind: Essays on Cosmology and Religion in Ugaritic and Old Testament Literature* (Bibleworld; London: Equinox, 2005), 170.

42 *How to Control Your Anxiety before It Controls You* (London: Robinson, 2019), 42.

inevitable doom. The sound of the roaring and foaming waters can be heard as the onslaught of threat and danger, as the overwhelming noise and distraction of anxious thoughts, as the periodic ebb and flow of worry. The cosmic collapse and narrowing of living space to which all of this amounts make a feasible expression for anxiety's complex bodily reactions, especially those that affect breathing and movement.[43] Here lies the therapeutic potential of this poetry: open language that each and every listener hears on their own, open images that resonate with a range of experiences, open words that can construct a literary dam to ward off the waters that know no limits.

From the uncontrollable forces of ebb and flow to the endless expanse of the horizon, from its sheer magnitude to its lack of any real boundaries, the Hebrew poets show how familiar features of the sea can speak meaningful words for the experience of the anxieties of life. But they also inspire their readers to plumb the depth of this imagery in their own creative ways. The blurred line between fear and anxiety, for instance, may be likened to the various oceanic stages that stretch from the surface to the abyss. In the ocean's upper regions, diffused sunlight still allows for some orientation. Near the shore, a quick ascent will permit a look at the firm ground outside of the waters. Yet, from the so-called Midnight Zone downward, complete darkness eliminates all sense of direction and clarity.

The Hebrew poets assure their readers that God will help them in their anxieties, yet they do not envision passivity. Communal voices, poetic expression, and the power of imagination all inspire action through language. Giving names to troubles and giving words to experience bestow a dose of agency to everyone who stands helpless at the shore. This is not to be confused with impatience, even less with taking matters into one's own hands. To the contrary, if such language can curb the chaotic waters, then all who speak it join God in the creative exercise of re-establishing boundaries within which life can flourish. Following in the footsteps of the psalmists and prophets, the reality

---

43 The image of a compressed universe resonates with the widely shared associations of anxiety: "Limited freedom of movement, that is, a tightness, is in many languages (lat. *anxietas, angustia*, engl. *anxiety*, frz. *angoisse*) the semantic core of fear. In situations of fear, all feeling of expanse and openness is eliminated;" Janowski, *Anthropologie*, 170 (my translation).

and the specific experience of anxieties may be articulated with reference to the water's sheer force ("I am washed away"; "I am swept off my feet"), the torrent's confusion and disorientation ("I am adrift"; "I am being pulled under"), or the sea's rage and swell ("I am powerless"; "It is too much for me"). Looking with the Hebrew poets out to sea, their words can express and inspire expressions for what otherwise might escape definition and throb on without a name. Here are words for all who suffer alone on their small islands, whose "collapse is as vast as the sea" (Lam 2:13), who need a language that neither covers their anxieties nor drowns their faith.

Finding Calm amid Chaos

The poetry of sea and waves allows readers of the Bible to say aloud what is happening under the surface of their lives, granting them a gift of articulation that can be inspiring, cathartic, and liberating. But the poetic dynamics of Psalm 46 are more than a model for emotional literacy. As the poem travels from the raging sea to the glad rivers, from the shaking ground to the stable city, and from the clamor of crumbling mountains to the voice of God, this compact composition articulates a proactive response to the complexity of anxiety. The chaos of the world will not go away; the tension of everyday living will not be laid to rest. But there are ways for living with, despite, and in the face of chaos, ways for limiting the tidal pull of exaggerated thinking. Psalm 46 does not promise an enduring equilibrium or a change of heart and mind, yet its imaginative narrative can create a stable resting place amid the frantic floods.

Imagining Tranquility

The palette of Hebrew poetry is fully employed in Psalm 46, interweaving repetition and variation, mixing sounds and scenes, shaping symbols and imagery. This latter dimension is foundational for the language of chaos, but it also stands at the heart of the poem's depiction of calm, joy, and stability. At the beginning of the middle section (vv. 4–5), the narrative of Psalm 46 arrives at the city of God, which is identified as a concrete expression of divine presence ("God is in her midst"). Far from merely providing a contrast to the arrogant waters, the joyful streams that "gladden the city of God" have their own place in the cosmic narrative of unrest, combat, and calm.

The parallel structures of verse 4 qualify the city as God's "holy dwelling," a description that moves the focus from walls and gates inwards to the temple. God's presence at the center of the sanctuary, the "holy of holies" (Exod 40:35; 1 Kgs 8:11), narrows the perspective of the poem yet further to the one point on the map where heaven and earth meet, where God dwells in the midst of humanity.[44] Ancient texts typically depict divine dwelling places as the center of all things and as a source of refreshing waters (e.g., Gen 2:10–14; Ps 65:9; Ezek 47) that overflow from the temple outward, filling the community, the city, and all the earth.

> Holy, holy holy, Lord of hosts!
> The whole earth is full of his glory!
>
> Isaiah 6:3

> For the earth is full of the knowledge of the Lord,
> like the waters that cover the sea.
>
> Isaiah 11:9

> Thus says the Lord:
> This is Jerusalem,
> in the midst of the nations I have set her,
> and lands are all around her.
>
> Ezekiel 5:5

Thinking of God's city as the "navel of the world" (Ezek 38:12) endows the particular image in Psalm 46 with a stability that is beyond any mundane, earthly quality.[45] The specific construction of stone and wood

---

44 Cf. L. Michael Morales, *Who Shall Ascend the Mountain of the Lord? A Biblical Theology of the Book of Leviticus*, NSBT 37 (Downers Grove, IL: InterVarsity Press, 2015), 52.

45 For the translation of Ezek 38:12, see Levenson, *Sinai and Zion*: "Geography is often, to the 'primitive' mind, simply the physical representation of

is a symbol for goodness, protection, and assurance that stands against the tumultuous, destructive waters of verses 2–3. That the relationship between chaotic sea and glorious city is not explicitly spelled out leaves a peculiar tension in the text. The waters rage at the shoreline of life; the mountains that hold up the heavens shake, yet here at the center of it all stands this city that "shall not be shaken."

This tacit coexistence of unrest and stability, of chaos and calm, resonates well with the dynamic worldview of the poem and reflects the fluid interaction of creation and order. There are the waters; there is the city. Inasmuch as the help of God is specifically anchored in an urban space, the city is not identified by name. Other poems, such as Psalms 2, 48, 76, 84, 87, and 122, speak explicitly of Jerusalem or Zion, yet the perspective of Psalm 46 suggests an international orientation. With five mentions of ארץ ('ereṣ) in the poem, the focus rests not just on Israelite territory but also more generally on the "land" or the "earth." The tension of stability is not restricted to one people or one political power, but is a universal reality that can be observed wherever the shoreline is crossed and wherever God is present.

This broad canvas of symbolic language and anonymous city poses an invitation for the imagination. Evoking the contours of everyday structures is a common therapeutic reflex in the Bible, leading its readers to conjure up before their inner eye, for instance, "a strong tower" (Ps 61:3; Prov 18:10) or a "rock and fortress" (Ps 31:3; Joel 3:16).[46] The open descriptions of these places and buildings prompt both ancient and contemporary audiences to fill in the missing details, to utilize their imagination, and to create in this encounter their own symbol of calm. This invitation extends both to the anxious feelings ("the miry bog") and to the renewed stand on solid ground.

---

transcendent reality. What is most important must stand at the center, as any artist knows;" 115.

46 Archie Smith Jr. provides some intriguing reflections in "Rock: An Unlikely Metaphor for Spirituality, Family Therapy, Mental Health and Illness," *Pastoral Psychol* 66 (2017): 743–756. As J. Gordon McConville notes, "the Psalms rest on the tacit premise that linguistic acts change things.... The act of language, in composition and use, is thus a component of the Psalms' capacity to transform;" *Being Human in God's World: An Old Testament Theology of Humanity* (Grand Rapids, MI: BakerAcademic, 2016), 200.

I desperately waited for the Lord.
   He reached out to me and heard my cry.
He raised me up from the pit of destruction, from the miry bog,
   and put my feet on rock, made firm my step.

                                            Psalm 40:1–2

Such images and the interactive dimension of the text can weaken the ruinous exaggeration of anxiety and perhaps even provide an anchor that allows for the focus that is washed away by the waves.[47] Even if the exercise of imagination might not push the ocean of worry behind its boundary line, it might just discover an island of calm that stands, like the city in Psalm 46, firmly amid the rolling waters.

Hearing God's Voice

Psalm 46 opens with a generic description of divine attributes to which the second half of the poem adds sharper contours. Shifting from portrayal to performance, God's presence is realized in the support of the city; God's power is put into action as the mighty divine voice thunders against the chaotic armies. This movement from general to specific infuses the doxology of verse 1 with drama and depth and involves all participants of the poem. The recipients of Psalm 46 no longer just hear about God's help but they see it at work. They hear the roar from on high. They witness God's power in the world. These sights and sounds feed into yet another transition, namely, the shift from descriptions to direct address in verses 8–9.

Come, look at the mighty works of the Lord!
   For he wrought desolations in the world,
bringing wars to an end everywhere.
   Bows he breaks, spears he shatters,
   chariots he burns with fire.

For the first time, the voice of the poem speaks directly to the audience. The imperatives "come!" and "look!" are plural forms that prompt their

---

47   "Anxious persons often report an inability to recall events of peace or success. Even when they do, they often struggle to hold onto those memories to calm or reassure themselves. . . . The brain is constructing too many alternatives or scenarios unsupported by reason or memory;" Hogue, "Fear, Faith, and the Human Brain," 667.

hearers to see with their own eyes the work of God.[48] That this work is defined as "desolations" may at first sight be alarming, yet the focus rests here not on an ecological crisis, but on God's crushing of military equipment, on God's breaking, shattering, and burning of human tools of terror. As the divine warrior is literally "laying to rest" (מַשְׁבִּית; cf. Gen 2:3) the onslaught of chaos, the cosmos can operate in peace and order, at least for a while. Founded on the story of opposition and order in verses 1–9, the poem gears up for its climax and conclusion. The statement in verse 10, which is likely the best-known part of Psalm 46, presents yet another shift, namely, a transition from invitation ("Come, look!") to expectation.

> *Let go, know that I am God!*
> *I will be exalted among the nations,*
> *I will be exalted in the earth.*

With a poem full of the noise of waters and armies, it is reassuring to hear that God has the final word. It is quite common for the divine voice to appear in the Psalms, especially toward the end of poems where it typically calls its hearers to draw out the consequences of the preceding material.[49] In the case of Psalm 46, this mode of application is complicated because it is not clear to whom God is speaking. Set in parallel with the imperatives of verse 8, the verbs in verse 10 ("Let go, know!") are plural forms and could address either the defeated nations or, as in verse 8, the universal audience of the poem.

Such ambiguity is a hallmark of the Bible's poetry, and the polyphony of speakers and hearers often is a fruitful place for reflections on inclusion, participation, and responsibility.[50] A closer look at the word pair in verse 10 suggests initially that the armies who oppose the calm city are the target of God's call. Contrary to the contemplative

---

48 A similar appeal to the senses appears in the neighbor poem Psalm 48—"As we have heard, thus we have seen, in the city of the Lord of hosts, in the city of our God"—that culminates in a tour of God's city. "Those who came to the city are invited to take in its entire imposing circumference, to 'count' its towers deployed in space so that they may 'recount' God's greatness for all future time;" Alter, *Art of Biblical Poetry*, 124.

49 See, e.g., Pss 2:6; 12:5; 50:7–23; 75:2–4; 81:6–14; 95:8–11; 132:11–18; cf. Jacobson, *Direct Discourse in the Hebrew Psalter*, 82–132.

50 For such reflections, see my "Speaker Ambiguity in the Psalms."

translations that are commonly offered (e.g., "Be still;" ESV, NRSV, NIV, NLT), the first verb speaks of submission and surrender, of accepting defeat and limitation.[51] To find a divine declaration of victory at the end of Psalm 46 makes for a meaningful conclusion to the poem's narrative, but the call to "let go" can also speak to the community who has come through the waters. Since God is the only active agent in the poem, it is possible to conclude with commentator Ellen Charry that verse 10 "counsels Israel to desist from military action and to wait for God to deal with its foreign enemies."[52] However, God's voice can also speak to the anxieties of life.

Judson Brewer, professor in psychiatry at Brown University, has taken a close look at the prevalent "'just stop it' mentality," which assumes that reasoning and rational thinking may be an effective strategy for breaking the absolutizing tendencies of anxiety.[53] But since "even low levels of persistent anxiety make it hard for us to think,"[54] this strategy is bound to clash with the protective impulses of the human nervous systems. Brewer instead promotes a better understanding of anxiety itself, especially in terms of its underlying motivations.

> Worrying may not feel rewarding—indeed, it's often downright unpleasant. But to our brains, it can serve as a suitable reward because it not only feels as if we're doing something—making plans, uncovering solutions—it also distracts us from the more distressing feeling of anxiety and thus offers the illusion of control.[55]

---

51 For other uses of the verb רפה (*rāpah*), see Deut 9:14; Judg 11:37; 1 Sam 15:16; Ps 37:8. The JPS translation is right on target: "Desist! Realize that I am God! I dominate the nations; I dominate the earth." Cf. Brown, *Seeing the Psalms*: "The command reflects a new reality, an equilibrium established by God's dramatic intervention in which the weapons of war are silenced and chaos subsides;" 116.

52 Ellen T. Charry, *Psalms 1–50: Sighs and Songs of Israel,* BTCB (Grand Rapids, MI: Brazos Press, 2015), 237. Reading Psalm 46 or hearing Luther's hymn as a battle cry misses the mark entirely: the weapons are broken in the poem and Luther's records show that he saw Psalm 46 "as a hymn of comfort;" Paul Westermeyer, "'A Mighty Fortress' and Psalm 46 in Context," *Word & World* 34 (2014), 401.

53 "We've Got Anxiety All Wrong," *PT* (July/August 2021), 31.

54 Brewer, "Anxiety All Wrong," 32.

55 Brewer, "Anxiety All Wrong," 33.

Excessive episodes of anxiety can have a wide and complex range of triggers and neither Brewer nor Psalm 46 blame their addressees for their troubles. Still, the divine voice in verse 10 raises the question of human limitation. As the Bible univocally assigns the ultimate responsibility for cosmic stability to God, the call to "let go" can be heard as a reminder that even the best efforts will not obliterate the raging waters. The elevation of God's superior stance in no way undermines the efficacy of human articulation and imagination. There is much that humans can say and do to find calm amid the waters, but the final word, in this poem and in this restless world, belongs to God.

The Calm of Community
The image of God's city and the resonance of God's voice can provide focus amid the turbulence of anxiety, yet both elements also break through the isolation that the anxieties of life can breed. In this poetic story, there is a place where a community dwells safely with God at their center; there is a voice that addresses each person directly; there is a circle of human beings who exclaim together "we will not fear" without belittling the shaking ground on which they stand. As a subtext to the noise of water and war, the shifts of scenery, the drama of combat, the city, the weapons, and the divine voice, this communal voice runs through all of Psalm 46. The opening confessions determine the pitch at which the chorus sings in verses 7 and 11.

> *The Lord of hosts is with us,*
> *the God of Jacob is a fortress for us!*

This statement is first proclaimed in response to God's defense of the city and, finally, in response to God's voice. The final word about chaos and creation belongs to God, yet Psalm 46 ends with the reminder that the struggle, articulation, and newfound posture toward the waves is a community project. To think about the human condition in terms of "us" and "we" is a natural inclination in the Psalms and this chorus of voices may be particularly important in a social environment where the cultivation of self is regarded as the highest ideal. The anxieties of life, of course, are expressed differently for anyone and the images of calm will be very personal constructions.

Rather than seeing a tension between each person's story and the story of the community, the Psalms suggest that they can be heard together. The individual lament of Psalms 42 and 43, for instance, shares many elements with the communal lament in Psalm 44.[56] Such coexistence of voices avoids a generic one-size-fits-all approach to life and it embeds each personal story in a larger narrative. That both are present and that both speak of trouble and comfort are healthy reminders that anxiety is "a deeply personal and existential reality, triggered to varying degrees, individually and collectively."[57] For communities that are aware of this complexity, the sharing of anxieties may become a haven of rest for speakers and hearers alike. Each on their own, the articulation of the particular waves that loom at one's personal horizon may put into words what otherwise may grow into a flood. In turn, such honesty can proclaim the liberating truth that each person shares in the universal narrative of chaos and calm, that everyone wanders through life on the same fragile shoreline.

Along with the images and narratives that the biblical writers have created, the communities who receive them can become places of calm.[58] The voice of the people in Psalm 46 is a hopeful sound, yet it remains to be heard in unison with the divine voice of verse 10. As David Firth noted in his study of the Psalms, the ebb and flow of lament and praise mean that in these texts "triumphalism is also marginalized because although God's reign is rightly celebrated, it is acknowledged that this reign is experienced only imperfectly in our world."[59] The potential for finding calm amid chaos depends to a large extent to a community's acceptance of this ingrained tension of life. Neither tragedy nor triumph, neither relentless rain nor sunny days without end, the human

---

56 See, e.g., references to God's command (צוה in Pss 42:8 and 44:4), presence (פניך in 42:5 and 44:3), and faithful care (חסד in 42:8 and 44:26).

57 Bingaman, "New Anxiety," 668.

58 "Our biblical narratives, the histories of our religious communities at their best, and our theological imaginations offer images that do indeed move in the direction of offering peace and reassurance, acceptance, and reconciliation. Stories of calmed storms, warm embraces of returning children, and the forgiveness of sin offer images of peace in place of the demands and threats of economic downturn, shattered families, and predatory institutions;" Hogue, "Fear, Faith, and the Human Brain," 668–669.

59 "Anxiety," 103–104.

experience in this unstable world is complex and ripe with questions and uncertainties. Psalm 46 and its many parallel poetic scenes of chaos and combat do not expect their readers to arrive at a place of permanent peace. To the contrary, they embrace each person who is troubled by their anxieties within the wider community of humanity and offer a language with which they can live in the world in which they find themselves.

Such poetry is a gift for living each chapter of life, but there is also an end to the story. Without losing sight of the challenges of being human, these poetic expressions and the mighty myth of God "who gives the sun as the light by day, the order of moon and stars as light by night, who shakes the sea and its waves roar" (Jer 31:35) provide the same language from which the biblical authors craft a perspective that reaches far, far beyond the horizon. Psalm 46 is but one scene in a much bigger story that will reach its conclusion when God will "kill the dragon that is in the sea" (Isa 27:1) or, as the New Testament has it, when "the sea is no more" and a new city opens its gates (Rev 21:1–2). Communities who anchor their shaky boats in these words can brave the rough sea of life together.

CHAPTER 2

The Lonely Bird on the Roof
Psalm 102 and the Reality of Life Alone

> *Full of tragedy,*
>> *my life reaches down to Sheol.*
> *Numbered with those who descend to the pit,*
>> *like a person without strength.*
> *Let go amongst the dead,*
>> *like the slain laying in the grave*
> *whom you remember no more,*
>> *who are cut off from your hand. . . .*
> *You have isolated me from my friends,*
>> *made me a horror to them.*
> *Shut in,*
>> *I do not go out.*

Psalm 88:3–5, 8

Wading through thick fog, each step is shrouded in gray silence. The world sits so small, all sounds muffled, all color soft and shy. Every so often life's walk at the shoreline steps into the bliss of perfect privacy, into a precious moment when the waves can no longer be seen and the land of worry and weakness is far away. Each solitary walk at the foggy sea whispers of freedom, yet these promises are usually beautiful only for a while. The fog will dissolve, the horizon will broaden again, color and company will return. For all the warmth that its velvety mantle can offer, life alone would soon grow cold without the restoration of the self to its surroundings. Being alone can be a welcome retreat amid the chaos of the calendar, but it can also feel like floating forlorn in the cold ocean or walking through a deep forest, lost for paths and pals. Loneliness is a complex matter. But whether it is embraced or feared, sought or avoided, it is a quiet companion of every human being. For even when the fog is gone and other swimmers emerge on the shore, the haze of loneliness never quite leaves.

As much as the human condition is negotiated on the thin line between calm and chaos, it also hangs in the balance of individual and social experiences. The poetic lines from Psalm 88 are all spoken from a first-person perspective that is full of agency, rich in articulation, and deep with awareness, but still the well-being of the speaker is tied up entirely with their relationship to other people and to God. The blend of determination and dependence is representative of the human experience at large. Yet in this ancient text both parts of the equation add up to a negative sum: friendless, God-forsaken, and sated with tragedy, the speaker of these lines disappears behind locked doors. The comparison with the "slain laying in the grave" is no mere figure of speech. Left "without strength" and kept from God's saving hand, the isolated life of Psalm 88 truly is touched by death invading life. The fusion of social, existential, and spiritual aspects points to a profound difference between ancient and contemporary worlds, yet the struggle with loneliness is no less an issue for human well-being today. Prolonged periods of loneliness and the pain of isolation that Psalm 88 articulates can still be matters of life and death, but both the ancient poet and the modern psychologist know that life alone is not only ever an extreme or even a problem.

From the loneliness of the first human in Genesis 2 to the isolation of prophets and psalmists, the Old Testament embraces loneliness as an essential part of the human condition that stretches across a full range of experiences. The reality of life alone is not the yoke of a few, nor is it resolved by human community. The Hebrew poets dispel all foggy misconceptions about lone living with their honest words and especially with the personal images of isolation that they place before their readers. Lady Jerusalem, the abandoned city who weeps while scanning the vast, empty horizon (Lam 1); Jeremiah, the God-forsaken prophet (Jer 15); a small bird that perches alone on a roof (Ps 102)—loneliness is given a face that is public yet flexible, that is raw yet reassuring.

When the fog lifts and life is still full of lonely days, the Hebrew poets point their readers to that small winged friend and invite them to listen to its solo song about speech, survival, and solitude. The melody of the lonely bird can be dissonant because it knows that life can play more themes than any solo performance can cover. But its trills and triplets can also lift the head of every lonely soul who stops and listens, curious to find its own voice and its own place amid the sea of society.

Life Alone

For all its universal reach, the experience of loneliness continues to be a difficult topic of conversation. The terminology is simply too slippery, the associations too relative. Being alone may be a welcome condition or just the status quo or thoroughly unpleasant. Someone may be alone because they have been abandoned, yet someone else may have abandoned a situation to be alone. In any of these scenarios, being alone is not necessarily the same as being lonely and the line between the two is not easily defined. Even solitude, which is usually a positive term, can become unpleasant; isolation, which is usually a negative term, may be actively sought out in the manner of Jeremiah who "sat alone" rather than in the "company of scoffers" (Jer 15:17; cf. Ps 1:1). Perhaps the real struggle with defining loneliness does not lie in the ambiguity of these words but in its pervasive presence in everyday life circumstances.[1] Loneliness is not just an extreme experience brought on by bereavement, illness, deficient social services, or imprisonment. It surfaces in every age group; in routine transitions like moving cities, going to college, or changing gyms; in marriages and churches; in disagreements at work or in feeling misunderstood by a neighbor. A normal part of life, the faces of loneliness are legion and not all of them are languishing.

As a recognition of the relative quality of life alone, psychological researchers define loneliness as perceived social isolation, as the negative experience of having less social interaction than desired.[2] This emphasis on the subjective nature of loneliness is a vital element in the

---

1   John G. McCraw detects at least ten different forms of loneliness, such as metaphysical, communicative, ethical, emotional, and cosmic; "God and the Problem of Loneliness," *RelStud* 28 (1992): 319–346.

2   See, e.g., John Cacioppo, James. H. Fowler, and Nicholas A. Christakis, "Alone in the Crowd: The Structure and Spread of Loneliness in a Large Social Network," *J Pers Soc Psychol* 97 (2009): 977–991.

interpretation of current sociological and demographic trends. The shift toward solo culture is a complex phenomenon that vibrates under the tidal pull of urbanization, the rise of digitalization, and the shifting sand of social norms.[3] Some people may choose to live alone for financial reasons or because of disappointments with traditional family life. Others live on their own because of family breakdowns or simply because they are new to a city.

A deep pool of personal stories and preferences simmers underneath the surface of statistics, swirling up often enough to wash over any undue conflation between life alone and loneliness. More specific surveys may not accommodate these complexities either, yet they capture the growing wave of loneliness with a sharper lens. In 2010, a study reported that more than a third of Americans aged 45 and older felt lonely.[4] In 2017, the Jo Cox Commission on Loneliness observed that more than 14 percent of Britain's population "often or always feel lonely." This segment of society is largely made up of elderly, unemployed, disabled, or migrant individuals, yet the UK Office for National Statistics also shows that 16- to 24-year-olds report feeling lonely more often than people aged 65 to 74.[5]

---

3 See, e.g., David Riesman with Nathan Glazer and Reuel Denney, *The Lonely Crowd: A Study of the Changing American Character*, abr. and rev. (New Haven, CT: Yale University Press, 2020). The 2021 UK census concluded that "the proportion of one-person households ranged from 25.8% in London to 36.0% in Scotland;" "Bulletin: Families and Households in the UK: 2021," https://www.ons.gov.uk/peoplepopulationandcommunity/birthsdeathsandmarriages/families/bulletins/familiesandhouseholds/2021). In Japan, single households make up 35 percent of society, marking a 10 percent increase from 1995 to 2015; cf. Bryan Lufkin, "The Rise of Japan's 'Super Solo' Culture," https://www.bbc.com/worklife/article/20200113-the-rise-of-japans-super-solo-culture.

4 G. Oscar Anderson, "Loneliness among Adults," https://www.aarp.org/research/topics/life/info-2014/loneliness_2010.html.

5 "Loneliness—What Characteristics and Circumstances Are Associated with Feeling Lonely?" https://www.ons.gov.uk/peoplepopulationandcommunity/wellbeing/articles/lonelinesswhatcharacteristicsandcircumstancesareassociatedwithfeelinglonely/2018-04-10#which-factors-independently-affect-loneliness. In the American context, Theresa O'Keefe speaks of a "systemic isolation" that results from higher social mobility and the decline of religious association and cross-generational living; "Growing up Alone: The New Normal of Isolation in Adolescence," *JYM* 13 (2014): 63–84. See also Ami Rokach, "Loneliness and Life: From Beginning to End," in *Psychology of Loneliness*, ed. Sarah J. Bevinn (New York: Nove Science, 2011), 69–89.

While lonely people stand, paradoxically, everywhere along the shoreline of life, their look at the horizon will differ immensely. Diagnostic questionnaires like the UCLA Scale of Loneliness are helpful for gauging the regularity of feeling lonely. Yet by their generic nature they are just as unable to take aboard the personal experience of loneliness as the statistics of demographic data. These limitations, however, well up from the essence of loneliness itself. Embarking on a psychological inquiry of life alone, Frieda Fromm-Reichmann reflected in 1959 on the "extremely uncanny experience" of loneliness.

> People who are in the grip of severe degrees of loneliness cannot talk about it. . . . This frightened secretiveness and lack of communication about loneliness . . . produces the sad conviction that nobody else has experienced or ever will sense what they are experiencing. . . . Most people who are alone try to keep the mere fact of their aloneness a secret from others, and even try to keep its conscious realization hidden from themselves.[6]

Joining forces with the diffuse and shapeless torrents of anxiety, the fog of loneliness hushes conversation and muffles connection. This lack of words can be isolating and costly. For instance, psychologists Louise Hawkley and John Cacioppo link social isolation to anxiety and hypervigilance: "lonely individuals see the social world as a more threatening place."[7] Other researchers have connected prolonged loneliness to a decline in cognitive functioning, to cardiovascular and inflammatory diseases, and to depression and sleep deprivation.[8] These observations

---

6 "Loneliness," *Psychiatry* 22 (1959), 5–6. The unspeakable nature of loneliness is not just a problem that faces psychologists but, as Olivia Laing points out, also a struggle for those moving cities: "Loneliness is difficult to confess; difficult to categorise;" *The Lonely City: Adventures in the Art of Being Alone* (Edinburgh: Canongate Books, 2016), 2.
7 "Loneliness Matters: A Theoretical and Empirical Review of Consequences and Mechanisms," *Ann Beh* 40 (2010): 218–227.
8 See, e.g., Adriano Winterton, et al., "Associations of Loneliness and Social Isolation with Cardiovascular and Metabolic Health: A Systematic Review and Meta-Analysis Protocol," *SysRev* 9 (2020): 1–7; Lara E. Caballero, et al., "Are Loneliness and Social Isolation Associated with Cognitive Decline?" *Int J Geriatr Psy* 34 (2019): 1613–1622. According to the Mental Health Foundation, 53 percent of 18- to 34 year-olds in the UK report having felt depressed because of loneliness and 57 percent of the general population report that they

show that the recent attention to loneliness is born out of a real challenge, that there can be a connection between being alone and being
unwell.

Loneliness is not contagious, neither does it explain each and every
problem.[9] A vast number of individuals simply enjoy extended periods
of alone-time and many teenagers and seniors thrive on their own. For
those who would enjoy more companionship than they currently have,
however, the challenges abound. Making friends or finding a partner is
not something that can be willed into existence. Yet underneath these
practical considerations lingers the unspoken and unspeakable grip
of loneliness itself. Misconceptions of life alone, a lack of expression,
feeling abnormal or weak, suffering from undue comparisons—a more
robust view of loneliness can be a starting point for alleviating these
social aches.

Pulling their listeners inland from the murky, misty sea, the ancient
poets of the Old Testament normalize the feeling of being forlorn. Their
words cut through the ropes of stigma and shame that entangle the
heart. They cut through these knots and tether loneliness to the broad
harbor of the human condition that is deep with expressions and sturdy
amid the storm. Because as long as there is no language for feeling
lonely, life on the island will only be more lonesome.

Loneliness and the Bible

As Fromm-Reichmann put it, culling and cultivating that kind of language is no small task. The secret and unspeakable nature of loneliness is, however, but one side of the problem. The constant spotlight
on romantic relationships and the cultural impulse to tie self-worth

---

isolate themselves from others when suffering from depression or anxiety; cf.
J. Griffin, *The Lonely Society?* (London: Mental Health Foundation, 2010), 21.

9   For a balanced view on loneliness, see Janet Batsleer and James Duggan, *Young
and Lonely: The Social Conditions of Loneliness* (Bristol: Policy Press, 2021),
14–21. John Swinton points to the autobiography of Monica Coleman, who
relates her struggle with a psychiatrist who "explained Monica's sadness via
a social model, as if Monica were somehow incapable of seeing the difference
between loneliness and the deep darkness she was going through;" *Finding
Jesus in the Storm*, 67. Cf. Monica Coleman, *Bipolar Faith: A Black Woman's
Journey with Depression and Faith* (Minneapolis, MN: Fortress Press, 2016).

to social status can aggravate the pain of lonely people. Not immune to either of these currents, the church navigates its own place in this social landscape. All honest efforts of inclusion and integration notwithstanding, the elevation of marriage, parenthood, and community in Christian living can easily be heard as a dismissal of congregants who prefer to spend more time alone than with others. It may also deepen the shame of those who feel lonely amid, or because of, their congregation.

Such feelings can, however, arise also in response to the biblical promises of a God who does not forget anyone (Isa 49:15), a savior who will be "with you always" (Matt 28:20), and a body of believers where everyone belongs (1 Cor 12:12–26). If loneliness prevails, if it lingers secretly under the outward appearance of a satisfying social life, the constant diet of these verses will likely make lonely worshippers lonelier and their sense of failure deeper. Since the human condition demands a more nuanced and caring language of life alone, it is encouraging to find that the Hebrew poets are aware and articulate enough to meet this need with imagery and words that ring as true as all their liturgies of life together.

The Sole Problem of Genesis 2

An unfortunate upshot of the boundless debates around creation and gender, the portrayal of the human condition in Genesis 1–2 is only rarely seen in its sweeping breadth. These spotlights may illumine central aspects, such as the steady chorus "good, good, very good!" of God's mastery of creation or God's gracious gift of life, land, and law to humanity. But they leave other parts out of the limelight, even if these occupy large proportions of the text. Keeping too close an eye on the goodness of Genesis 1, for instance, can overshadow the fact that about a third of Genesis 2 is devoted to something that is "not good" in the world: Adam is alone (Gen 2:18).[10] However the narrative in Genesis 3

---

10 Whether Genesis 2 is read as a complementary version of day 6 or whether the similarities and differences are left standing as they are (e.g., in Genesis 2, human life appears on earth before the plants), Genesis 1–2 is a prime example of the Bible's parataxis, of offering two takes on the same topic—often one poetic and one prosaic one—without harmonization. The breadth of viewpoints that can exist even within one particular theological community bears

is read, the archetypal crisis of the human species is not pride or selfish-
ness, but being alone in the world.

Adam–Alone is a catastrophe amid the ordered cosmos that calls
for immediate divine attention. One verse suffices for Adam becoming
a "living being" (Gen 2:7), two for the fateful tree of knowledge (Gen
2:16–17), yet the writer commits a total of seven verses to God's remedy
of Adam's condition. The entire animal kingdom is surveyed, a slow
and enormous parade that yields no suitable match but surely "allows
us to feel the man's loneliness."[11] Taking matters a step further, God
performs a drastic surgery, building Eve from the raw matter of Adam's
flank.[12] With a sigh of relief ("at last!"), Genesis 2 ends happily ever after
with Adam's poem about Eve. These are the first human words in God's
world, yet instead of praising the creator, these lines celebrate human
companionship.

In Jewish and Christian tradition, the canonical primacy of Genesis
1–2 imbues this text with a foundational significance for how humans see
themselves, each other, and God in this world. These two chapters offer
a generous vision of humanity's place, privilege, and power; the sacred
task of world-keeping (Gen 2:15); the splendor of divine gifts; and the
mythology of marriage. Adam's loneliness likewise speaks to the deep
realities of creature and creator, yet it also attends to the down-to-earth
conditions of its ancient audience. That the solitary individual needs a
"helper" highlights the fragility of each human being who, as Ecclesiastes 4 warns, has slim chances to make it on their own when injured, cold,
or attacked. Adam's key problem is survival. The remedy is to grow the
herd through marriage and procreation. The lone wandering of Jacob,
Moses, or Elijah likewise should raise concerns about their sustenance,
not about their souls or search for meaning.[13] All in all, Genesis 2 shows

---

out this interpretive openness; cf. J. Daryl Charles, ed., *Reading Genesis 1–2:
An Evangelical Conversation* (Peabody, MA: Hendrickson, 2013).

11   Gordon J. Wenham, *Genesis 1–15*, WBC 1 (Nashville, TN: Thomas Nelson,
1987), 68.

12   The word צלע (ṣēlaʿ), which is commonly translated as "rib," refers everywhere
else to a "side" (ca. 40 times), especially in building constructions (see, e.g.,
Exod 26:20–35). The verb in Gen 2:22 is neither "create" (ברא), "make" (עשׂה),
nor "fashion" (יצר), but "build" (בנה).

13   As the theologian Miroslav Volf notes, the travel-bound Abraham "is not
a lonely modern self, restlessly roving about;" *Exclusion and Embrace: A*

less explicit concern for the divine–human relationship—there is, for instance, no dialogue between Adam and God—than for the safety, sustenance, and survival of the human species.

To the extent that Genesis 1–2 is read in its own world, the text will not yield the troublesome conclusions that it seems to suggest. God's assessment of Adam's situation, for instance, does not mean that the lives of unmarried and childless people are "not good." In an environment in which survival depends on family ties and where honoring father and mother (Exod 20:12) is a bare necessity, life alone is risky. But in societies with equal work opportunities, social services, and pensions, the generic call to "be fruitful and multiply and fill the earth" (Gen 1:28) no longer carries the same gravity. For Christian communities, at least, the tension between these verses and Jesus's life as a single, childless man should cause as much pause for reflection as Paul's recommendation to stay unmarried (1 Cor 7:27, 40).[14] A related problem in reading Genesis 1–2 concerns the idea that marriage will cure loneliness, that spouses become "one flesh" in every single respect.[15] Adam's poem is a beautiful and balanced composition, but perhaps the excessive focus on his new partner (×3 זאת, "this one") raises the expectation to a level of fulfilment that no relationship can deliver. In any case, Genesis 2 does not record a response from Eve and Genesis 3 immediately shatters all illusions of eternal bliss by revealing married life to be brimming with potential for fear, blame-shifting, and alienation.

Those Who Sit Alone

As with the concept of creation and the relationships of women and men, the Bible's brief preface cannot answer all questions. There is more to human life on earth than can be said in two chapters, more to the reality of life alone and the rewards and risks of life together. The poetic books of the Old Testament reveal a more robust view of loneliness

---

Theological Exploration of Identity, Otherness, and Reconciliation (Nashville, TN: Abingdon, 1996), 42.

14 For a brief reflection on celibacy and Genesis 1:28, see R. R. Reno, *Genesis*, BTCB (Grand Rapids, MI: Baker Academic, 2017), 58.

15 "It is, perhaps, a solitude mitigated but not entirely removed by the creation of woman;" Robert Alter, *The Art of Biblical Narrative* (New York: Basic Books, 1981), 30. See further Jayne V. Clark: "Singleness is not the cause of loneliness;" "Struggling through Loneliness" *JBC* 29 (2015), 10.

that captures its presence and pain in more depth than the narrative about Adam's quick fix. The shunned and shut-in speaker of Psalm 88, for instance, shows that the struggle of lonely people is not promptly resolved by divine intervention. On the contrary, the absence of God and others is lamented bitterly, the pain of "being counted among the dead" is not silently borne, but expressed. Behind these words—and behind Eden's euphemism "not good"—lies the widespread ancient perception that separation from others was akin to standing with one foot in the grave.[16] The guidance for leprosy in Leviticus 13:45–46 reflects exactly this worldview.

> As for the person with the mark of skin disease, his clothes shall be torn and his head shall be disheveled. His moustache he shall cover and 'unclean, unclean!' he shall cry. All the days on which the mark is on him, he is unclean. Unclean he is and he shall sit alone. His dwelling shall be outside of the camp.

This instruction seems to protect others from contagious ailments. Yet, the particular skin disease in Leviticus 13 does not change hosts in a medical sense. Rather, "its impurity is contagious."[17] Purity and uncleanness in the Bible have to do first of all with the presence of God. The sanctuary needs to be kept pure for the holy God to indwell it; therefore, all that is impure needs to be distanced from it or cleansed. Leviticus's discussions about unclean animals, people, and objects often associate impurity with death (e.g., cadaver-eating animals, loss of blood). The scaling of the skin is a sign that the affected person is disintegrating and crossing from life to death (see Num 12:10–11). The shredded attire and unruly hair indicate a state of mourning (e.g., Lev

---

16 Alexander Fischer observes for Egyptian society that "a human being isolated from their social mode of existence and separated from their society is equivalent, quite simply, to dying;" *Tod und Jenseits im Alten Orient und im Alten Testament: Eine Reise durch Antike Vorstellungs- und Textwelten*, SKI.NF 7 (Leipzig: Evangelische Verlagsanstalt, 2014), 32 (my translation). The following paragraphs develop my "'I sat alone:' The Language of Loneliness in the Hebrew Bible," *ZAW* 133 (2021): 512–525.

17 Jacob Milgrom, *Leviticus 1–16*, AB 3 (New York: Doubleday, 1991), 805.

10:6; Ezek 24:17). The diseased sufferer "experiences a living death"[18] because of the physical disintegration and also because of the exclusion from the sanctuary and the community.

Alone at the edge of society, loneliness emerges in Leviticus 13 as a liminal space between the center and the periphery that confines individuals, if only for a short time (Lev 14:1–9), in the "forecourt of death."[19] This passage demonstrates that the ancient texts of the Bible regard "sitting alone" not just as a sad episode but also as a serious struggle. This same bodily posture appears in poetic passages that lend speech to this struggle, that offer images to express the hard edges of life alone.

> *How can this be?*
> *She sits alone,*
> *that city who was full of people.*
> *She has become like a widow,*
> *that lady among the nations,*
> *that princess among the provinces.*
> *She has become a slave.*
>
> Lamentations 1:1

The personal overtones of the personified city are tangible and tragic, yet Lamentations 1 employs the language of loneliness primarily as a political metaphor. Most of the chapter speaks about Jerusalem's enemies and the allies who have abandoned her. As in Eden, it is striking to see that loneliness, rather than destruction or shame, is chosen by the poet as the primary problem. It is above all else the loss of relationship with the nations, her inhabitants, and her God that show how vast Jerusalem's collapse truly is. Her pain is unspeakable, her condition unthinkable—"How can this be?"—leaving the poet with images and comparisons. The prophet Jeremiah suffers a similar fate, albeit with a complex twist.

---

18 Gordon J. Wenham, *The Book of Leviticus*, NICOT 3 (Grand Rapids, MI: Eerdmans, 1979), 201.

19 Erhard Gerstenberger, *Leviticus: A Commentary*, OTL (Louisville, KY: Westminster John Knox, 1996), 167.

Your words were found and I consumed them.
Your word became to me a joy and a delight for my heart,
    for your name is called out over me, O Lord God of hosts.
I do not sit in the circle of those who laugh aloud,
    nor do I exult in triumph.
Because of your hand, I sit alone,
    for you have filled me with indignation.

Jeremiah 15:16–17

The prophet sits alone because of his commitments to God but his anti-social silence may also be read as a critique of the people around him (cf. 16:1–8).[20] Regardless of whether one focuses on his piety or his protest, the determination "not to sit" with the scoffers morphs in the very same verse into a dreadful burden. He may be complaining that his share in God's wrath has isolated him from society (cf. 6:11)[21] or he may interpret his loneliness as divine punishment; either way, Jeremiah sits alone because of God's hand.

These tensions between choice and imposition resonate with the rest of this passage, which sets the prophet's joy over God's word (v. 16) alongside his most provocative challenge. "Are you, after all, like someone who would lie to me, like waters that cannot be trusted?" (v. 18). Having left everyone to stay true to God's call, Jeremiah's lament of loneliness ultimately confronts God's absence. In contrast to Psalm 88 and Lamentations 1, this distance is resolved by a divine word that is comforting but also makes communion conditional: "If you return, I will restore you" (v. 19).

These three passages reveal that loneliness is no stranger to the Hebrew poets. Whether in the priestly instructions, in the political crisis of exile, or in the ministry of Israel's prophets, life alone is a real problem that affects God's people in tangible ways. Unlike Genesis 2, these passages do not equate being alone with being without other people. The community is not far from the ill person in Leviticus

---

20 See my reflections on Jeremiah 15–16 in "When Words Become Too Violent: Silence as a Form of Nonviolent Resistance in the Book of Jeremiah," *BibInt* 29 (2021): 187–205.

21 "The weight of this kind of message meant that Jeremiah became isolated within his community;" Terence E. Fretheim, *Jeremiah*, SHBC (Macon, GA: Smith & Helwys, 2002), 238.

13,[22] there are children left to Lady Jerusalem (see Lam 1:4, 11), and Jeremiah enjoys the company of Ahikam (Jer 26) and Baruch (Jer 36). Loneliness rather is an existential and spiritual issue. It is presented as death invading life, as being far from God who is the source of life (cf. Jer 2:13).

In the portrayals of Lady Jerusalem and Jeremiah, this crisis is met head-on with articulation and accusation, with images of widowhood and murky waters, with personal outcries about commitments and culprits. Even as these solitary figures sit alone, their spoken words reach beyond their small islands, longing for an open ear, breaking the silence of loneliness. The shattered princess and the privileged yet perplexed prophet invite their hearers to sit with them and to learn from them that even those with power, beauty, and divine favor are not immune to the lonely side of being human.

A Lonely Bird: Imagery and Isolation in Psalm 102

These lonely individuals and Adam's experience in the garden assign to human companionship a place that the divine–human relationship does not seem capable of filling. The impulse to elevate God beyond everyone else resonates with many biblical passages and remains a valid theological sentiment.[23] Yet, in Genesis 2, God's presence does not suffice for the lone human to live in sync with the good structures of the world. Even if this were the case, God's absence in Jeremiah and Lamentations is not easily overcome. Christian readers face a similar challenge in the narratives of Jesus's final days. Alongside his unspeakable physical sufferings, the gospel writers portray Jesus's social and spiritual pains that cannot be resolved because God and disciples have disappeared. But Matthew, Mark, and Luke know where to find words for this struggle. Jesus's prayer in the garden echoes Psalm 42, the cry on the cross is taken from Psalm 22, and much of Jesus's language

---

22 Martin Noth suggests that the lepers' families were responsible for providing them with food; cf. *Leviticus,* rev. ed., trans. J. E. Anderson, OTL (Philadelphia, PA: Westminster Press, 1977), 106.

23 "Ultimately, then, 'loneliness' is a God-shaped vacuum within us;" James M. Houston, "Continent of Loneliness," *Crux* 46 (2010), 12.

resonates with Jeremiah's poetry of isolation and rejection.[24] These links invite weighty theological reflections,[25] yet hearing this language ring forth at Gethsemane and Golgotha also suggests that loneliness is indeed everyone's cross to bear. Instead of promoting a posture of silently waiting, the Hebrew poets and the New Testament writers alike model a language for life alone that is raw, real, and radically honest.

The significance of the Psalms is reflected in these applications of the New Testament but this is only one example of their enduring legacy. This collection of 150 poems has inspired countless hymns of praise and birthed grand visions of kingship, yet its anonymous and generic language also has given utterance to hard times. From illness to slander, from anxieties to politics, the Psalms paint their picture of human life across a vast canvas of pain and problems. Although not as urgent as the opposition of enemies or the destructive strain of wicked speech, the experiences of loneliness, isolation, and abandonment surface often.[26] These three concepts are not identical. They overlap and each poem will focus more on one dimension than on another. Taking its place alongside the forsaken cry of Psalm 22 and the shut-in speaker of Psalm 88, the first-person lament in Psalm 102 offers a particularly nuanced language for loneliness, even if it frames this language amid a more complex crisis.

The first eleven verses capture the struggle with life with a variety of vivid descriptions: "my bones cling to my flesh" (v. 5), "I am like a lonely bird on the roof" (v. 7), "I wither away like grass" (v. 11). The heading of Psalm 102 suggests that these phrases describe illness, yet

---

24 The connection between Jeremiah and Jesus runs deeper yet; see, e.g., Mark F. Whitters, "Jesus in the Footsteps of Jeremiah," *CBQ* 68 (2006): 229–247; Michael Knowles, *Jeremiah in Matthew's Gospel: The Rejected-Prophet Motif in Matthean Redaction*, JSNT Sup 68 (Sheffield: Sheffield Academic Press, 1993).

25 "He alone is able to take upon himself the indescribable totality of what it means to be forsaken by God;" Hans-Joachim Kraus, *Psalms 1–59: A Commentary*, CC (Minneapolis, MN: Augsburg Publishing House, 1988), 189.

26 "Personal distress is often tied up with a sense of isolation. The distressed psalmist feels beleaguered, cut off from family and friends, distant from temple and community, and often far removed from God himself;" Philip S. Johnston, "The Psalms and Distress," in *Interpreting the Psalms: Issues and Approaches*, ed. David G. Firth and Philip S. Johnston (Downers Grove, IL: InterVarsity Press, 2006), 66.

their figurative and generic nature must not limit its application to the sickbed.[27] As in other laments, the direct address in verse 12 ("But you, O Lord") signals the turning point of the composition. Indeed, the hymn that runs until verse 22 soars in a different register, singing praises about God's reign and the deliverance of the destitute. It would be typical for a lament psalm to end on such a positive note,[28] but the personal narrative that unfolds in Psalm 102 returns in closing to the dismay where it began.

> He has troubled my strength on the way,
>   cut short my days.
> O my God, I say:
>   'Do not take me away in the midst of my days!'

These agonized words in verses 23–24 are heavy with the pain of the current experience and cannot easily by redeemed with a nod to verses 25–28 that extol God's ever-lasting existence to the safety of future generations.[29] Caught between lament and lament, the upbeat hymn at the center of the poem offers only partial, temporary comfort. The speaker raises their head above the waves and catches a glimpse of light at the horizon before plunging back into dismay.

For some readers, this brief ray of sunshine or the assurance about a better day may be comforting. But Psalm 102 does not wash away all troubles or land at a new shore of companionship. In the place of a divine response or a recognition of closure by the speaker, its words

---

27 "The language used to describe the needs of those who pray was generated in the experience of a span of troubles: physical affliction, social affliction, warfare. But its function in these psalms is symbolic, metaphorical, analogical, for the many forms that the human predicament of helplessness can take;" James L. Mays, *The Lord Reigns: A Theological Handbook to the Psalms* (Louisville, KY: Westminster John Knox Press, 1994), 27.

28 Note, for instance, the divine comfort at the end of Psalms 12:5, 60:6–7, and 132:15–18, and the closing crescendo of praise in Psalms 10:16–18, 22:22–31, and 43:4. The following section develops my "'I am a Lonely Bird:' Psalm 102 and the Psychology of Loneliness" *BTB* 53 (2023): 68–76.

29 "What needs to be pointed out right away is that the individual prayer, who expresses themselves in their fear of death in verses 2–12.24–25a, gains nothing from this horizon of salvation that is situated at such a far distance;" Hans Odil Steck, "Zu Eigenart und Herkunft von Ps 102," *ZAW* 102 (1990), 363 (my translation).

themselves are a friend to the forlorn; its honest language and imagery are its response to loneliness. The poem offers a liberating script for those who feel alone in their loneliness and who lack words to express the pain with which they live. In particular, the image of a lonely bird that sits on its roof (v. 7) speaks of the acknowledgment and acceptance of this human experience. Psalm 102 is a tumultuous text, yet this winged word sits, speaks, and sings amid its many dark words, ever eager to open the lonely ears and eyes of all who gaze up to its warm plumage.

Circling the Roof

The poem opens with a set of stereotypical pleas. Though the appeal "do not hide your face from me" and the references to the "day of trouble" are common (e.g., Pss 13:1; 50:15; 86:7; 119:19), they take on their own significance in Psalm 102. The psalmist's concern for their "day" frames the entire lament in verses 3–11.

> All my days are spent in smoke,
>> my bones are scorched in the furnace. (v. 3)

> My days are stretched like a shadow,
>> I wilt away like grass. (v. 11)

The movements of rising smoke and stretching shadows are unstoppable, as is the approach of destruction that the speaker fears. Beyond mere anticipation, however, death appears to be already present rather than just around the corner. The Hebrew of verse 3 reads "in smoke" rather than "like smoke" (NRSV, NIV, ESV), starting the lament with something more urgent than a mere comparison. This disintegration is expressed also by the triad "my days," "my bones," and "my heart" across verses 3–4. Each of these pillars of existence is pulled away, and to make matters worse, the speaker's struggle to eat ("I forget to eat my bread," v. 4) is identified as the result of this condition: a vicious circle with no good end in sight.

The longer the poem goes on, the more the afflicted speaker diminishes, dwindling from "my bones" (v. 3) to "my bone" (v. 5), reducing in stature and in speech ("my groaning," אנחתי). The verb אנח (ʾānaḥ) can denote audible sounds (cf. Lam 1:21; Ezek 21:7), yet none of its thirteen occurrences entail intelligible expressions; moreover, in Joel 1:18 it is not humans who groan, but animals. This collapse of human speech hints at the loss of life and identity that emerges in sharper contours in verses 9–10. Unable to eat or speak, the psalmist comes so close to death that their name is used as a curse word.

> *All my enemies taunt me,*
>   *those who deride me curse by my name,*
> *because I eat ashes for food,*
> *because of your indignation and your wrath,*
>   *for you have taken me up*
>   *and you have thrown me down.*

As in Psalm 88, somatic and social pain interweaves with spiritual agony. The deeper Psalm 102 penetrates the abyss of self and society, the louder becomes the question for God. Aside from the pleas in verses 1–2 and 24, the psalmist addresses God only in verse 10 where the fourfold "you" raises sharp accusations of divine wrath and confusion ("taken up"/"thrown down"). The Old Testament offers a far more nuanced picture than any simplistic equation of "sin = suffering" or "suffering = judgment" would allow.[30] Yet in a worldview that knows God to be active and involved in human affairs, the terrible situation in Psalm 102 is as much the speaker's reality as it is God's responsibility. Biblical laments never shy away from holding God accountable (see, e.g., Pss 44:23–26; 83:1) but such articulations are signs of resilient faith rather than rebellion. They acknowledge God's power to effect change and, by extension, they complain about God's lack of action.

The Lonely Bird on the Roof

The words, speech, and development of verses 1–11 depict a human being who regards themselves and who is regarded by others as having

---

30 Robert Culley points out that verse 10 "may imply that the suffering is a punishment for sin but this is not said so explicitly. Nor do sin and punishment become issues in the resolution of the problem of the sufferer;" "Psalm 102: A Complaint with a Difference," *Semeia* 62 (1993): 27. See also Fredrik Lindström, *Suffering and Sin: Interpretations of Illness in the Individual Complaint Psalms* (Stockholm: Almqvist & Wiksell, 1994).

crossed the line between life and death already. In contrast to the modern mindset, ancient views of the world characterize death not just as a place, but as a power that can invade the realm of life.[31] The extreme experiences of life, such as illness, threat, or isolation, routinely are described by the Hebrew poets in the liminal language of life and death, God and grave, speech and silence. The sufferer of Psalm 102 speaks from this blurred space. Caught in the tension between light and darkness ("my days are stretched like a shadow," v. 11), the text presents its speaker as a phantom whose time, essence, and speech are coming undone.

Such severe suffering, however, does not mean that death has already triumphed, that all agency and life has succumbed to the forces of the underworld.[32] Like the speaker of Psalm 88 who prays and protests against God's absence, the poet of Psalm 102 is well enough to express their experience with a profound degree of self-awareness, emotional literacy, and articulation.

> *I am like an owl of the wilderness,*
>   *I am like an owl of the wasteland.*
> *I stay awake.*
>   *I am like a lonely bird on the roof.*

The identity of these three birds is troubled by their rare appearance and the vast distance to Israel's ancient fauna. Whereas the first bird, the *qāʾāt*, is rendered by most translations as a "(desert) owl," some Bible editions follow the Greek Septuagint and read here a "pelican" (NKJV; JPS); again, others opt for a "vulture" (RSV). The *qāʾāt* appears outside of Psalm 102 only among the wild beasts that haunt the ruins of Edom (Isa 34:11) and Nineveh (Zeph 2:14) and in the lists of unclean animals

---

31 "To the ancient Near East, the empirical world, as manifestation and symbol, points beyond its superficial reality. A continuous osmosis occurs.... This openness to the spheres of divine-intensive life and of bottomless, devastating lostness is probably the chief difference between ancient Near Eastern conceptions of the world and our own;" Keel, *Symbolism*, 56.

32 "Any illness or misfortune is a partial experience of death's power and of underworld conditions.... Psalmists vividly describe their distress as if they were in Sheol, cut off from Yahweh. But they know that they are still alive, and able to pray;" Philip Johnston, *Shades of Sheol: Death and Afterlife in the Old Testament* (Leicester: Apollos, 2002), 97.

in Leviticus 11 and Deuteronomy 14. These two lists, incidentally, also record the only other mentions of the *kôs*, the second bird in verse 6.

These parallel passages and the presence of the birds in Psalm 102 as a pair suggest that the question of their symbolic value is more important than the classification of their species. That both the *qāʾāt* and the *kôs* are identified as unclean animals and that both flutter among the eerie ruins of crumbled cities suggests that this pair is a stock phrase, a symbol for spaces that are hostile to human flourishing. Bernd Janowski, a biblical scholar well-versed in ancient anthropology, has analyzed biblical death metaphors and has noted that comparisons with objects, such as wax, broken pottery, or smoke, as well as comparisons with animals and plants, usually entail a kind of cross-fertilization.[33] The statement "I am like an owl of the wilderness" is no innocent comparison, but an appropriation—a mode of seeing-oneself-as—that breaks down the boundary between human and animal.

The speaker of Psalm 102 makes an existential declaration about their sense of self and their alienation from their own nature, humanity, and health. This portrayal resonates with the consuming fire and withered grass of verses 1–11 and is deepened further by the concession "I stay awake" in verse 7. The troubled situation of the speakers may suggest a case of insomnia, yet the Hebrew verb in this verse always describes an active wakefulness (e.g., Ezra 8:29; Ps 127:1; Jer 5:6). If all were well, the psalmist would sleep, but the liminal space of life and death allows no peace, the confusion of identity no sense of self, and the tiresome existence between day and night no rest.

The "lonely bird," the *ṣippôr* of verse 7, appears more frequently in the Old Testament (×40, esp. in Lev 14) and is often clad in a positive garb that contrasts strongly with the *qāʾāt* and *kôs*. The *ṣippôr* is among the clean birds (Deut 14:11), enjoys some protection in Israel's laws (Deut 22:6), and, as Job 41:5 suggests, even makes a suitable playmate for children. In Psalms 84:3 and 104:17, these animals are promised divine protection and Isaiah 31:5 goes as far as to compare God's

---

33 "The images used here are not aesthetic ornamentations of reality, but expressions of an understanding of reality.... The lamenting supplicant appropriates part of the nature of the respective subject of comparison;" *Arguing with God: A Theological Anthropology of the Psalms*, trans. Armin Siedlecki (Louisville, KY: Westminster John Knox, 2013), 237.

protection of Jerusalem to a hovering *ṣippôr*. On its own, the psalmist's identification as a *ṣippôr* would be positive, but the incongruity with the other two birds creates a curious, inner tension.

Even if there is some family resemblance, the psalmist's words artic- ulate a struggle of identity: owl/bird, death/life, accompanied/alone. Psalm 102 parses loneliness in terms of internal alienation but also with the pain of not belonging to others. The two birds of death are men- tioned first and outnumber the clean bird, pushing the *ṣippôr* and all its positive colors to the edge of the roof. Transfixed spatially between heaven and earth, existentially between human and animal, and tem- porally between day and night, the psalmist is portrayed as belonging nowhere at all and, therefore, as lonely as possible.[34] Situating the bird on a roof rather than on a tree provides an ideal stage for putting the pain of loneliness in plain sight and, fueled by the smoke and ashes of verses 1–11, for expressing its close kinship with death. By means of its liminal dimensions, the loneliness of Psalm 102 fragments time, space, and company—the very foundations that sustain human life.

The Lonely Bird and Its Song of Loneliness

The poetry of the Old Testament offers a complex mix of lonely crea- tures who each in their own way fill Adam's silence with words and images. The poets who stand behind these solitary scripts are forerun- ners of the recent rise of "loneliness literature" in contemporary culture. Nicholas Dames, a scholar of comparative literature and novel writing, has described this "New Fiction of Solitude" as marked by monologues, memoirs, and self-expression. In the place of dialogues and story, this self-conscious literary mode thrives on a "stubbornly solitary voice [that] may be welcome, even necessary, for telling us what it means to be human."[35] This voice speaks of the reality of loneliness, yet it is not

---

34 "The psalmist suffers isolation, even derision. Through metaphor, the psalm- ist's distress is given a distinctly social nuance insofar as the imagery of unclean birds associated with lamentation is expressive of isolation (both in the wilderness and on the housetop!) and vulnerability;" Brown, *Seeing the Psalms*, 146.

35 "The New Fiction of Solitude," *The Atlantic* (Apr 2016), 101. From among the many examples of this genre, I warmly recommend Katherine May, *Wintering:*

content with raising awareness and breaking stigma. Instead, the lonely speakers in these novels and biographies courageously look at loneliness itself and embark on the challenging task of living with it rather fleeing from it. The lonely bird of Psalm 102 sings alongside these contemporary voices, and its melody, similar to theirs, travels through the dark register of the pain and confusion of lonely days, hits the familiar notes of being human, and rings in the higher octaves of new discoveries.

A Language for Life Alone
From the ritual purity of Leviticus 13 to the metaphorization of a capital city, from the correlation of isolation and death to the ancient associations with owls and wild places, the Bible's portrayal of loneliness stands at a considerable distance from today's look at life. Some stretches of this overt gulf will not be breached because worldviews and perceptions of self and society have so drastically changed. At other sections, however, the stream that divides original and contemporary readers is shallow enough to wade across. For instance, feeling alienated by the company of others and struggling with disorientation are present realities in the world of Psalm 102 and in today's world.[36] Likewise, feelings of loneliness are embedded in the poem just as today in a complex web of questions about self-worth, well-being, mortality, and God. When it comes to the pain and the destructive power of loneliness, psychologists and poets, however, take a step closer yet. They may start from entirely different shores but they meet on the same sandbank in the midst of the river. The Bible's cosmology and social organization identifies loneliness as a hazard for healthy living as much as scientists' cognitive analyses. Text and therapist know it to be part of the human condition as well as a problem.

The struggle with life alone, of course, does not always take place in the extreme territories of life and death. Whether episodic or often, whether endless or occasional, the wide continuum of experiences weaves loneliness deeply into the fabric of living while also resisting an extreme view of its impact and explanatory value. The reality of

The Power of Rest and Retreat in Difficult Times (London: Rider, 2020); Kate Bowler, *No Cure for Being Human* (London: Rider, 2021).

36 As Fromm-Reichmann observes, "while alone and isolated from others, people feel threatened by the potential loss of their boundaries;" "Loneliness," 7.

life alone needs neither to be downplayed nor demonized. Yet, like other difficult experiences, it needs to be put into words. For reaching far and inviting many, a meaningful language of loneliness should be non-specific and inclusive; it should be honest and honor the pain of being human without promising easy solutions. Psalm 102 does not define human experience narrowly but paints it across a broad canvas of comparisons, images, and emotive expressions. For instance, the loss of boundaries, the sense of alienation from self and others, and the uncanny feeling of disorientation can be captured then as well as today with the description of days "stretching like a shadow" (v. 11). When every day feels like the next and when time becomes empty, the human heart indeed can be "struck down like grass" (v. 4) and the declaration "I wither away like grass" (v. 11) can put words to the weariness of life alone.

Poetic speech allows its hearers to express their vague, painful, and personal experience of "I am lonely" by way of sights and objects that are concrete. In the Old Testament, such comparisons take loneliness out of one's inner world and articulate it in the creative form of lament that aims "to create a situation that did not exist before the speech, to create an external event that matches the internal sensitivities."[37] Biblical poetry about the self expands the limitations of language and can create some critical distance, reflection, and communication. Metaphors and similes, such as the grass, shadow, and bird of Psalm 102, are vital for lonely people because, as Fromm-Reichmann observes, "one cannot break through their isolation with abstractions."[38] These natural elements can become meaningful images of isolation because they are concrete and because they are flexible. A bird on a roof is a real object in the world rather than a theoretical description, yet still it remains open to the individual imagination.

In the same way in which this particular image will bring to mind different associations for each person—birds come in any color, size, and posture—the connections between one's loneliness and this small animal likewise are open-ended. Fromm-Reichmann's honest concession about the limits of scientific description—"many poets and

---

37 Ingvar Fløysvik, *When God Becomes My Enemy: The Theology of the Complaint Psalms* (Concordia Academic Press, 1997), 30.

38 "Loneliness," 9.

philosophers have come closer to putting into words what loneliness is than we psychiatrists have"[39]—speaks precisely in support of this kind of language. A little bird can sing a song that is real to life, that can help lonely humans to articulate their part of the universal experience of life alone.

The Lonely Choir of Bird-Watchers

An important aspect of this music is its first-person expression. Psalm 102 does not speak in the style of Proverbs 26:2 ("Like a ṣippôr bound to wander. . . so a needless curse will go nowhere"), but as a personal, direct statement: "I am like a lonely bird." The speaking voice of this poem allows other individuals to speak its words as their own, but apart from this application it also highlights the need for letting loneliness speak on its own terms. The first-person expression in Psalm 102 goes to show that loneliness is never an abstract or general reality but that it is always personal, always someone's loneliness. Adam's situation is as different from Jeremiah's as that of the leper from Lady Jerusalem's.

The colors of life alone shine with as much variety as the bird's plumage. For one person, the aspect of being lonely in the company of others will stand out most from the three birds on the roof. Someone else might find more resonance between their lonely, dark hours and the sleepless nights of the psalmist. To someone else, the bird's physical location may be most meaningful as they stand and work alone in a public space. Time, space, company, silence, confusion, disorientation—the bird on the roof holds together a wide scope of personal associations that can lend words to what otherwise may remain unspeakable.

All imagery in the Bible deserves careful reflection about such connections, yet the art of metaphor is just as strong, if not stronger, in its incongruity. For all that one could say about loneliness and Psalm 102, likely the simplest observation is that the expression "I am lonely" is parsed with reference to a bird and not to a human being. Such cross-species comparisons are a foundational aspect of biblical anthropology and can take on quite nuanced dimensions (see, e.g., Isa 1:3; Jer 8:7; Prov 30:18–19).[40] In Psalm 102, the presence of a bird endows

---

39 "Loneliness," 8.

40 Cf. Benjamin A. Foreman, *Animal Metaphors and the People of Israel in the Book of Jeremiah*, FRLANT 238 (Göttingen: Vandenhoeck & Ruprecht, 2011);

this poem with a wider applicability. The portrayals in Jeremiah 15 and Lamentations 1, after all, are highly specific and each carries its own gendered language for loneliness. Whether the prophet is imagined as a heroic hermit or as the old, pensive sage from Michelangelo's famous painting, the male figure emerges as a solitary radical who withstands the scoffers. In stark contrast, the loneliness of Lady Jerusalem is presented in the overtly feminine colors of the abandoned wife, the bereaved mother, and the weeping princess. The stereotypical contours of each depiction limit their appeal in a way that is unknown to the bird. Regardless of gender, age, social standing, income, and accomplishments, anyone can speak the first-person expression of Psalm 102 as their own words. This thoughtful choice of comparison makes the lonely bird on the roof a universal icon of loneliness.

Shout It from the Rooftops!
This broad appeal comes into focus also in the bird's location. The winged creature is not hiding in the forest, not nestled away in a bush, not absorbed in a colony of other birds. Its seat on the roof lends loneliness a public platform and draws attention to itself. Whether it is the destructive connotations of the two owls or the unhealthy patterns of eating ("I forget to eat my bread," v. 4) and sleeping ("I stay awake," v. 7), the poem creates a stage on which loneliness can be seen in action. The bird's public position can inspire private reflection as well as open conversation about a topic that concerns all because it is part of everyone's life. The lone bird confidently takes its place in the Bible and in the midst of human habitation to show all who pass by that loneliness is a natural aspect of life, that

> to be lonely is to be human, perhaps even when trying to be a more genuine human being, or a more honest Christian. Indeed, sharing our feelings and experiences of loneliness may be analogous to taking an imprint of our fingerprint; it expresses who we really are.[41]

Katharine J. Dell, "The Use of Animal Imagery in the Psalms and Wisdom Literature of Ancient Israel," *SJT* 53 (2000): 275–291.

41 Houston, "Continent of Loneliness," 7.

This normalizing of loneliness is good news for everyone, yet perhaps it speaks louder in some professions and age-groups than in others. For instance, the pastoral office, similar to other leadership positions, can be a lonely role and particularly prone to undue expectations of wholeness. Henri Nouwen's classic reflection *The Wounded Healer* is among the few books that address this particular vocational loneliness. Rather than silencing the reality of life alone, Nouwen encourages pastors to embrace "their own loneliness as a source of human understanding."[42] The biblical narratives of leadership provide some company for this challenging posture (besides Jeremiah and Jesus, see also Moses in Exodus 19:14),[43] but it is especially the Bible's poetry that expresses the tension, burden, and steady presence of loneliness. The first-person expressions and the images for reflection can invite pastors to come to see and articulate their own loneliness and by extension to invite those in their care to hear the song of the lone bird for themselves.

> So we see how loneliness is the minister's wound not only because he shares in the human condition, but also because of the unique predicament of his profession. It is this wound which he is called to bind with more care and attention than others usually do. For a deep understanding of his own pain makes it possible for him to convert his weakness into strength and to offer his experience as a source of healing to those who are often lost in the darkness of their own misunderstood sufferings.[44]

From the pulpit—not unlike the roof a place both lonely and public—or in private conversation, a pastor's honest embrace of life alone can be a liberating word for all whose shame and secrecy about their experiences isolate them yet further. Such silent suffering will be part of every

---

42 Henri J. M. Nouwen, *The Wounded Healer* (London: Darton, Longman and Todd, 1979), 85. For a case study of pastoral loneliness, see Greg Scott and Rachel Lovell, "The Rural Pastors Initiative: Addressing Isolation and Burnout in Rural Ministry," *Pastoral Psychol* 64 (2015): 71–97.

43 These figures often are abandoned by their people and also by God. On the intersection of horizontal (i.e., social) and vertical loneliness in the prophetic office, see Udo Tworuschka, "Einsamkeit—Ein religionswissenschaftlich vernachlässigtes Phänomen," *ZMR* 59 (1975), 40.

44 Nouwen, *Wounded Healer*, 87.

corner of a congregation, including married and young worshippers who, by all appearance, may not struggle with feelings of loneliness. Church communities are not immune to the rising challenge of youth loneliness and can benefit from the insights of public research initiatives. The UK-based project *Loneliness Connects Us*, for instance, offers a helpful list of recommendations, such as

- Name and recognise loneliness among young people as a natural dimension to life and growing up—do not treat it as something to be ashamed or afraid of.
- Work to reduce stigma of feeling lonely, normalise being alone and promote attitudes and experiences of solitude.
- Recognise how difficult it may be for young people to acknowledge that they need help and/or to articulate and ask for it: make it easier for them.[45]

These statements highlight the need for a language of loneliness as well as for the acknowledgement of life alone in every stage of life. Pastors, parents, youth, and youth workers who struggle with such vulnerability may find in the poetry of the Old Testament a starting point for such conversations and reflections. The sleepless bird, the heartbroken city, the confused prophet, and the savior who stands alone before garden and cross are good company for embracing and expressing loneliness today. The language that each of these speakers offers will not heal life alone. But it humanizes the experience of loneliness and makes space for it within the fullness of the human condition, within the life of a community, within the relationship with God.

The Gift of Life Alone

The language of loneliness that Psalm 102 and other biblical poems impart to their readers can still be a meaningful expression of the

---

45 Batsleer and Duggan, *Young and Lonely*, 177–178. The full list of recommendation pays special attention to poverty, racism, and the pressures of the education system. The study ran from October 2016 to July 2019 and was conducted by Manchester Metropolitan University and 42nd Street, a charity supporting mental health among young people.

human experience today. It can give words to the pain of a broad range of situations in which loneliness becomes a burden.[46] Beyond this gift of acknowledgment and articulation, however, the poetic materials in the Bible also make space for thinking about loneliness in a slightly more positive way. At the most basic level, several of the key passages keep the return to social interaction in view. Jeremiah's lone stance, for instance, is met by a renewal of God's presence and the isolated speakers in the psalms often find themselves toward the end of their poems in the company of their congregation (see, e.g., Pss 3:8; 11:7; 28:9).[47] The frequency of these reversals offers some hope that life together is always still a possibility, but the consistent ebb and flow across the Psalms also identifies loneliness as a recurring issue. The Bible is not naive about the social dimension of the human condition, nor does it suggest that other people will eradicate the pain of being alone altogether. On the contrary, the foundational account of human relationship in Genesis 2–3 as well as many other passages leaves no doubt about the destructive potential of human companionship (see, e.g., Ps 141:4; Prov 13:20). As Psalm 1 and Jeremiah 15 go to show, there are many times when it is better to be alone than "to sit with the scoffers."

Sitting in Solitude
Still, loneliness and withdrawal have more to offer than damage control. If only ever as a hard-won journey through crisis, the positive side of life alone surfaces in the subtitles of current books on the topic, such as Francesca Specter's *Alonement: How to Be Alone and Absolutely Own It* (2021) and Olivia Laing's *The Lonely City: Adventures in the Art of Being Alone* (2016). Given the social organization of ancient communities and the close associations of death and isolation, such celebrations

---

46 See, e.g., Caroline Blyth, "'I am alone with my Sickness': Voicing the Experience of HIV- and AIDS-related Stigma through Psalm 88," *Colloquium* 44 (2012): 149–162, and John E. Colwell's reading of Psalm 22 and the struggle of bi-polar disorder in *Why Have you Forsaken Me? A Personal Reflection on the Experience of Desolation* (Milton Keyes: Paternoster, 2009).

47 Kristin M. Swenson traces this journey through Psalm 22, which "turns from complaint and terror marked by loneliness and alienation, to praise and confidence told among family and friends," *Living through Pain: Psalms and the Search for Wholeness* (Waco, TX: Baylor University Press, 2005), 164.

are unlikely to occur in the Bible.[48] There is, however, one poem that
departs from the "not good" condition of Genesis 2 and frames the pain
of those who "sit alone" in a different perspective.

> *Good is the Lord to the one who waits for him,*
> > *to the life that seeks him.*
> *Good it is to wait silently for the salvation of the Lord.*
> > *Good it is for a man that he would bear the yoke in his youth.*
>
> *Let him sit alone and in silence, for he shall bear it upon himself.*
> > *Let him put his mouth in the dust—perhaps there is hope!*
> *Let him show his cheek to the one who strikes him.*
> > *Let him be filled with insult.*
>
> Lamentations 3:25–30

The sixty-six verses of Lamentations 3 are organized as an acrostic
poem in which each stanza begins with a successive letter of the Hebrew
alphabet.[49] The three statements in verses 25–27 are joined together by
the letter ט and the word "good" (טוב) that describes the patient silence
of an unidentified human being. The advice that follows—"Let him sit
alone"—shares in this recommendation of submission.

In view of Leviticus 13, Jeremiah 15, and Lamentations 1, the call for
this posture is, at best, surprising. The threefold instruction carries overtones of punishment and the mention of dust and physical harm adds a
destructive dimension to this demand for quiet suffering ("why should
anyone who is alive complain?" v. 39). It has become common practice
amongst interpreters to receive this section of the chapter as one voice
amid a complex polyphony in which many different positions coexist. Scholar Balu Savarikannu, for instance, hears in verses 25–30 the
"Voice of Tradition" that speaks from the "underlying assumption that
God is sovereign, working in ways that are beyond our understanding,

---

48 "Loneliness as a longed-for benefit that gives active pleasure is alien to the
Old Testament;" Hans Walter Wolff, *Anthropology of the Old Testament,* trans.
Margaret Kohl (London: SCM Press, 1974), 217.

49 Acrostics appear elsewhere in the Old Testament (see, e.g., Pss 9–10; 119; and
Prov 31). For more details on the poetic constitution of Lamentations 3, see my
"Language of Loneliness," 521–522.

hence it is better to endure such distress."[50] But as Savarikannu points out, this posture is but one response to tragedy. Most of Lamentations 3 is quite forthright about God's excessive judgment and the chapter ends with a cry for divine assistance. The goodness of sitting alone is but part of a larger reflection on the fall of Jerusalem in 587 BCE. Some readers may find it cathartic; others may find it troubling.

Inasmuch as the correlation of "good" and "alone" in this text troubles a straightforward celebration of life alone, Lamentations 3 raises the question about the Bible's attitude toward meditation and solitude. According to scholar Mark Davies, defining solitude can be as complex as defining loneliness since some writers use the two words interchangeably and across diverse ascetic, religious, and secular contexts. Promoting a holistic approach that accepts the many sides of life alone, Davies speaks in favor of solitude because it "invites people to turn and face their loneliness head on" and because it allows "individuals the opportunity to become better connected to self, to God, and others."[51]

Although Davies's observations do not speak about the Bible directly, they resonate with individual Psalms whose speakers can be found "meditating" (הגה) on God's word and character (e.g., Pss 1:2; 63:6; 77:12; 143:5). Each of these voices speaks in a solitary, prayerful setting and their lone musings breed comforting thoughts and new perspectives. Even if the modern concepts about self and personal time with God cannot be read back into these ancient texts,[52] they envision sitting alone as a good place for humans. Left to oneself without comparison or group orientation, personal memories may rise to the surface and God's presence may be found anew. The bird on the roof gets to see things from up there that it will never see on the ground or in company

---

50 "A Polyphonic Reading of Lamentations 3," *JAET* 20 (2016): 32.

51 "Solitude and Loneliness: An Integrative Model," *JPT* 24 (1996), 8.

52 The reciting of the Psalms would have been at first a public event at the temple (see, e.g., Ps 63:3). The practice of personal prayer grew out of the transformation of sacrifice that was brought on by the distance to the temple during the Jewish diaspora (see, e.g., "The sacrifice acceptable to God is a broken spirit" [Ps 51:17] and the "living sacrifices" of Romans 12:1); cf. Shaye S. Cohen, *From the Maccabees to the Mishnah*, 2nd ed. (Louisville, KY: Westminster John Knox Press, 2014), 54–64.

and that no other bird may ever notice.[53] With nobody distracting its wandering gaze or attracting its eye, its loneliness bristles with the hope of a new vantage point that can be won no other way.

Together Alone

For all the goodness that individual prayers grant to life alone, however, they never lose sight of life together. The balance that is articulated by the interweaving of individual and communal psalms also appears, of all places, in Dietrich Bonhoeffer's *Life Together*.

> We can only be alone when we are in community and we can only live in community when we are alone. Both need each other. Each on its own is beset with deep danger. Whoever wants community without being alone, will plummet into the emptiness of words and emotions, and whoever wants to be alone without community will perish in the depths of vanity, self-absorption, and despair.[54]

The Hebrew poets and the German theologian spoke at very different times and to very different audiences, yet each on their own assigns the experience of being alone its rightful place in life. The Bible does not portray the sorrow of Lady Jerusalem and the sufferings of Psalm 102 as an enjoyable experience or as a spiritual discipline. The positive dimension of these texts lies, simply, in that they are what they are: honest words that minister to lonely hearts as they resonate with the deep pains of the human condition.

Whoever speaks these words and hears the lone bird's song as their own tune comes face-to-face with the reality of human existence. A life that is bent on quenching and conquering life alone, so Bonhoeffer, will be at risk to "plummet into the emptiness of words and emotions," to speak in a way that does not do justice to the complexities of life. The poetic voices of widow, prophet, and bird beckon all who hear them

---

53 Swenson points to these revelatory dynamics in Psalm 22: "After his journey through pain and loneliness, the psalmist is able to contribute something uniquely valuable to his community, the voice of one who 'knows,' and on account of his special knowledge is able both to bring hope and encouragement to others;" *Living through Pain*, 157–158.

54 *Gemeinsames Leben* (Gütersloh: Gütersloher Verlagshaus, 2006), 66 (my translation).

to integrate their tune amid their hymns about life even as they themselves stand surrounded by peers and partners. Psalm 102 is not only a
poem for the lonely. Its raw words and its helpless perspective compel
all who read it to look beyond the comfortable edge of their warm nest.
Besides every lonely bird, after all, there are always at least two other
birds on the roof.

Creative Loneliness
Whether as a script for speaking about loneliness, as an inspiration
for articulation and awareness, or as an appeal to look out for lonely
voices, the poetry of Psalm 102 sounds forth in many keys. The question of how to hear, speak, and preach these texts is an ongoing exercise
for all who gather under the lonely bird's roofline, yet the presence of
the little winged creature itself is a matter for reflection. Sprung from
the observing and imaginative heart of an unnamed Hebrew poet, the
association of bird and life alone is a testimony to the productive and
creative power of lone hours. Like all other items in the human library,
like any other project that has required prolonged periods of reflection,
study, planning, and design, this poem elevates the creative dimension
of loneliness. For all her remarkable insights into the devastation of isolation, Frieda Fromm-Reichmann's analysis is fully aware that

> nearly all works of creative originality are conceived in such states of
> constructive aloneness; and, in fact, only the creative person who is not
> afraid of this constructive aloneness will have free command over his
> creativity.[55]

Resonating with the Psalms' and Bonhoeffer's evaluations of the need
and benefits of life alone, this assessment embraces it from yet another
dimension. Not only can personal loneliness promote the betterment
of self and others, it can also be an unparalleled space for original
thought and creativity. Without losing its shadow side of disorientation
and strain, time spent alone has yielded and continues to yield much of
humanity's most treasured literature, artwork, architecture, and inno-
vation. Far from pushing lonely people to the fringes of society, this

---

55 "Loneliness," 2.

reality of human productivity honors loneliness and makes it an equal of life together. The wider community may offer the lonely people in their midst companionship and orientation, yet the loneliness of each creative effort can offer humanity authentic expressions of life. Human creativity, in Psalm 102 and all its other expressions, is loneliness at its best.

How observation, experience, reflection, and expression work together in these lonely moments is an impossible knot to untie. How loneliness can be one of the most dreadful feelings of the human condition and at the same time one of the most driving forces of the human story likewise remains an unspeakable and astonishing fact of life. Settled above everyone's head, slightly out of reach and so easily overlooked, the bird of Psalm 102 may hold an answer, but it will never yield it to the human desires for analysis and understanding. Its melody captures the pain of days stretching like shadows, the sleepless nights, the alienation from others, and the fear of death. Genesis 2 emphatically rules out that animals are fitting companions for human beings. Yet birds can be good teachers (Job 12:7–8) and yield wisdom (Matt 6:25–26). When the pain of life becomes unspeakable, when one's island has become too strange to share with another human being, these quiet friends may be the only ones to listen and understand. Those who open their eyes to the natural world may not just find that their feelings of loneliness are soothed by its inhabitants.[56] They may also discover an acceptance of their humanity and a sense of belonging that is at times hard to find at the crowded beaches of human society.

---

56 See, e.g., R. Hammoud et al., "Lonely in a Crowd: Investigating the Association between Overcrowding and Loneliness Using Smartphone Technologies," *SciRep* 11 (2021), Article number 24134. I warmly recommend Søren Kierkegaard's superb reflection on the birds and lilies in Matthew 6 in *Spiritual Writings: Gift, Creation, Love. Selections from the Upbuilding Discourses*, trans. George Pattison (New York: Harper Perennial, 2010). "The bird and the lily are visible and external images of what a human being is to become invisibly and inwardly, namely, the site of an unconditional affirmation of existence;" Peter Kline, "Imaging Nothing: Kierkegaard and the *Imago Dei*," *Anglican Theological Review* 100 (2018), 699.

CHAPTER 3

Words of Woe
Jeremiah's Articulation of Despair

> *The old have left their post at the gate,*
>   *the young their music.*
> *Joy has left our heart.*
>   *Our dancing has turned to grief,*
> *The crown has fallen from our head,*
>   *woe is us for we have sinned!*
> *Because of this, our heart is ill.*
> *Because of these things, our eyes are dark.*
>
> Lamentations 5:14–17

For all its complexity, human life usually unfolds in a rather small universe. The immediacy of tasks and relationships settles the eye on what is nearest and keeps all else at a distance from the island of this moment. But beyond the shoreline, the unstable world knows little of such rest and routine. Seismic shifts set events in motion that are impossible to anticipate; waves mount slowly and escalate as quickly as they approach, leaving those who spot them at the horizon in woeful resignation. Hands droop, heads hang low, and eyes grow dark as the comfortable and familiar circle of existence comes undone. The desperate search for hope drives the human heart to the edge of its island, away from anguish and eager to lay hold of a new perspective. Looking back inland, there is no longer music but only misery. But looking out across the vast, dark sea offers no new horizon either because dark eyes only see darkness and despair.

As the music stops and the dancing ceases, the final chapter of Lamentations entertains the terrible thought that this darkness will not again give way to a new day. Christian readers may know this little poetic book best for its hopeful hymn about God's new mercies that swills brightly at its center. Yet even there the look at the future is fragile, tentative at best. "Perhaps there will be hope" (Lam 3:29). As in the biblical text, the uncertainty of this "perhaps" remains a reality in the world today. Then and now, the loss of perspective and the collapse of hope are firmly at home at the shoreline of the human condition. When the sages offer no counsel in the gate and the delightful distraction of youthful tunes has faded away, when even God remains silent, the poetry of the Old Testament steps into the breach to speak for darkened hearts.[1]

This task of offering a new vision is associated primarily with the biblical prophets who are commonly understood to be concerned with the future. In reality, however, the contents of books like Isaiah and Ezekiel deal far more with the fears of the present than with the glories of the future, more with the trauma of today than with tomorrow's healing. The book of Jeremiah especially keeps its eye on the wreck of Jerusalem's vast collapse and speaks about it with the rawness that the clash of confession and experience demands. The traditional association of Jeremiah and Lamentations is born out of a shared struggle of finding words for the depths of despair. Jeremiah's harrowing poems allow their readers, both then and now, to articulate the pain of the hopeless present. The inarticulable eclipse of the horizon is desperately in need of language, not only because it is part of being human but also because such speech can be the starting point for discovering that hope may not be found on sunken islands, but in an entirely new land.

Despair and Being Human

The reality of despair, sadly, owes its recent entry into the public conversation to economics rather than to social consciousness. The so-called "deaths of despair" crisis in the United States captures the sharp rise

---

1 "God's absence forces us to attend to voices of grief and despair," Kathleen O'Connor, *Lamentations and the Tears of the World* (Maryknoll, NY: Orbis Books, 2002), 86.

of suicides and of self-inflicted and substance-related deaths among people in their late 40s and early 50s.[2] Psychologist William Copeland and his team set out to find a more precise understanding of despair, yet this task proved to be rather difficult because the most common descriptions at hand tended to blur the lines with other human struggles. For instance, feeling hopeless is also symptomatic of depression; helplessness and feeling sorry for oneself are also associated with suicidal thinking.[3] Despair comes in many shades and seasons and its reach is broader than clinical diagnosis, including, for instance, living with a chronic illness, the breakdown of relationships, the loss of a job, or the death of a loved one. It is a lived reality for many people and can be a real threat to human flourishing,[4] yet it remains a phenomenon that is hard to put into words.

In search of a definition, the Latin root of the word "despair" perhaps provides a good starting place as it suggests that despair is the opposite of hope ("spes"). Hope is not something that arises on a sunny day but during a crisis that longs for a change, for a resolution toward a better future. Expressions of hope can vary from optimism and confidence ("I'm sure this will get better!") to dire words of survival ("We need this to get better!"). The domain of despair, however, occupies a stratum that is deeper yet, that houses all those painful situations that have no perspective of improvement at all. "I cannot see any way forward," "there is nothing anyone can do to solve my problems."

---

2 The phrase was first introduced in the economic analysis of Anne Case and Angus Deaton (Princeton University), which paid particular attention to the systemic dimensions of despair, for instance, in the correlation of suicide and education, race, and poverty. Cf. *Deaths of Despair and the Future of Capitalism* (Princeton, NJ: Princeton University Press, 2020).

3 Cf. William Copeland et al., "Associations of Despair with Suicidality and Substance Misuse among Young Adults," *JAMA Netw Open* 3 (2020): e208627. doi:10.1001/jamanetworkopen.2020.8627. See further Bruce Bower, "'Deaths of Despair are Rising. It's Time to Define Despair." https://www.sciencenews.org/article/deaths-of-despair-depression-mental-health-covid-19-pandemic.

4 According to Lilly Shanahan, psychology professor at the University of Zurich, despair manifests itself across the entire spectrum of human functioning. Cognitive despair, for instance, "refers to thoughts indicating defeat," emotional despair involves excessive sadness, irritability, and hostility and can lead to "risky, reckless, and unhealthy acts that are self-destructive." Despair can also affect sleep, appetite, and concentration; "Does Despair Really Kill? A Roadmap for an Evidence-Based Answer," *AJPH* 109 (2019): 854–858.

The Jesuit priest William Lynch hears in such words "the sense of
the impossible."[5] The futility of despair stifles human feelings and narrows the horizon of possibilities. "What is the use? There is no goal, no
sense, no reason; and so I do not hope or wish or will. . . . I therefore do
not move. I stand still."[6] The old citizens of Lamentations 5 leave their
places in society, the young no longer sing, the dancing has stopped and
the community at large, in its despair, cannot envision a new day or a
new tune. This collapse of perspective is crucial to take into consider-
ation because it marks the fine line between scenarios that are hopeless, such as an impossible event or task, and full-blown despair. In the
words of philosopher Anthony Steinbock,

> hopelessness pertains to the experience of the impossibility of a specific
> occasion; . . . . I turn the car key and the car will not start; I try over and
> over again; it is hopeless. . . In despair I experience directly the *ground
> of hope* as impossible. . . . I do not just give up doing this or that (hope-
> lessness), but I give up altogether.[7]

The language of the "ground of hope" takes on particular significance
for people of faith whose foundation of hope is not themselves or the
world around them, but their God ("despair grips me at the level of my
spiritual being").[8] In the Old Testament and in the life of faith, hope
is not a human prognosis about the future or positive thinking, but
ultimately a trust in God who is "Israel's hope and savior in trouble"
(Jer 14:8). The despair of which Lamentations and Jeremiah speak is
thoroughly theological and fully in keeping with its own categories of

---

5 *Images of Hope: Imagination as the Healer of the Hopeless* (Montreal: Palm
   Publishers, 1965), 48.

6 *Images of Hope*, 48. "In despair, we not only abandon, relinquish, and
   renounce hope, but also resign, surrender, and yield to the bleakness of our
   inner worlds. . . . Despair can be expressed in a precipitate and headlong manner which contrasts with the ability to await, depend, look, trust, and expect;"
   Jeanne Bailey, "From Hopelessness to Despair," in *Hopelessness: Developmental, Cultural, and Clinical Realms*, ed. Salman Akthar and Mary Kay O'Neil
   (London: Karnac, 2015), 139.

7 "The Phenomenology of Despair," *Int J Philos Stud* 15 (2007), 446–447 (emphasis original). Steinbock charts a continuum across inoperative hope, despera-
   tion, pessimism, hopelessness, and despair.

8 Steinbock, "Phenomenology," 448 (emphasis original).

divine agency, absence, and antagonism. The Bible's desperate mode of "giving up altogether" flows from the ancient community's experience of being given up by God.

These initial thoughts may raise some eyebrows even among casual Bible readers. The Psalms, after all, brim with confidence that "hope in God" can calm the downcast soul (Ps 42:5; cf. Pss 71:5; 78:7; 130:5), Isaiah hopes in God even as God is hidden (Isa 8:17), and the apostle Paul describes hope to be unshaken and reliable (2 Cor 1:7; Rom 5:4). Even in affliction, Christians are only "perplexed, but not driven to despair" (2 Cor 4:8). These and other verses are readily available and can be a source of comfort when despair threatens to overwhelm individual lives. But the quick referral to the Bible may not always be the best response to such real life experiences. The reminder that "we always have hope" can belittle the sharp pain of the present, it can suppress emotions, and it can lead to talking at others rather than listening to them.

But this is only half the problem. Whereas depression or loneliness are hardly ever identified as sins, despairing about the future and about God can easily be understood in this way, both by the people who are in despair and by those around them. In her book *Despair: Sickness or Sin?*, the theologian Mary Bringle unpacks the mixed responses that this question has received across the history of the church.[9] This wider historical perspective allows for a healthy balance and conversation, yet Bringle's work never strays far from the particular human experience of despair that she sees reflected, shared, and embraced in Jesus's life.

> A focus on the cross discloses what a discussion of the sinfulness of despair can otherwise easily overlook—namely, the fact that despair is an integral part of being human, a dimension of our humanness that even God Godself did not spurn to embrace. Too much talk about

---

9 Augustine and Aquinas, for instance, would speak of sin if someone despairs of God's ability and willingness to forgive. Other thinkers, such as Luther and Kierkegaard, place despair instead in the wider context of humanity's alienation from God. As Bringle summarizes, "a despairing mood may not be, in the strictest sense, *a* sin; nonetheless, it gives evidence, in the severest sense, of Sin itself," *Despair: Sickness or Sin? Hopelessness and Healing in the Christian Life* (Nashville, TN: Abingdon Press, 1990), 106 (emphasis original).

either the impiety or the pathology of despairing can cause us to negate
our own experience—to deny the real painfulness of our living.[10]

This concrete reality of a despairing human being allows for a practical
starting point and shifts the conversation from diagnosis to the tasks
of acceptance and articulation. This warming attitude toward despair
is a necessary counterweight to the absolute claims of hope because it
meets people where they are and honors their experience. As Lynch
proposes, making space for the posture that "it is all right to despair, or
to be without hope" can play a vital part in responding well to a crisis.[11]
Moreover, including despair as a part of the human condition avoids
the construction of categories that would alienate the people who most
need a listening ear and erode the guilty feeling that "such and such
a thought—hopelessness, for example—is not Christian."[12] Accepting
despair is ultimately about accepting oneself and other people.

> Hopelessness is a more usual and more human feeling than we are
> wont to admit. The plain fact for all of us is that many things are with-
> out hope, many people we are inclined to depend on cannot give hope,
> and many isolated moments or periods of life do not themselves con-
> tain hope. . . . It is critically important to know that this *is* the human
> story, for otherwise we would think ourselves inhuman whenever we
> encountered hopelessness in our lives.[13]

The perspective that Lynch and Bringle offer is a hopeful voice amid
the loud choirs of culture and church whose songs about endless possibilities, unshakeable convictions, and unlimited expectations tend to
drown out the reality of despair. Hope is real and good and comforting.
But "hope is not absolute in its range. Part of reality belongs to hopelessness."[14] Despair is a universal aspect of human living because everyone encounters hopeless situations. The task is not to hope for all
things all the time, but "to mark off the areas of hopelessness and to

---

10 *Sickness or Sin?* 154. See also Christian D. Kettler, *The God Who Rejoices: Joy,
    Despair, and the Vicarious Humanity of Christ* (Eugene, OR: Cascade, 2010).
11 *Images of Hope*, 55–56.
12 *Images of Hope*, 66.
13 *Images of Hope*, 53–54 (emphasis original).
14 *Images of Hope*, 66.

acknowledge them directly."[15] However, this is not easily done. As hard as it is to define despair, it is just as difficult to put that sense of the impossible into words, to express the disorientation of crumbled foundation, and to articulate that overwhelming darkening of life's horizon.

Jeremiah's Poetry and the Language of Despair

Aware of the inarticulable quality of despair, Bringle structures her work not on theories or taxonomies, but around two literary characters. Narrated in the first person, the lives of Isabel, a lapsed Irish Catholic from Mary Gordon's *Final Payments*, and Celie, a Southern Black woman from Alice Walker's *The Color Purple*, "offer an imagistic and invaluable entry" into the evasive nature of despair.[16] Isabel, for instance, loses her father and her lover and with it "her own purpose and identity";[17] she expresses this despair with "moans and outcries of pain but ultimately, by a stultifying silence."[18] Celie responds to her own abandonment likewise with "anesthetic silence" and resolves that "resignation seems safest."[19] The two novels portray the women's despair in painful details of failing self-esteem, loneliness, and lifelessness.

Bringle's blend of literature, psychology, and theology prompts the question whether or not the Bible may also contain such language of despair. This search is troubled initially by the lack of a Hebrew equivalent. The standard lexicon entry is יאשׁ (*yāʾaš*), which appears in 1 Samuel 27:1 (David's hope that Saul would "despair of seeking me" should he move to Philistine lands), in Job's description as a "despairing man" (6:26) and in the reflection on work and death in Ecclesiastes 2:20. These three texts touch on aspects of futility and hopeless actions, but neither offers an expression for articulating despair or touches on the existential and theological struggle of losing life's ground of hope.

---

15 *Images of Hope*, 62.

16 *Despair: Sickness or Sin?* 24.

17 *Despair: Sickness or Sin?* 26.

18 *Despair: Sickness or Sin?* 32.

19 *Despair: Sickness or Sin?* 32–33. For a similar approach, see Eve Holwell, "Literary Depictions of Hopelessness: A Short Story, a Novel, and a Poem," in *Hopelessness*, 85–105.

Metaphors of resignation and defeat likewise remain descriptive.[20] For discovering a more nuanced and expressive language for despair, the book of Jeremiah promises to be a good candidate not just because of the mode of crisis that reverberates through all its chapters but also because of its raw first-person speeches and its insistence to speak about the desperate clouds of life without taking the eyes off that faint, frail glimmer of sunrise at the horizon.

Reading Jeremiah as Trauma Literature

Jeremiah is no easy reading. The book exceeds Genesis and the Psalms in length, contains in its first twenty chapters barely any historical reference points, and shows overall little concern for chronological order. Its fifty-two chapters shift abruptly from poetry to prose, from accusation to symbolic action, from personal questions to political crisis. If this literary tangle were not enough, the book also overwhelms its readers with stark scenes of divine judgment and violence. Many of Jeremiah's interpreters have come in recent decades with fresh eyes to this turbulent literary landscape and have read it as a retrospective digestion of military, social, and theological trauma. The book looks back at the fall of Jerusalem (cf. 1:1–3) and engages in an effort of meaning-making for a defeated and disillusioned people. It lends words not so much for predicting or recording Judah's crisis, but rather for explaining, processing, recovery, and healing.

A hermeneutic of trauma attempts to read every element in Jeremiah as an articulation of the unspeakable pain of exile.[21] For instance,

---

20 For instance, the word רפה (rāpah) appears in 2 Samuel 4:1 when Ish-Bosheth's hands sink upon hearing of Abner's death. In Isaiah 13:7, the hands of God's enemies become feeble (see likewise רפה in Jer 6:24; Ezek 7:17 and כהה, "fading," in Isa 42:4 and Ezek 21:7). Elsewhere, people's "hearts melt" (מוג + לב) in an awestruck encounter with God (e.g., Exod 15:15; Ps 46:6; Nah 1:5). This semantic overview and the exegesis that follows are developed from my ""Woe Is Me!": The Book of Jeremiah and the Language of Despair," *JBL* 139 (2020): 479–497.

21 "Wounds of such destructive depth do not arrive with roadmaps, blueprints or disaster dictionaries to lead victims through the morass that faces them. But trauma and disaster studies help name the injuries, point to processes of survival, and set societies onto some new form new form of life. . . . They bring to the fore the creative, imaginative words that reveal wounds that refuse to be healed;" Kathleen M. O'Connor, *Jeremiah: Pain and Promise* (Minneapolis,

the outcries of the prophet can legitimize laments and complaints toward God, the people's confessions and prayers can serve as a script for acknowledging one's own part in the crisis (e.g., 3:22–25; 14:20–22), and the images of divine warfare can offer theological explanations for Babylon's victory and a hope for liberation. Isaiah may be more concerned with Zion's future and Ezekiel with the identity of God's people abroad, but Jeremiah stares right into the desperate disaster and speaks with no reservation about the collapse of the very ground of hope.

> *Why do we still sit here?*
> *Gather up and let us go to the fortified cities*
> *and let us perish there.*
> *For the Lord our God has doomed us to perish.*
>
> Jeremiah 8:14

The question cannot be answered; the posture has resigned itself to an unchangeable future. The speakers of these words have lost hope not just about the event of deliverance but also about God's favor as such. Inasmuch as searching Jeremiah for scenes of despair is an open-ended exercise, the book contains six passages that join Lamentations 5:16 by calling out "Woe is me!" or "Woe is us!" in the face of overwhelming disaster. Because of its archaic character, the word "woe" may perhaps be translated as "trouble" or "disaster." What makes this word such a good candidate for despair, however, is not its precise translation, but its self-reference ("disaster comes my way," "I am overwhelmed," "trouble is mine") and its expressive quality. The Hebrew poets sound out the experience of despair with a deep, guttural "oy," a woeful exclamation that elevates the need of expressing despair and, at the same time, manifests the lack of words for just that articulation.

Each of the six passages in which this moaning cry sounds forth includes a dense web of other words and expressions that construct a

MN: Fortress Press, 2011), 27. For Jeremiah and trauma, see, e.g. also Louis Stulman, "Reading the Bible as Trauma Literature: The Legacy of the Losers," *Conversations with the World* 34 (2014): 1–13; L. Juliana Claassens, "Preaching the Pentateuch: Reading Jeremiah's Sermons through the Lens of Cultural Trauma," *Scriptura* 116 (2017): 27–37; "Jeremiah: The Traumatized Prophet," in *The Oxford Handbook of Jeremiah*, ed. Louis Stulman and Edward Silver (Oxford: Oxford University Press, 2022), 358–373.

well-rounded lexicon for despair. The woes of the people, the city, the prophet, and the scribe unfold across the book as a poetry of despair that speaks for its own day as well as rings true as a meaningful template for articulating the reality of human despair today.

The Powerless Despair of the People

The first woe in the book appears in one of its most turbulent sections. The poetry of Jeremiah 4 plunges straight into war and destruction. Eight of the fifteen words in verse 5 are commands, the people run scared ("Let us go into the fortified cities!"), God announces judgment, and Israel's leaders collapse (vv. 6–9). The prophet Jeremiah, himself a member of the terrified community, finds his own voice in this dramatic script and holds nothing back as he cries out to God.

> *Surely, you have terribly deceived*
> *this people and Jerusalem, saying:*
> *'Peace will be to you!'*
> *But the sword reaches up to the throat!*
> *At that time it will be said to this people and to Jerusalem:*
> *'A scorching desert wind comes toward my people,*
> *not to winnow nor to purge,*
> *a wind stronger than these people comes for me.*
> *Now it is I who speaks judgment over them.'*

                                                            Jeremiah 4:10–12

The audacious accusation in verse 10 marks the first response to despair in this passage. Instead of asking for an explanation, Jeremiah puts words to the sharp conflict between God's promise of peace and God's pronouncement of war.[22] Although there is no rebuke from God to the prophet's protest, the verdict of verses 11–12 speaks for itself. Judgment is inevitable and unstoppable, blowing like a scorching wind toward city and people. That this blow will strike "at that time" only underlines

---

22 For more details, see my "Quoting the Words of God: Language and Theology in Jeremiah 4.10 and 32.25," in *From Words to Meaning: Studies on Old Testament Language and Theology for David J. Reimer*, ed. Samuel Hildebrandt, Kurtis Peters, and Eric N. Ortlund, HBM 100 (Sheffield: Sheffield Phoenix Press, 2021), 132–138.

the inevitability of destruction, yet along with the passive verb "it will be said," it also adds an unsettling anticipation to this tumultuous scene. But even before these details can sink in, the scene shifts once more and spotlights in verse 13 the people's desperate "woe is us" at the sudden rise of armies.

> Look, he rises like clouds,
> his chariots like storm,
> his horses swifter than eagles!
> Woe is us, for we are shattered!

These military references suggest the Babylonians as the catalyst for this despair, yet strong winds, clouds, and storm appear elsewhere in God's arsenal against chaos (e.g., Exod 15:8; Pss 18:16; 97:2; Isa 30:28; Zeph 1:15). The parallel expressions of "swords reaching the throat" in verse 10 and Jerusalem's "evil reaching up to your heart" in verse 18 suggest that the corruption of people and city has gone so far that God's mandate as creator demands radical action. The people are helpless to withstand the attack, yet under normal circumstances they might survive the invasion. However, if God who previously fought for Judah now turns against them, the very ground for hope no longer bears any weight and the people resign themselves to their powerlessness and uncertainty. If not even their prophet can get a hearing, how will they change the divine decree? As the leadership collapses, surely there is no hope left for ordinary people.

The poetic turbulence of Jeremiah 4 amasses to a gripping display of the chaos of its day. Voices, images, cries, and questions rattle against each other and act out the trauma of an inscrutable God and the overwhelming destruction that had to be endured. The text captures the paralyzing feeling of an approaching disaster, a reality that Jeremiah 6 takes yet a step further. The ring of warfare is tightening, the invading soldiers are so close that they can be heard, and the community stands surrounded and in hopeless anticipation of its destruction. As the enemies rise, plan, and prepare and as the clock ticks on and the shadows lengthen, the people have no option but to surrender themselves to the woe that has befallen them.

Prepare war against them!
   Arise, and let us go up at noon!
     'Woe is us, for the day turns,
       for the shadows of evening stretch out!'
   Arise, and let us go up by night,
   let us destroy their palaces!

Jeremiah 6:4–5

Jerusalem's Desperate Attempts

Closed in with no way out, the people in Jeremiah 4 are robbed of any perspective toward change. As they find their leaders crushed and their God turning against them, despair comes upon them as an unpredictable and sudden realization. The woe of Jerusalem in 4:30–31, who is personified here as in Lamentations 1 as a woman, is expressed with language that is just as dire and just as desperate.

And you, O desolate one,
   what will you do?
Even if you dress in scarlet,
   if you adorn yourself with golden decor,
   if you widen your eyes with paint,
in vain you make yourself beautiful!
   Your lovers have rejected you and seek your life!
A voice I hear, like a woman in labor,
   distressed, like a woman who bears her first child,
   gasping for breath, the voice of Daughter Zion.
   She stretches out her hands:
     'Woe is me! For I faint before murderers!'

Seeking to evade the destruction, Jerusalem tries to take control of her fate but fails miserably. Her lovers, likely a cipher for political allies (cf. Jer 2:33–37), have become her murderers and any effort to keep up the façade is "in vain." The language of costly dress, golden ornaments, and attractive makeup is set in jarring contrast to God's address ("O desolate one"). Jerusalem is depicted as self-assured, deluded, and blind to her lack of power. As with the people, God plays a crucial role in the sudden plunge into despair by revealing the irrevocable downfall that looms at the horizon.

This juxtaposition of hopeful masquerade and desperate breakdown is expressed by the shift of images from the beautiful woman to the woman fainting in labor. Jerusalem may once have been in control and hopeful about her future, yet like the people in 4:13, her sense of self, world, and God change in an instant. Jerusalem's despair sounds forth when her presumption crumbles under the weight of the real world. Her despair sounds forth in front of the mirror ("a voice I hear") as she stands abandoned and sees nothing else but the broken remains of her existence.[23] In Jeremiah 10:19, Jerusalem's second woe, this realization shifts to a resignation that is expressed with a lonely lament.

> Woe is me—my collapse, my terrible wound!
> So I had to say: 'Surely, this is what I suffer and I must bear it.'

Jeremiah's Woe of the Absolute

One of the features that sets Jeremiah apart from the other prophetic books is its extensive participation of the prophet. Jeremiah's agency takes its cue from the book's first conversation: "Ah, Lord God! Behold, I do not know how to speak, for I am only a youth" (1:6). Despite this reasonable cry of resistance, the prophet must resign himself to his calling. This situational dread of having no choice slowly shifts toward despair as opposition, confrontation, and frustration take hold of Jeremiah. His response is verbal and blunt, bringing his troubles before God in outright protest (4:10), in sheer bewilderment (12:1–4; 14:13), and in laments that border at times on bitter resentment. Life is too much for Jeremiah, and the conflicted prophet longs to undo the event of his own birth.

> Woe is me, O my mother, that you bore me!
> A man of strife, a man of quarrel—to all the land!
> I have not lent, nor have I borrowed—all of them curse me!
>
> Jeremiah 15:10

---

23 Steinbock's description of despair resonates well with Jerusalem's lonesome portrayal: "This absolute distance from the ground of hope is the experience of being abandoned, being alone, and being left to myself in the present;" "Phenomenon," 449.

In contrast to all other woes in the book, only this expression of despair is explicitly addressed to somebody. Jeremiah reaches in his loss of perspective for a hearing ear even if this cry is not answered. The poem in Jeremiah 15 highlights the need of the desperate individual for articulation and community, but it also offers a tragic picture of the nature of despair. The present situation is so unbearable that no future can be imagined. Consequently, an escape must be sought in the past, however unreasonable this might be. With its desperate gaze at a past that cannot be relived, Jeremiah 15 is a parade example of the ways in which despair traps the sufferer in the hopeless present and narrows the horizon to an inescapable dead-end.

Jeremiah's sense of self is captured in terms that are entirely negative ("a man of strife, a man of quarrel"). There is no indicator that these are titles that others have given him; this is how he speaks of himself. Moreover, the parallel arrangement of verse 10 pronounces Jeremiah to be in conflict with "all the land" and with the entire population—"all of them!"—who is collapsed into one faceless crowd of opposition. Whereas the previous passages draw a connection between despair and the illusions of power and security, the poetry of Jeremiah 15 shines a spotlight on the tendency of despair to feed on what Lynch describes as the "absolutizing instinct" in whose presence

> each thing loses its true perspective and its true edges. . . . But above all, everything assumes greater weight than it has, and becomes a greater burden. . . . The absolutizing instinct is the father of the hopeless and adds that special feeling of weight that hopelessness attached to everything it touches.[24]

From the prophet's viewpoint, any hope of change or help is ruled out. The poet who penned Jeremiah 15 has captured in but a few words the hopeless posture of the prophet, yet the passage also gently pushes back against the absolutizing assessment of its speaker. The total perspective of "all the land, all of them" is called into question by Jeremiah's address to his mother, who supposedly would support rather than curse him. In the broader contours of the book, other supporters, such as

---

24 *Images of Hope*, 106–107.

Ahikam (ch. 26), Ebed-Melech (ch. 38), and Baruch (ch. 36), come to the prophet's aid and right away in chapter 15 God responds with a new word of support (vv. 19–21).

But instead of skipping too quickly to God's affirmation, the tension must be endured and Jeremiah's "woe is me!" must be heard for what it is: a painful showcase of the paradoxical enclosure of despair. Once the prophet is in its grip, he extrapolates and absolutizes his pain, yet at the same time he is unable to look beyond the shoreline of his dark island to discover the beacons of hope that remain alive in the storm that tosses around him.

Baruch's Shattered Hopes

The final woe of the book belongs to Baruch, who is introduced in chapter 36 as Jeremiah's scribe. Speaking in restless anguish and physical strain, Baruch's words engage in a similar attempt at blame-shifting ("The Lord has added") that was voiced by the prophet in Jeremiah 4. This time, however, God responds immediately with a rebuttal and puts the onus on Baruch's expectations rather than on divine lack of favor.

> Thus says the Lord, the God of Israel, to you, O Baruch:
> You said:
>> 'Woe is me!
>> For the Lord has added sorrow to my pain!
>> I am weary with my groaning
>> and rest I do not find.'
> Thus you shall say to him:
> Thus says the Lord:
>> Behold, what I have built, I am breaking down,
>> and what I planted, I am plucking up—the whole land!
>> But you, do you seek for yourself great things?
>> Do not seek them, for I am bringing disaster upon all flesh!
>
> Jeremiah 45:2–5

Jeremiah 45 is the shortest chapter of the book, yet still the structures of communication are quite complex. Baruch's "woe" in verse 3 appears in a quotation by God ("You said"), who rehearses the scribe's despair. The passage then shifts to the divine answer that reprimands Baruch for "seeking great things." A first reading might suggest that the "great things" for which Baruch had hoped concern his personal life or the honor of his family (cf. Jer 32:12). But a comparison with other verses in Jeremiah (cf. 29:3; 33:3; 50:4) shifts the focus to the bigger stage of national restoration. God's sharp reply exposes Baruch's ambitions to play a heroic part either in averting judgment altogether or in somehow affecting a quick restoration.[25] The scribe seems to have shared some of the mistaken ideas about Israel's security that had imploded with such force in Jeremiah 4 and 6. Any such ambition is broken asunder by the language of breaking-down in verse 5, which reaffirms the divine resolve that the new day of building will not dawn before the darkest of nights has passed (cf. 1:10; 18:7–9; 24:6; 29:5).

The Open Ears and Eyes of Despair

Exhibiting a range of shared elements, Jeremiah's six woes formulate a nuanced perspective on despair. The people and the city are overwhelmed by the sudden realization that neither their leaders nor their allies can save them. Baruch and Jerusalem are gasping in pain and restlessness, ready to give up altogether as they realize that the nation's collapse will not be averted through their efforts. The portrayals of Jeremiah and Jerusalem identify isolation as a key ingredient of despair and highlight the speakers' struggle to negotiate their self-identity in light of the world around them. Finally, both prophet and scribe stand helpless before their God who has become inscrutable. Words and postures of resignation stand side-by-side with extrapolation and blame-shifting (4:10; 15:10; 45:3), and all scenes of despair are as personal as they are painful.

Jeremiah's despair speaks in its own culture and language (e.g., God as chaos-warrior; Jerusalem as woman) and into its own historical trauma of the invasion of 587 BCE. The six scenes of woe do not allow for an easy connection to contemporary economic, social, and

---

25 Fretheim comes to the same conclusion: "Baruch had hoped that Israel, which had been built up and planted, could be saved from destruction," *Jeremiah*, 573, as does Pamela J. Scalise, "Baruch as First Reader: Baruch's Lament in the Structure of the Book of Jeremiah," in *Uprooting and Planting: Essays on Jeremiah for Leslie Allen*, ed. John Goldingay, LHBOTS 459 (New York: T&T Clark, 2007), 305.

psychological challenges. The walls may not crumble around today's readers and armies may not besiege them, but the sense of the impossible and the problem of seeing with fresh eyes beyond the rubble is as much a part of being alive today as it was in Jeremiah's day. Because of the expressive quality of Jeremiah's poetry, the reality of lost hope that it articulates can still speak for all who face an overwhelming crisis, though it likely will carry most weight in situations in which faith, hope, and assurance are washed under by the roaring waves of despair.

The Acceptance and Agency of Despair

For all its judgment and efforts at explanations, Jeremiah does not diagnose despair in any way. The book does not criticize it as a posture that is sinful or a sign of weak faith, neither does it dismiss despair as a sickness or failure. Rather, Jeremiah simply portrays the loss of hope as something that can strike anyone regardless of their closeness to God (Jer 4:10), their social and political connections (Jer 4:31), their efforts to serve other people (Jer 15:10), or their good intentions (Jer 45). With no regard for education, gender, and social standing, despair cuts across the human community. In the place of condemnation, Jeremiah's woes invite careful reflection on how to accept and articulate despair. Instead of despairing over feelings of despair, this prophetic poetry pleads for expressing it, for becoming literate and liberated to speak of the impossible aspects of life.

But Jeremiah's language of despair is not a monologue. All six passages of "Woe is me!" place this cry in a complex scenario with many speakers and listeners around. The desperate war poems in chapters 4 and 6 switch constantly between the voices of people, God, and prophet. In Jeremiah 15, the prophet addresses his mother. Baruch's woe is heard and quoted by God. What these scenes of communication suggest is that the success of any speech about despair depends largely on the response and acceptance of those who stand around the desperate speaker. Prophetic in the true sense of the word, the sharp tone of Jeremiah's woe interrupts and criticizes any reading that is interested only in keeping up a facade of piety and self-control.[26] Like the prophets'

---

26 "Complain, protest, resist.... Communicate all that is shattered, despair-creating, and spirit-defeating. Lay it out so you can see it yourselves and can see each other in this deep, unending wound;" O'Connor, *Pain and Promise*, 90.

critique of self-serving worship (e.g., Isa 1:10–17; Jer 7:1–10), the honesty of Jeremiah's despair challenges any quick equation of despair and sin and makes space for everyone whose life says "I am facing the impossible," "I give up," "trouble is all I see." God shows Lady Jerusalem the real danger of her stance (4:30), calls Jeremiah to return (15:19), and challenges Baruch about his ambitions (45:5), yet none of these desperate speakers is reprimanded, dismissed, or condemned for putting their experience of hope's end into words.

Acceptance and articulation are significant responses for the hopeless heart because they can unleash pent-up emotions and allow the unspeakable cloud of pain to take a shape that is at least somewhat concrete. The Hebrew poets and prophets model such language across a wide scope of situations. Alongside the poetry of Lamentations 5 and Jeremiah, the woe of despair sounds forth also in Isaiah's realization of his "unclean lips" before God's holy throne (Isa 6:5) and by speakers who are caught in an overwhelming battle (1 Sam 4:7–8), betrayed by others (Isa 24:16), or stuck at a hopeless distance away from land and temple (Ps 120:5). All of these passages come with their own storylines of loss, yet all ascribe an encouraging measure of agency to shattered human beings.

Each of these woes is uttered as a first-person outcry that participates in the effort of making sense of the situation, keeping one's voice alive, and struggling for survival. Even in the people's siege (6:3) and Jerusalem's resignation (10:16), the desperate sufferers use the one thing that is under their control, namely, their voice. The paradox of a claim on agency and a lack of control emerges perhaps nowhere with more friction than in Jeremiah's wish not to have been born. Hanne Løland Levinson has studied Jeremiah 15 and its related passages (e.g., 1 Kgs 19; Job 3; Jer 20; Jonah 4) and concludes that

> in uttering their death wishes, the biblical characters strive to gain control of their situations; the death wishes are, therefore, rhetorical strategies for survival. . . . The biblical characters claim agency and autonomy by uttering a death wish because they try to make something happen, regardless of whether they negotiate or cry out in despair.[27]

---

27 *The Death Wish in the Hebrew Bible*, SOTSMS (Cambridge: Cambridge University Press, 2021), 144.

Even if the horizon is dark, even if words are impossible, the mere act of saying something at all keeps the characters in Jeremiah's poetry alive. "You hear me, therefore I am." This honoring of voice, identity, and agency is part of the book's processing of Jerusalem's traumatic fall and strategy of survival. Insofar as it inspires humans then and now to open their mouths, it is meaningful all on its own. It may, however, be yet more special when, as often in Jeremiah's polyphony, God alone is the listener to these voices.

The Sounds of Despair

The cries and conversations across Jeremiah's poetic portions articulate a dissonant chorus of despair that lends the book an unmistakably personal and emotional character. If this prophetic composition is primarily interested in blaming Israel for their sin or in justifying God's righteous judgment, it is hard to understand why these voices are included and why they sound forth with such raw force. Jeremiah's poetry wants its readers not just to know what has happened but also to hear and to feel the despair of the many parties involved. Hearing Jeremiah's first-person expressions rather than more detached, third-person descriptions (e.g., "Behold, the people are giving up!") can counter the persistent instinct of repression.

For readers who find no words on their own or are unsure if they may use them, the "Aahhh" or "woe" (English) or "oiiii" (Hebrew) of Jeremiah's poems can strike a chord precisely because of their inarticulate nature. A version of what Kathleen O'Connor has identified as a "breakdown of language" in other literary works, these open sounds often suit the unspeakable reality of being human more accurately than well-crafted statements.

> Physical and emotional pain destroys language because severe pain is "unshareable." In Shakespeare's *King Lear*, the wordlessness of the old king's shock makes his entrance with his dead daughter Cordelia in his arms so pitiful. All he can say is 'Howl, howl, howl'—unbearably expressive and beyond words.[28]

---

28 *Pain and Promise*, 23.

Inasmuch as Shakespeare's royal howling and Jeremiah's prophetic woe speak no intelligible word, they offer release for pain and pressure.[29] The many shouts and intimate expressions in the Bible's poetic material can inspire their hearers to speak and shout and sob likewise, yet they need to be heard also as an important reminder that screaming can be more appropriate than explanations, that sounding out problems can sometimes matter more than hearing solutions. As the question-and-answer patterns in Jeremiah 8:12–16, 16:10–13, and 22:8–9 suggest, stoic explanations of disaster were already a mainstream response in the aftermath of Jerusalem's fall. "Why has the Lord brought all this evil upon us?" "Because you have forsaken his law and worshipped other gods!" It is one of Jeremiah's most precious accomplishments to combine such analyses with evocative visions of what "all this evil" may have felt and sounded like.

Jeremiah's loud "Woe is me! Woe is us!" imparts to its first readers a testimony that their suffering has not gone unnoticed, that it is real, and that feelings of despair are an appropriate reaction. "We could not have done any different; we really had no control over what happened; if we could go back, the same thing would come to pass; woe and trouble truly were upon us." Though far removed from the politics and problems of Jeremiah's day, the book that bears his name still invites its readers to look back and see those painful moments in their past for what they truly were: an overwhelming struggle, an impossible situation, a genuine reason for despair. Hearing this poetry and heeding its invitation for speaking it is an exercise that can allow some readers a new sense of emotional literacy and liberty amid their unspeakable memories and their dark outlook at the future.

Despair and Disillusion

Jeremiah's language of despair resounds amid a complex blend of historical crisis, literary artistry, and theological reflection that each in

---

29 Aaron Schart's observations on Hebrew *hôy* hold true in many ways also for the *'ôy* of Jeremiah's despair: "Such a sound spontaneously escapes a physically or mentally injured person, and without this scream the person could not adequately express the pain. . . It gives some measure of relief to the overly stressed nerve system;" "Deathly Silence and Apocalyptic Noise: Observations on the Soundscape of the Book of the Twelve," *Verbum et Ecclesia* 31 (2010), 2. See further Rhiannon Graybill, "'Hear and Give Ear!' The Soundscape of Jeremiah," *JSOT* 40 (2016): 467–490.

their own way leave their mark on the biblical text. The therapeutic dimensions of acceptance, agency, and articulation are at the heart of this language. An authentic expression of their own experience of being human, the Hebrew poets who are responsible for this prophetic book long to open their readers' mouths and ears but they also strive to grant them a new vision. Each poem of woe centers around a shocking moment of insight, of a new awareness of self, world, and God. The people and the city in Jeremiah 4 realize that their self-security and control are mere illusions, the prophet must accept that his words of judgment make him unpopular, and Baruch's ambitions to be part of those "great things" and the hero of the hour are broken asunder. These beliefs about human possibilities and power collide one after another with the bitter reality of failed political manipulations, prophetic inefficacy, and human limitations.

In each passage, despair ruptures the routines of life precisely at the moment when the speakers see the world as it is rather than how they assumed it to be. With sudden and startling force, Jeremiah's woes characterize despair as a moment of revelation in which people and prophet alike can no longer avoid seeing their limitations and presumptions. Sharing in the terrible experience of Lady Jerusalem in Jeremiah 4, these literary scenarios hold up a mirror for Jeremiah's readers. Whether it is a domesticated certainty about God's course of action, a self-assured conviction that good looks and connections will achieve deliverance, or a plan to heroically swoop in and save the day, Jeremiah's scenarios suggest that the clash between expectation and experience can take many forms. What they share, however, is the sobering message that any over-confident posture can crumble any minute into wide-eyed resignation.[30]

These portrayals and their implications for today's look at life are not easy to digest but they are foundational to one of Jeremiah's most daring attempts to reach beyond the dark horizon and to see something positive, indeed hopeful, even in despair. The strange transformation

---

30 "All of us struggle against the constraints placed on our bodies, our commitments, our ambitions, and our resources, even as we're saddled with inflated expectations of invincibility.... I must accept the world as it is, or break against the truth: my life is made of paper walls. And so is everyone else's;" Bowler, *No Cure for Being Human*, 186.

from wound to wonder, from injury to insight, participates in the same poetic tension that resonates through God's job description for the prophet.

> *See, I have set you this day over nations and over kingdoms,*
> *to pluck up and to break down,*
> *to destroy and overthrow,*
> *to build and to plant.*

Jeremiah 1:10

The three word pairs liken God's judgment and restoration to the work of a builder and a gardener; they involve design and care, planning and patience. The imbalance of the six verbs tilts toward destruction, yet the longer they weave through the book (e.g., 18:7–9; 24:6; 29:5; 45:5), the more the act of breaking and re-making becomes a joint venture. Breaking and building are two sides of the same coin and Jeremiah's expressions of despair are not merely the bad news before the good news. Rather, they are a gift of language that can open eyes to realities that might otherwise remain unseen. It can reveal the reality of the human condition in all its fragility, dependency, and limitation;[31] it can break down the presumptions that stand in the way of new insights.

In political and personal struggles alike, Jeremiah's poetry sees some positive potential in despair. Its ability to shatter unhealthy illusions and to disclose life with all its edges and limits does not diminish its woeful pain or redeem its sting. On the contrary, only those individuals who say "this is impossible" or "this is out of my control" are on the path of learning a truth about being human that cannot be found any other way. Few things in life will confront the self with its boundaries and barriers like the school of despair. In Mary Bringle's words, the challenge that flows from this confrontation means "taking control

---

31 Since both the prophet and the scribe are included in Jeremiah's woes, Arthur Gross Schaefer's and Steve Jacobson's testimony to the gift of despair is worth hearing in the context of pastoral and other leadership: "When we as clergy find ourselves disillusioned and despairing, we can seek to identify what illusion we have lost and what reality we might now find in its place. . . . By actively seeking 'disillusionment'—by dedicating ourselves to reality—sometimes our experiences of despair will turn to epiphanies;" "Surviving Clergy Burnout," *Encounter* 70 (2009), 48.

over those parts of one's life, however minor, which can be changed, all the while recognizing the incontrovertible limits within which no change can realistically be expected."[32] Calm and chaos, perspective and darkness, control and limitations—life at the shoreline is indeed a hopeful place in spite of, yet sometimes because of, its ebb and flow of despair.

Imagining Hope

Swimming the mile out to Jeremiah's particular island is never a comfortable exercise, but every sore stroke and salty breeze is well worth the effort. For all who can leave their categories of sin and sickness behind, the language of Jeremiah's world opens a broad horizon for speaking about the overwhelming crises of life. Jeremiah normalizes situations in which God's people want to give up altogether, have lost their sense of self, and can no longer believe in a new day. Beyond acceptance and articulation, this prophetic book instills despair with a revelatory power. In practice, the shift from standing in the midst of suffering to seeing the precious insights of despair will never come easily, especially when one's woes echo without response across the vast sea of human struggle.

The journey with despair requires travel companions who remind the desperate heart that hope is always only a relational concept, something that must be given rather than generated. Amid the dominant narratives of today—"our civilization tends to associate a sense of shame with the need for help, as if all real 'life' must come from within"[33]—this is no easy task. Self-sufficiency is often the first response to crisis, making even the warmest words of encouragement a victim of deaf ears. Striking a balance with its relentless poems of death and destruction, Jeremiah offers two case studies that expose the problem of hope (Jer 29) and model the ministry of hope (Jer 30–33).

---

32 *Despair: Sickness or Sin?*, 50. A thoughtful reflection on cultural narratives of power can be found in Konrad Grossmann, "Macht und Ohnmacht. Von der Schwierigkeit, das eigene Leben zu beeinflussen," *Systemische Notizen* 19 (2006): 4–11.

33 Lynch, *Images of Hope*, 40.

The Hurdles of Hope

The impulse to help those who have lost all hope comes naturally to most people and has been a key element all through the Judeo–Christian tradition. The legacy of the Hebrew poets is continued in the words of Jesus and Paul, yet all across the Bible speaking a word of hope is a tricky business. This challenge, ironically, is seen in quite striking colors in the context of Jeremiah 29:11, the number one stop for many readers who search the Bible for a word about a hopeful future.[34] The popularity of this verse comes from its crisp combination of God's plans, good intentions, and reassurance.

> *For I know the plans that I plan for you, declares the Lord,*
> *plans of peace, not of disaster,*
>   *to give you a future and hope.*

Presented as a letter from Jeremiah, God's word is addressed in Jeremiah 29 to the first wave of Israelites whom the Babylonians had forcefully deported from Jerusalem. The comforting tone and God's gentle promises make no mention of the trauma of the lost homeland; indeed, the call to build houses and plant gardens (v. 5) signals that God's work of restoration has begun, even away from home and under foreign rule. The break with the past is total; the reality of sin and judgment is at best implicit in the address to the exiles who are asked to wait a full seventy years until God will turn their fate around (v. 10). God's plans are good, yet living on foreign soil and knowing the golden future to be more than a generation away is likely not the good plans for which one would hope.

These dimensions and details make God's promises of the future somewhat complicated. But Jeremiah 29 articulates a more shocking message yet. After the two statements of new life, divine help, and a coming restoration (vv. 4–7, 10–14), the readers learn that the exiles reject God's good plans.[35]

---

34 In 2021, this verse held first rank of the verses that users of YouVersion shared, bookmarked, and highlighted most often in Germany, Indonesia, Nigeria, the United Kingdom and several other countries; cf. "YouVersion 2021 Downloadable Stats," https://docs.google.com/spreadsheets/d/1G0NLDOyN5PHNCmKhlPzjBc_BvGha5qd1v0AS16yfMjM/edit#gid=0.

35 Most Bible translations separate the quoted response in verse 15 from verses 10–14 (see, however, the 2003 version of the *JPS* translation). The reading

> *I will be found by you, declares the Lord,*
> *and I will restore your fortunes.*
> *I will gather you from all the nations where I have scattered*
> *you, declares the Lord,*
> *and I will bring you back to the place from where I have*
> *exiled you.*
> *But you said:*
> *'The Lord has raised up prophets for us in Babylon!'*

Jeremiah 29:14–15

Far from accepting the conditions outlined in the letter, Jeremiah's recipients prefer the message of their own prophets who, like their counterparts in Jerusalem (cf. Jer 27:16), offer the hope of a much quicker return. God's plans may be good, yet the people have better plans. Inasmuch as the communication between God and people is tender up to this point, after the response that is quoted in verse 15, the tone shifts from comfort to outright condemnation that especially targets particular prophetic figures (vv. 21, 24). When read as a whole, Jeremiah's letter to the exiles cannot be characterized as a message of hope and peace. The focus of the chapter rests instead on the same struggle for prophetic authority that already dominates Jeremiah 23–28. The chapter is as much a stage for the clash of expectation and reality as it is a showcase for human self-reliance. This commitment to internal resources instead of trusting in outside help continues in the aftermath of Jerusalem's fall (Jer 40–44).

Reading Jeremiah 29:11 in its context elevates once again the need for articulating and accepting despair. The radical break from scorched lands to new gardens speaks a theological message about God's new initiative, yet its abruptness and the eclipse of the traumatic past is no wholesome response to despair and loss. Speaking hope into situations of loss and overwhelming disaster is tough in the best of circumstances, yet it will only be harder if no space is made for despair and for the grief of disillusionment. The failure of the prophetic word in Jeremiah 29 reminds its recipients that encouragement is not a one-way street. The chapter also troubles the idea that citing a single Bible verse can produce lasting change, no matter how hopeful it may be.

---

presented here follows my "Are God's 'Good Plans' not Good Enough? The Place and Significance of Jer 29:15 in Jeremiah's Letter to the Exiles," *JSOT* 45 (2021): 561–575.

Imagining with

Inasmuch as Jeremiah's scenes of despair utilize the whole range of Hebrew poetic art, its therapeutic language of hope likewise weaves lines, voices, images, and expressions into a dense tapestry. The poems in Jeremiah 30–33, the so-called "Book of Comfort," share many formal and lexical aspects with Jeremiah 1–20 but the connection runs much deeper.[36] In contrast to Jeremiah 29, these four chapters do not block out the painful past but sketch their new horizon against an honest assessment of the crisis that echoes and expresses the community's despair with undiluted force.

> *We hear a voice of panic!*
>   *Terror—and no peace. . . .*
> *Why is every face turned gray?*
>
> Jeremiah 30:5–7

> *Incurable is your collapse,*
>   *terrible your wound!*
> *There is no support for your cause,*
>   *no medicine for your wound,*
> *no healing for you.*
>
> Jeremiah 30:12–13

> *A voice is heard in Ramah,*
>   *lamenting and bitter weeping!*
> *Rachel is weeping for her children,*
>   *refusing to be comforted for her children,*
>   *for they are no more.*
>
> Jeremiah 31:15

Adding to these dire lines the raw memory of "the whole valley of the corpses and ashes" outside Jerusalem (31:40), Jeremiah's word of hope

---

36 For a sample of parallels, see Barbara A. Bozak, *Life "Anew:" A Literary-Theological Study of Jer. 30–31*, AnBib 122 (Rome: Editrice Pontificio Istituto Biblico, 1991). The composition of Jer 30–33 holds together by the artistic phrase "I will turn their fortunes" (*šabtî šĕbût*) that occurs in 30:3, 18, 31:23, 32:44, and 33:7, 11, 26.

often speaks with the same language as its word of hopelessness and shows itself to be just as aware of the reality of despair. The frequency and detail of such woeful poetic fragments suggest that the talk about shattered assumptions is part of the book's hopeful speech. As in the poems of despair, a firm look at the tragedy is necessary to create a firm foundation for moving forward. Without such acceptance any new vision will crumble under the unspoken ballast of the past. It is only with the deep wounds as part of the conversation that the poetry can move on to proclaim that

> God has made a new move. It is a move made only in the midst of the candid diagnosis. It is not a word spoken by Yahweh in ignorance about the real pathology of Judah. It is rather a word of "second truth" that comes only with and after the first word of truth. It is a word of second possibility as the first possibility of old life is read to its harsh ending.[37]

This "second truth" unfolds in Jeremiah 30–33 not by way of timetables or calls for faithful endurance. Far from such specifics and demands, these chapters imagine, envision, and unveil Israel's future. They expand the narrow and dark horizon of defeat. They pull up to shore those who are lost on their silent seas. They place the hearers on the colorful stage of life. They proclaim and sing and dance.

> *The city will be built on its mound,*
> *and the palace will stand in its place.*
> *From them will come forth songs of thankfulness*
> *and the voice of bright singing!*

Jeremiah 30:18–19

> *Again you shall adorn yourself with tambourines*
> *and you shall go out with dance and bright song....*
> *Then the young women shall rejoice with dance,*
> *the young and the old men together!*
> *I will turn their mourning to joy!*

Jeremiah 31:4, 13

---

37 Walter Brueggemann, *Hopeful Imagination: Prophetic Voices in Exile* (Philadelphia, PA: Fortress Press, 1986), 39.

Without proper attention to the poetry of trauma that is strewn amongst these scenes it would be easy to dismiss them as wishful thinking. Yet Jeremiah's therapeutic use of words operates with honesty and hope. This balance accepts despair but it does not understand despair as the final word of the human condition. The songs and dances in Jeremiah 30–33 paint a graphic scene before its readers; they stimulate memories; they awaken sights and scents; they plaster the way on which Israel has walked into exile and envision how the people will travel this road in the opposite direction (31:21). Jeremiah's poetry invites its audience to taste new harvests (31:5), to hear fresh brooks of water (31:9), and to think of their very lives as a "watered garden" (31:12).

Reading strategies that approach prophetic restoration promises with a keen eye for messianic glories will read right past the pastoral and psychological power of this language. The traumatic context of crisis and the vivid language of Jeremiah 30–33 indicate that the biblical prophets are not so much concerned with the future as with the misery of those to whom they speak in the present.[38] Just like the prophetic laments and retrospective tales of doom, their prophecies of restoration speak in the immediate and intimate register of crisis literature. Such prophetic poetry lends sights and sighs to those who have lost their vision and voice because it is deeply aware that

> hope not only imagines; it imagines *with*. . . . What happens in despair is that the private imagination, of which we are so enamored, reaches the point of the end of inward resources and must put on the imagination of another if it is to find a way out. . . . Despair lies exactly in the constriction of the private imagination.[39]

Jeremiah's poetry is a companion in suffering, a friend who, somehow, can see a horizon when all thoughts of the future have become

---

38 The same observation applies to Isaiah 40–55 and Ezekiel 33–48: "It would hardly be correct to state that the prophet Second Isaiah is 'eschatological.' *His* language is that of metaphors and poetic artistry, the purpose of which was to lend support and comfort to his fellow country men in one of the most difficult periods in their history;" Hans M. Barstad, *A Way in the Wilderness: The" Second Exodus" in the Message of Second Isaiah*, JSSM 12 (Manchester: University of Manchester Press, 1989), 106 (emphasis original).

39 Lynch, *Images of Hope*, 23 (emphasis original).

impossible. Imagination will triumph in such conversations over information, creativity will do more good than calculation and control, metaphor and images will breathe new life into dry bones.[40] The recipients of these visions, then and now, may take on the role of the unnamed speaker who awakes from slumber in Jeremiah 31:26 and looks around at the comfort, the possibilities, and the hope that have broken into their dark world from without.

The Character of Hope

For all the power of such speech, the prophetic ministry of hope presents no naive automatism of hearing and healing. Words bear weight and can make a change all on their own, yet they are strongest when they rest on the character, care, and authority of the one speaking. This is prophetic hope: God speaks. Right away in Jeremiah 30:1–5, the readers are pointed to God as the initiator of this new and permanent word of hope ("Write on a scroll all the words I have spoken to you"). The human voices mix and shift constantly after this introduction, but in the final chapter only God speaks.

The assurance in Jeremiah 33 of "health and healing" (v. 6), the vision of new music and marriages (v. 11), and the promise of new leaders and covenant (vv. 14–22) all come from God personally. The disaster is still in view (vv. 4–5) and not ignored. But from God's vantage point, the crisis is not the end but the beginning of a new narrative that is not based on illusions of power but on a powerful God,[41] that is not stuck in the past but starts the slow turn to new life. No longer do the scoffing words of the enemies define Israel (30:17; 33:24) but the community is now named as God's dear servant (31:10). Jerusalem likewise, though shattered and disillusioned, is now given the privilege to be God's "name of joy, a praise, and a glory before all the nations of the earth" (33:9). Inasmuch as this gift of new names

---

40 "Rational argumentation could not give the people this kind of hope... the rhetor strives to produce not so much a new opinion as a new way of viewing the world;" Michael V. Fox, "The Rhetoric of Ezekiel's Vision of the Valley of the Bones," *HUCA* 51 (1980), 7.

41 "Jeremiah believes that God is able to do an utterly new thing which violates our reason, our control, and our despair;" Brueggemann, *Hopeful Imagination*, 29–30.

highlights the book's ambitions of transformation, it also serves to
characterize its giver.

> For I will restore health to you
>   and your wounds I will heal, declares the Lord,
> because they called you:
>   'Outcast! That is Zion, nobody cares for her!'

Jeremiah 30:17

> Is not Ephraim my dear son,
>   my darling child?
> Even as I speak of him,
>   I fondly remember him.
> Therefore, all that is in me yearns for him,
>   I will surely have mercy on him!

Jeremiah 31:20

God is portrayed in these first-person speeches not as detached analyst
or a problem solver, but as an involved carer. Jeremiah's therapeutic
words are powerful because they are spoken by a God who sees and
hears and feels, who shares in the struggle of people and prophet. The
scenes of "woe" themselves are testimonies to this divine participation.
The tragedy of 4:13, for instance, is followed in 4:19–21 by a heartfelt
lament of God weeping alongside Jerusalem and its inhabitants ("O my
anguish within! I tremble! O the walls of my heart! My heart is restless").[42] Jeremiah's hopeless grasping for the past is met by a renewed
divine promise of protection (15:19–21). As yet another mark of the tensions of breaking and building, the same voice that pronounces harsh
endings also speaks with empathy. Jeremiah's hope is rooted in the
character of God.

---

42 Cf. J. J. M. Roberts, "The Motif of the Weeping God in Jeremiah and Its Back-
    ground in the Lament Tradition of the Ancient Near East," *OTE* 5 (1992): 361–
    374. The divine speech in Jeremiah 31:20 shares several aspects with Jeremiah
    4:19–21, which is a highly ambiguous text "that compels the reader to hear
    the mourning of prophet, city, and God *all at once*—an acoustic panorama,
    a tri-dimensional lament, a cumulative response to the historical disaster;"
    Hildebrandt, "Speaker Ambiguity in the Psalms," 204 (emphasis original). See
    also Hosea 11:8–9; Micah 1:8–9; and Isaiah 16:9–11.

The prophetic approach to despair concerns the identity of the despairing sufferers and the identity of the one who imagines new possibilities with them. This task is a divine as well as a human responsibility because the language of hope cannot be a monologue and it cannot be learned on a lonely, desperate island.[43] The narrative in Jeremiah 32:1–15 that floats freely amid the imagery and voices of Jeremiah 30–33 acts out this social and communicative dimension, yet it also shows that the language of hope is not only expressed with words. Imprisoned in the royal palace, the prophet Jeremiah acts upon God's directive and purchases a field in his hometown Anathoth, which lies about 5 kilometers north of Jerusalem. Symbolic actions are common in the book, yet they usually carry a negative message. Spoiled clothes symbolize Israel's spoilt calling (Jer 13); broken jars mirror the shattering of people and city (Jer 19). The purchase of the field, however, is a parable of hope through and through that turns even the mundane legalities of paperwork into a token of a brighter future.

> *Thus says the Lord of hosts, the God of Israel:*
> *Take these documents. . . and put them in a stone jar*
> *so that they may last for many days.*
> *For thus says the Lord of hosts, the God of Israel:*
> *Once again houses and fields and vineyards*
> *will be bought in this land.*

Jeremiah 32:14–15

For the apostle Paul, "hope that is seen is not hope" (Rom 8:24) and this holds true for the day of liberation and peace that Jeremiah's field eagerly awaits. Yet in Jeremiah 32, these few square meters of dirt, weeds, and worms inspire hope precisely because they are visible. By looking at this piece of land, everyone who is left behind in the ruins can take heart and, like Jeremiah from his prison cell, imagine and act toward a new future. The desperate people of Anathoth need not have answers to the "how" and "when" of that day. They may be as confused about the whole affair as Jeremiah himself (v. 25). But the purchase of

---

43 "Hope cannot be achieved alone. It must in some way or other be an act of a community, whether the community be a church or a nation of just two people struggling together to produce liberation in each other;" Lynch, *Images of Hope*, 24.

the field can remind them of the prophet who rose from their midst and painted with his words bright pictures of music and dance, who imagined a horizon beyond the empty gates and silent cities that Lamentations 5 mourned with such woe and weariness. When the ground of hope collapses, when giving up altogether is the only choice left, the creative words and small deed of a fellow human being can make real the hope that remains, nevertheless.

CHAPTER 4

A World Undone
Job 3 and the Language
of Shattered Assumptions

Who can make my life like those months of old,
  like those days when God kept me safe,
when his lamp shone above my head,
  giving its light when I walked in darkness?
Just like when I was in my autumn days,
  when the friendship of God was upon my tent. . . .
Then I thought that I would pass away in my family nest:
  like sand, I would have expanded my days,
  my roots expanded to the waters,
  dew nestling on my branches.

Job 29:2–3, 18–19

Familiar, stable, and tame. Many of the islands that human beings inhabit are little havens. The sun rises; the sun sets. The world is good; life has meaning. Vast as a golden stretch of sand, human life expands tenderly and predictably through time with its roots, refreshments, and routines in plain sight. Privileged and blessed, many stories may begin like this but then there is that surprising, terrible bend in the road that brings even the best life to its knees to draw a line in the sand. Where there was but time, now there is a before and an after. Where there were expectations and assumptions—"Then I thought"—now reality has washed away the warm sand, dried up the tender dew, and snapped off branches and roots. A sudden catastrophe and the traumatic crisis of its aftermath can call everything into question, leaving dear beliefs and hopes in shambles. In a blink of an eye, after one dark night at sea, the autumn days of the human experience can become unfamiliar and fragile, strange and chaotic.

Readers often come to the book of Job with questions about evil and justice, yet this giant among the Hebrew poetic works speaks just as much, and perhaps a bit more, to the basic challenges of life on earth. Job is no theoretical treatise, no argument for one particular theodicy.[1] At its center stands a human being whose core beliefs about self, the world, and God are upended. The traumatic shift from life to death, from light to darkness, confronts Job's readers nowhere more sharply than in the joint effort of narrative and poetry across chapters 1–3. The portrayal of Job in these chapters and, above all, in his first-person poem in chapter 3, creates a mirror for its readers where they may discover their own assumptions and recognize the psychological and theological turmoil that they met when their world came undone. Job's life and language arise from the book in sharp tones, but neither condemns its hearers nor confronts them with a negative role model. The poetry in Job 3 instead normalizes the human struggle between expectation and reality, offers language to articulate the agony of unveiled assumptions, and prepares the way toward a new view of the world that can stand on both sides of that grim line in the sand.

Assuming Reality

By means of observation and experience, people construct from a young age a set of generalized ideas about the world. To develop and live by these basic assumptions is as natural as it is necessary. The presence of such assumptions and the need for their shared acceptance is evident, for instance, in social interaction. The baseline expectation in every-day conversation is that speaking will be met with listening and with a response. Such assumptions, however, do not merely form a conceptual system that enables human cooperation but amount to fundamental convictions about the shape of the world and one's place within it.

---

1 Katharine J. Dell lists ten possible answers to the question of suffering that readers may draw from Job; *Shaking a Fist at God: Struggling with the Mystery of Undeserved Suffering* (Chicago, IL: Triumph Books, 1997), 96–98.

In the pioneer study of "our assumptive world," Ronnie Janoff-Bulman identified three core assumptions: "the world is benevolent; the world is meaningful; the self is worthy."[2] Her fieldwork as a professor of psychology led her to conclude that most people are generally optimistic about their future, entertaining even a "sense of invulnerability."[3] Such assumptions are not irrational or naive, but part of the human operating system that "guides our interactions in the world and generally enable[s] us to function effectively."[4] In view of how central they are in everyday living, it is startling to consider that the reality of people's assumptive worlds only ever comes to the fore when these worlds collapse.

> The essence of trauma is the abrupt disintegration of one's inner world. Overwhelming life experiences split open the interior world of victims and shatter their most fundamental assumptions. Survivors experience "cornered horror," for internal and external worlds are suddenly unfamiliar and threatening.[5]

Other researchers have questioned and developed Janoff-Bulman's three core assumptions, yet her pioneering work has established itself as a foundation in trauma theory and her questionnaire-styled World Assumption Scale remains a helpful tool for self-reflection.[6] Given the severe trauma of war and deportation that gave rise to so much of the Bible, Janoff-Bulman's basic framework of conviction and crisis promises to be a fruitful hermeneutic lens for the prophetic books, for Lamentations, and especially for Job.

---

2   Ronnie Janoff-Bulman, *Shattered Assumptions: Towards a New Psychology of Trauma* (New York: Free Press, 1992), 6.

3   *Assumptions*, 19. See further Tali Sharot, *The Optimism Bias: Why We're Wired to Look at the Bright Side* (London: Constable & Robinson, 2012).

4   *Assumptions*, 5.

5   *Assumptions*, 63.

6   See, e.g., Donald Edmondson et al., "From Shattered Assumptions to Weakened Worldviews: Trauma Symptoms Signal Anxiety Buffer Disruption," *J Loss Trauma* 16 (2011), which finds problems with the "retrospective reporting on pretrauma worldviews" (p. 360). See also V. van Bruggen et al., "Structural Validity of the World Assumption Scale," *J Trauma Stress* 31 (2018): 816–825. There is unfortunately little indication in Janoff-Bulman's book that the core assumptions of a life overshadowed by neglect and abuse will look very different than those of a life that is privileged with "positive interactions with caregivers" (p. 21).

Always a favorite text in the study of psychology—both psychologists Carl Jung and Sigmund Freud made extensive reference to Job—it is not surprising that Janoff-Bulman uses "Job's innocence and Job's sorry lot" as an illustration for her theories.[7] In 2014, Bible scholar Kirsten Nielsen developed these tentative connections with more depth, suggesting, for instance, that God's blessing and the affirmation of God's just punishment (e.g., Job 8:1–7) can be seen as evidence that the world is good and that actions have meaning.[8] In conversation with Janoff-Bulman's ideas about cognitive conservatism, Nielsen further highlights that Job "is unwilling to give up his belief in a just God" until he receives the "new information" that God discloses in chapters 38–42.[9]

Nielsen's reading of Job is an exemplary exercise of how the Bible and psychology can speak with one another. Whereas earlier analyses in the twentieth century routinely attempted to tap into the subconsciousness of Job or his author,[10] Nielsen's analysis remains descriptive and inspires a range of further reflections. For instance, since ancient communities would likely not have shared Janoff-Bulman's assumptions of personal self-worth, the theological and communal dimensions of Job's crisis demand more attention. Nielsen's descriptions of Job in the text further raise the question of how Job's readers may encounter and negotiate their own journeys from shattered assumptions to new reality.

---

7   *Assumptions*, 8. See, e.g., C. G. Jung, *Answers to Job*, trans. R. F. C. Hull (Cleveland, OH: Meridian Books, 1960); Marshall H. Lewis, *Viktor Frankl and the Book of Job: A Search for Meaning* (Eugene, OR: Pickwick, 2019).

8   "Post-Traumatic Stress Disorder and the Book of Job," in *Trauma and Traumatization in Individual and Collective Dimensions: Insights from Biblical Studies and Beyond*, ed. Eve-Marie Becker, Jan Dochhorn, and Else K. Holt, SANT 2 (Göttingen: Vandenhoeck & Ruprecht, 2014), 63.

9   "Post-Traumatic Stress Disorder," 65. "Our fundamental need for stability in our conceptual system is largely reflected in our tendency to maintain rather than change our theories about the world and ourselves;" Janoff-Bulman, *Assumptions*, 42.

10   See, e.g., Katz, "Psychoanalytic Comment." "Psychologically informed criticism can describe the qualities of a *character* as he or she is presented in the text, but must take care neither to presume that those characterizations are historical nor go beyond the text by 'filling in' details;" Kille, "Psychology and the Bible," 130 (emphasis original).

This interaction between the ancient book and the world in front of the text, then and now, seems to be encouraged by the characters and the story itself. In contrast to most key figures in the Old Testament, Job has no genealogy and lives outside of the land of Israel, meeting readers today still as a human being "representative of all who have felt their lives and their assumptions evanescing around them."[11] Finally, it remains to unpack how Job's language—and especially the poetry in chapters 3 and 38–42—articulates the breakdown of assumptive worlds and the rebuilding of new reality. To stand before the fragments of the world that one once inhabited is unsettling enough. But to endure the storm alone, to cling to the shipwreck, and to drift at sea in silence is unbearable. When the familiar havens of life have become unreliable and when the language that has always rolled off one's lips with ease no longer bears any meaning, the hope that remains often is found at new shores where different words and worldviews dwell.

Assumptions and the Reader in Job 1–3

The book of Job is often described as a literary masterpiece, yet as with all literature worthy of such acclaim, its profound insights require patient reading and study. Challenges abound from the interplay of narrative (chs. 1–2 and 42:7–17) and poetry (chs. 3:1–42:6) to the purpose of the endless dialogues, from the heavenly throne room to the darkened depth of Leviathan's realm, from the dense theological reflections to the frustrating failure of human conversation. Across each of these aspects, the poets responsible for composing Job major in one of the Bible's favorite literary maneuvers, namely, in placing impressions and arguments side-by-side without much guidance for how they connect. A hallmark especially of wisdom literature, this technique of parataxis suggests that the book is not out to provide plain information or answers. Instead, the act of reading is itself part of its pedagogy and the readers' observations, questions, hypotheses, and connections contribute to its meaning.

---

11   Philip S. Thomas, *In a Vision of the Night: Job, Cormac McCarthy, and the Challenge of Chaos* (Waco, TX: Baylor University Press, 2021), 13.

The third-person perspective of the book's opening verse ("A man lived in the land of Uz, Job was his name") puts Job's reader in the role of observer. As the narrative unfolds, the readers are privileged to witness the interaction in the heavenly court (1:6–12; 2:1–6) which, though a key ingredient to Job's terrible situation, is never revealed to him. The readers are also privy to Job's private conversations with his wife, friends, and God. In all these scenes, they are never passive recipients but prompted to interpret what Job's author puts before them. This participation begins immediately with the first two statements of the book.

A.   Job is blameless and upright, he fears God, and he turns away from evil (v. 1).

B.   Job has seven sons and three daughters. He has thousands of sheep, camels, oxen, and donkeys, as well as a host of servants. He is greater than all the men of the East (vv. 2–3).

If these verses are but the introduction to the main character, it is odd that they remain silent about Job's age, lineage, and profession. Some Old Testament passages make the dynamics of retribution more explicit—there are rewards for a God-fearing life (see, e.g., Deut 28; Ps 84:11; Prov 11:19–20)—but here the reader needs to put the pieces together. Since there is no connecting word, such as "therefore" or "because," the exact connection between Job's piety and possession remains unstated. The poetic openness of these parallel items may affirm ancient and modern readers alike in their assumptions about God and gifts, or it might prompt them to question whether there is or should be any connection at all.

From its first verses, then, the book taps into unspoken assumptions about investment and return, about effort and expectation, about faith and fairness. For readers who, like Job, live their lives trusting in God, some basic convictions about these word pairs will readily linger under the surface. Every healthy relationship, after all, includes responsibilities and expectations. Ecclesiastes's impossible balance between toil and gain, the injustice of wicked people getting rich ("All in vain have I kept clean my heart!" Ps 73:13), and the older son who works faithfully in the father's field all speak to this posture (Luke 15:29). It is only because assumptions of this kind are reasonable and based on previous experience that the turnover of Job's situation strikes home with such force. Cruel robbers obliterate his thriving business and a windstorm leaves him to bury all his children (cf. 1:13–19). The innocent, prayerful father is not struck by satanic intervention, but by human evil and natural disaster, which, to make things worse, sound like a covenant curse (cf. Deut 28), like a divine judgment for sin. How any reader will respond to this violent clash between the assumed and the actual world depends on how verses 1–3 are thought to connect. Should God-fearing people expect God's protection? Is faith a guarantee for material blessings?

The introduction draws out the presence of assumptions and illustrates how these are maintained. Immediately after the tacit connection of piety and possession, the book offers in verses 4–5 a window into how Job's upright attitude translates into religious practice. With only five verses to set up the main character, the detail that is given to the feasting of Job's children and his intercession deserve close attention.

> Job sent and consecrated them and he rose early in the morning to offer
> burnt offerings for them as many as they were, for Job said:
> 'Perhaps my children have sinned and cursed God in their heart.'
> Thus was Job's routine all his days.

Sacrifice, consecration, and prayer are widespread practices for pursuing divine protection. The longevity of these rites gives ample reason for assuming their effectiveness, both in Job's day and in the life of faith today. But while such convictions are neither arbitrary nor illusory, they remain part of a deeply ingrained belief in an "action–outcome contingency" that acts out the "assumption that we can directly control what happens to us through our own behavior."[12]

Job's intercession brings to the surface a whole range of unspoken ideas about controlling outcomes as well as about parental responsibility and the predictability of divine forgiveness. But verses 4–5 also illustrate the length to which humans will go to uphold their assumptions. Job's stealthy sacrifices suggest a lack of trust in his own children and cast some doubt over his example for their godly living. The excessive, preemptive ("Perhaps") offerings moreover betray a nervous attitude

---

12 Janoff-Bulman, *Assumptions*, 9–10.

toward God, revealing Job's faith to be more complicated than verses 1–3 might indicate. Whether Job's readers see here a model for good parenting and a reliable way to ward off disaster—perhaps even "a transaction through which the universe is made stable and predictable"[13]—or whether they dismiss his efforts as neurotic and naive, each response reveals its own set of assumptions of how self, God, and world work together.

Identifying assumptions in Job 1–2 is challenging because none of them are stated explicitly. The first-person perspectives of the poetic speeches in chapters 3–37 offer far more insights into the assumptive worlds of Job and his friends, yet even here the readers are often left to draw their own conclusions. The final two verses of chapter 3 display this tension of revelation and response.

> *For the terror I have always dreaded—it has come upon me!*
> *What I feared has come for me!*
> *I am not at ease, I am not quiet, I am not at rest!*
> *Turmoil has come.*

The specifics of Job's fear are not identified, but the admittance of some deep-seated anticipation of disaster suffices to trouble his initial characterization. The two perfect verbs ("I dreaded"/"I feared") reach back to the stable life before the tragedy, prompting all who were rather impressed with the Job of chapters 1–2 to revisit their first reading. Such an honest retrospective is as rare as it is revealing. If a blameless man like Job manages to hide his doubts about God—though his sacrifices offer a clue—any of Job's readers might likewise carry some dread underneath their polished outward appearance. Conversely, if this exemplary person lives in both faith and uncertainty, Job's readers may find some solace in their doubt-filled faith.

Reading across chapters 1–3, the two bookends of 1:1–5 and 3:24–26 spotlight and challenge the core assumptions of Job and his readers. The introduction points to some of the fundamental principles of Job's

---

13 Isabelle Hamley, "Patient Job, Angry Job: Speaking Faith in the Midst of Trauma," in *The Bible and Mental Health: Towards a Biblical Theology of Mental Health*, ed. Christopher C. H. Cook and Isabelle Hamley (Norfolk: SCM Press, 2020), 86.

worldview that the end of chapter 3 then calls into question. Seeing both at work is an important guard against caricatures of Job's heroic faith and, in turn, against unrealistic expectations about the faith of Job's readers. Everyone has assumptions about oneself, the world, and God; everyone carries certain beliefs and fears into their daily life. This is no sign of weakness or unfaithfulness but a plain reality of the human condition. The tacit link of righteousness and riches, the complexity of Job's character, the self-talk and the desperate outburst, all in their own ways confront Job's readers with their own assumptions and anxieties.

This challenge does not unfold as a word of judgment, but rather as a therapeutic gesture that normalizes the tension between faith and fear, between piety and practice, and between the assumed and the actual worlds. Meeting its readers which such honesty, the literary genius of Job 1–3 takes everyone by the hand who, like Job, has reached the point when acceptance—"The Lord gave and the Lord took" (2:21)—will no longer hold at bay the agony of overturned assumptions.

Job 3 and the Language of the World Undone

In view of the drastic change in literary style, tone, and characterization that occurs between chapters 1–2 and chapter 3, it is possible that an earlier version of the book consisted just of a short narrative about suffering and restoration (chs. 1–2 and 42:7–17) that was later combined with the poetic dialogues. Such expansions are not uncommon in the biblical materials that carry within themselves the questions and concerns of the communities who first recited, recorded, and reworked them. The shift from narrative to poetry is central to the history and shape of the book, but it also speaks of the human need for introspection and expression, a need that the euphemisms in chapters 1–2 hardly seem to meet.

> 'Naked I came out from my mother's womb,
>   and naked I will return.
> The Lord gave and the Lord took.
>   Let the name of the Lord be blessed.'
> In all this, Job did not sin or scorn God.

> Job 1:21–22

'Even though we receive goodness from God,
should we not also receive disaster?'
In all this, Job did not sin with his lips.

Job 2:10

These two statements are typically elevated as signs of Job's strong faith, yet such a reading is only compelling if readers agree that God can "take" anything at any time and that any "disaster" should be met with acceptance. Once these generic words are replaced with the cruel reality of dead children and bankruptcy that hides behind them, citing Job 1–2 as a model for trusting God becomes difficult.

According to Janoff-Bulman's study, humans are "biased towards assimilation rather than accommodation."[14] The two parallel phrases "in all this" and "Job did not sin" are an apt illustration for this kind of cognitive conservatism. As if nothing had happened, Job continues in his reverence and parses his personal nightmare in a generic framework of blessing and disaster. This tendency to "preserve already established beliefs" and to adhere to a "unified conceptual system in order to impose order on a complex, confusing world" is entirely reasonable given the sudden force of traumatic events.[15] It is the logical first response but, as Job 3 reveals just a few verses later, it is but the initial stage of grief and meaning-making. The change in words from Job 1 to Job 2 suggests already some kind of development, yet these brief expressions hardly prepare the reader for the explosion of chapter 3. The opening two verses immediately indicate a radical breakaway from pious acceptance.

After this, Job opened his mouth and cursed his day.
Job answered and he said:

---

14 *Assumptions*, 30.
15 *Assumptions*, 26. "He salves his hurt by quoting a pious proverb, which he has learned from religion. It is that popular faith which accepts that God can and may do anything because He is God. . . This corresponds rather well to the category of denial;" Walter Vogels, "The Spiritual Growth of Job: A Psychological Approach to the Book of Job," *BTB* 11 (1987), 78. Such denial, at least initially, need not only be negative but can be "a useful and valuable process that reflects the survivor's extraordinary psychological predicament. . . . Denial enables the survivor to more gradually face the realities of the victimization;" Janoff-Bulman, *Assumptions*, 98.

Job no longer blesses (1:21), but curses. He abandons his passive role of receiving messages of doom, cuts through his friends' silence (2:13), and takes control. The focus on Job's mouth is carried over from 1:22 and 2:10—four of the nine Hebrew words in 3:1-2 speak of speaking—but the wounded speaker now responds very differently to his tragedy. In a situation in which God makes no sense anymore and in which even the closest friends fail to speak words of comfort, Job's language breaks forth against all odds. The poetry of chapter 3 is addressed neither to God nor to any human ear. It stands complete on its own as a therapeutic turn to words, as speech for the sake of speech. Job opens his mouth not in praise or with pat answers, but with an authentic cry that cuts through the agony of divine absence, through the silence of human helplessness, and through the crashing collapse of his assumptive world.

Creating an Impossible World

The poetry of Job 3 is laden with expectation because of its connections to chapters 1-2 but also because it marks Job's first speech. The remainder of the book unfolds in three cycles of dialogues between Job and his three friends before various smaller poems and Elihu's speeches in chapters 32-37 prepare the way to God's voice from the whirlwind. Placed at the head of these conversations, Job 3 introduces many foundational aspects and its language of darkness and death resurfaces in many chapters. The poem is often praised for its imagery, wordplay, and structure, but these literary qualities must not create a wrong impression of what suffering sounds like. These finely tuned lines are not the immediate response to trauma but the imaginative version of how Job's author would hear a courageous and honest expression of a world come undone.

> *Let the day perish on which I was begotten,*
> *the night that said: 'A man was conceived!'*
> *That day, let it be darkness!*
> *Let God not search for it from above,*
> *let no radiance shine on it!*
> *Let darkness and deep shadow redeem it, let the clouds dwell upon it,*
> *let the shadows of day fall upon it!*

That night, let gloom seize it,
let it not be numbered among the days of the year,
among the number of months, let it not come!
See, that night, let it be barren,
let no cry for joy come into it!
Let those curse it who curse the day,
those who are ready to rouse Leviathan!
Let the stars of its twilight be dark,
let it hope for light, but have none,
let it not see the eyelids of dawn,
because it did not close the doors of my womb,
and did not hide trouble from my eyes.

Job 3:3–10

These two opening stanzas unpack the announcement in verse 1 that Job "cursed his day." Although the seven statements and the command "let it be darkness" sound some overtones to the creation account in Genesis 1,[16] the frame of verses 3 and 10 puts the focus more narrowly on the day on which Job was born. Still, there is a sense in which the eclipse of "that day" and "that night" stretches beyond his birthday. As Job takes an honest look at his newfound reality, he wishes not to have been part of the world at all, neither on his first day nor on any day since.

Job's gaze at the helpless present and the unthinkable future leave this desperate grasping at the past as his only option. Little is gained by pointing out that the wish not to have been born is irrational or that it is too extreme given that his assumptions had proven justified until the first message of doom had arrived. To the contrary, the very impossibility of his wishes speaks to the traumatic force with which his assumptions have been shattered. The all-inclusive scope of his curse must be extreme because his tragedy is extreme, casting a long shadow over his existence and over his previous beliefs all at once. Job has arrived at an impossible place where all assumptions have been overturned and where all life experience, past and present, has become unreliable. Since he must, however, continue to live in that place, he musters what is left to him: the force of emotive speech, the agency and freedom of human

---

16 Michael Fishbane, for instance, sees in Job 3 "an absolute and unrestrained death wish for himself and the entire creation;" "Jer IV 23–26 and Job III 3–13: A Recovered Use of the Creation Pattern," *VT* 21 (1971), 153.

language. Job has nobody to turn to—the friends are silent, God is mentioned only in abstraction (vv. 4, 20, 23)—and so his words all on their own must offer relief, somehow.

The poem begins with two passive verbs ("I was begotten"/"A man was conceived") that highlight the lack of choice and agency that marked Job's entry into the world. In a startling personification, Job dehumanizes his birth by having "the night" rather than his parents announce his arrival. Darkness attended his life even before he was born and darkness still reigns as he utters this poem. Contrary to Jeremiah 15, Job in his despair does not confront his parents or hold God accountable for his birth. This restraint and the focus on his birthday make his poem highly personal. This is truly and only his crisis. Rather than trying to put the cosmos right or justifying how humanity can continue to live in the world that he now inhabits, Job embarks on a personal vendetta with "that day" and "that night." Personified as entities in their own right—the day should be terrified, the night barren—Job's poetry creates a target to attack. From the four words for "darkness" in verses 4–6 to the excessive length of the poetic lines,[17] from the call for God to withdraw his saving light from "that day" (see תופע in Pss 50:2 and 80:2) to the silencing and blinding of "that night," Job's language unleashes an astounding, destructive force.

Even across the distance to this text and its world, the cathartic qualities of this fierce act of articulation can be heard. Especially the resolved imperatives ("Let it perish! Let it be darkness!") restore a small dose of agency to the beaten speaker. The force and freedom of this language is vital to appreciate for its own sake, but Job 3 reaches for something larger yet. Speaking from within the tension of not wanting to live in this world but having no other choice, the poem creates a new cosmos that accurately represents the world into which Job had been born. Contrary to Genesis 1, this particular world can only be created with curses, not with blessings. Its defining characteristics are not light and daily rhythms, but expansive darkness and a fractured calendar. Positive words, such as "redeem" or "dwell" (v. 5), are used

---

17   "Unusually, verses 4–6 each have three clauses, as if the vigour and viciousness of Job's curse cannot be contained within the normal two-part structure of a poetic line;" Ortlund, *Piercing Leviathan*, 22.

toward a negative effect;[18] the shadowy pockets of the day consume the daylight that remains, and stars no longer sparkle at night (v. 9).

Job is not reversing creation, cursing God, or damning the human species. He is creating his own, honest version of reality, starting with his birthday and reaching up to his present day. His language constructs a world that is true to the shattered assumptions of his old world. It is a dark world, a living space where life cannot exist. But this is where Job finds himself alive and breathing.

Job's Grave New World

The second half of chapter 3 further develops Job's perspective of being trapped in this impossible world. As the curse on his conception has run its course, the poem grasps in its despair at the next potential solution. Job's words about the womb and infant death in verse 11 demonstrate how far he has travelled from his acceptance in 1:21 ("Naked I came... naked I will return") and mark an appropriate entry to the eulogy of death and underworld that follows.

> *Why could I not have died at birth,*
>   *come forth from the womb and pass away?*
> *For what reason did the knees receive me,*
>   *and why the breasts that I would nurse?*
> *Oh I could be laying down now, be at peace, sleep!*
>   *Then there would be rest for me.*
>
> *With the kings and counsellors of the earth,*
>   *who rebuilt ruined cities for themselves,*
> *or with princes who had gold,*
>   *who filled their houses with silver,*
> *or like a stillborn child, buried and I would not be,*
>   *like infants who never see the light.*
>
> *There the wicked cease raging,*
>   *there the worn-out rest.*
> *Captives are altogether at ease,*
>   *they do not hear the voice of the slave-driver.*
> *The small and the great, there they are,*
>   *the servant released from his master.*

---

18 "Job wishes that the powers of darkness would 'redeem' his day from light into endless darkness;" Christopher Ash, *Job*, Preaching the Word (Downers Grove, IL: Crossway, 2014), 72.

Why does he give light to one who is troubled,
    and life to those whose living is bitter,
to those who long for death, but it is not here,
    though they search for it more than hidden treasures,
to those who would be joyful and in bliss,
    would rejoice if they found the grave,
to a man whose way is obscured,
    whom God has hedged in all around?

Job 3:11–23

These four stanzas must be heard as a whole, with the parallel why questions in verses 11 and 20 setting the tone for the entire section. If his world is as dark and troubled as verses 3–10 describe, it seems cruel that Job must live in it. But these wishes, and the chapter as a whole, reach beyond a mere exit.[19] The heart of Job 3 paints a picturesque image of the world of the dead, the realm of those who, unlike Job, "have found the grave" (v. 22). The threefold "there" across verses 17–19 fix Job and his readers on that place below, that epitome of tranquility where he would "lay down, be at peace, sleep, rest" (v. 13).

The evocative language in this section creates a counter-version to that dark world above the ground. Job's glorification of death and the impossible desire of having been born "a stillborn child" (v. 16) continue his resilient effort of making sense of his broken world. His shattered assumptions about God's care and goodness do not give way to resignation, but spark the search for an alternative world in which robbers and winds no longer kill. It is this hope for a livable environment that gives rise to the utopian society of verses 14–19. The wicked, the kings, the slaves, the princes, everyone alike enjoys a peaceful life in Sheol! Free of hierarchy and trouble, the grave, new world below is superior to

---

19 To the extent that the language of Job 3 and its parallel in Jeremiah 20 are, specifically, concerned with the desire not to have been born, it seems reasonable to conclude with Levinson "that neither Jeremiah nor Job qualifies as suicidal. These characters show no intent to end their own lives. They do not even ask God to end their lives," *Death Wish*, 117. On the book's "logic of suicide," see further Dan Mathewson, *Death and Survival in the Book of Job: Desymbolization and Traumatic Experience,* LHBOTS 450 (New York: T&T Clark, 2006), 80–82. The conversation between Bible and suicide is a complex topic in its own right. See, e.g., Yael Shemesh, "Suicide in the Bible," *JBQ* 37 (2009): 157–168; Paul Cantz and Kalman Kaplan, "Biblical Narratives for Positive Psychology and Suicide Prevention: An Evidence-Supported Approach," *MHRC* 20 (2017): 654–678; Steve Austin, *Hiding in the Pews: Shining Light on Mental Illness in the Church* (Minneapolis, MN: Fortress Press, 2021).

humanity's earthly existence with all its illusory promises of rewards. For that reason, too, stillborn children are better off because they get to bypass the pain of disillusionment altogether. The poem's endearing sketch of death is no gothic fantasy, but the logical consequence of seeing life's foundations broken asunder.[20] Before the catastrophe, Job's basic assumption was that he would "pass away" in his family nest in old age. Now that his eyes are open, he wishes he had "passed away" at birth (cf. גוע in 3:11 and 29:18).

But Job's death poetry goes yet deeper. What unfolds in Job 3 is not just a compromise but an outright celebration. Usually, people should seek wisdom like "hidden treasures," not death (v. 21; Prov 2:4), but here finding death is a delight and a reason for rejoicing (v. 22). These associations sharply break away from other biblical portrayals that see death as an enemy (e.g., Ps 18:4; Jer 9:21) and the underworld as a place of limitation and inactivity (e.g., Isa 14:11; Ezek 32:21). In addition to the negative aspects that modern readers associate with death, such as pain or loss, the Old Testament highlights the separation from God as the real problem. Since "Sheol is at the opposite theological extreme to Yahweh,"[21] the destitute who are near death routinely pray for God's renewed attention (e.g., Pss 30:3; 49:15). Against this backdrop, Job's joyful longing for death indicates that he is wishing to escape not just from this world but also from God.

The final stanza confirms this suspicion. Although the Hebrew text of verse 20 unmistakably uses a third-person verb ("Why did *he give* light to the one who is troubled?"), almost all Bible translations opt for the passive form "Why is light given." This rendition might make more sense in a poem that hardly mentions God, yet it obscures Job's theological crisis of having to carry on as "a man whose way is obscured, whom God has hedged in all around" (v. 23).[22] Job's core assumptions do not so much concern his self-worth or his right to wealth and health. Rather, the hardest blow of his shattered world pertains to his relationship with

---

20 "With his Sheol fantasy, his belief that life is to be found in death, Job rediscovers a symbolically coherent world," Mathewson, *Death and Survival*, 82.

21 Johnston, *Shades of Sheol*, 75.

22 As in verses 3–10, everything that was previously a good gift from God—Psalms 5:11, 91:4, and 140:7 use "hedged in" (סכך, v. 20) in a positive, protective way—now is unbearable.

God. As his world has become dark and unliveable, God's presence, power, and promises are altogether irrational and irritating, making the prospect of being as far away from God as possible a reason for great joy.

A Nightmare Come True
Job's words about birth and Sheol are powerful but, in the end, they remain impossible wishes. The very fact that he can utter them means that he did not die at birth. This impossible character of the poem needs to be embraced as its very heartbeat. When the failure of his assumptions can no longer be ignored, theologized, or explained in the manner of chapters 1–2, Job's words ache with existential tension. He must live, against his will, as one whose "way is obscured" (v. 23). The poem ends with a profound expression of this particular agony, which is only made worse because it had been anticipated.

> *For before my bread comes my sighing,*
>   *poured forth like water are my roars.*
> *For the terror I have always dreaded—it has come upon me!*
>   *What I feared has come for me!*
> *I am not at ease, I am not quiet, I am not at rest!*
>   *Turmoil has come.*
>
> Job 3:24–26

The substitution of food for sighing is common in other laments (e.g., Pss 42:3; 102:9), as is the "roaring" of verse 24 (Pss 22:1; 32:3). The clustering of words of unrest and chaos, however, suggests that "roaring" is not just an audible release of pain in Job 3. The "turmoil" (רגז) on which the poem ends is more literally a quaking or trembling, a term that is often used to describe the chaotic waters that threaten to undo the created order (e.g., Ps 29:3; Isa 17:12–13; Hab 3:2). This cosmic language and the threefold negation in verse 26—"not at ease, not quiet, not at rest"—demonstrate just how much Job's shaken world has shaken him.[23] But still he refuses to give up by "roaring" like the divine warrior (e.g., Isa 5:29; Jer 25:30; Joel 3:16) amid and against this chaos, ever in the

---

23 "It is not only the external world that is perceived as threatening, but the internal world as well: It is in a state of chaos. Victims cannot derive any equilibrium from prior assumptions, for they are no longer adequate guides to the world;" Bulman-Janoff, *Assumptions*, 65.

pursuit of a new perspective that restores, somehow, what he previously believed to be true about God, the world, and himself.

Poetry for a Collapsed World

Job 3 is one of the most profound poems in the Old Testament. From its structure to its imagery, from its sounds to its questions, the building blocks of Hebrew poetry amass here a composition that is never fully heard or comprehended. But what Job 3 bestows upon its readers lies not just in its literary marvel but in its raw language. The Bible nowhere else provides such an intimate and irritating portrayal of personal disillusionment. The poem begins in darkness and ends in chaos, creating along the way a litany of curse, confrontation, and question that is distressing, but that will only offend those who are living in the first five verses of the book. Resolving this chapter by turning to other parts of scripture means a tragic loss for all who know that line in the sand all too well, who live like Job in an unliveable world. If, however, Job 3 is heard on its own, this tumultuous poem can give license to readers today to put their shattered assumptions into words and to articulate their own experience of a world in turmoil.

Job Opens His Mouth

The first few words of Job 3 may look like a mere transition but they carry a vital message. Studies on trauma routinely emphasize the need for personal space and time, for an initial period of grieving and of processing. Job's mourning posture on the ash heap and the seven days of silence may be seen as stations of this kind, yet the more pronounced therapeutic contribution of Job's early chapters lies in their restoration of agency. The development of Job's character across chapters 1–3 can be read as a journey from repression and a resistance to change, to a silent period of processing, to the initiative of speech.[24] This progression is not normative, as if everyone has the luxury of sitting with friends in silence or the strength of finding new words after just a week. But Job's journey is hopeful because it speaks of change. The length and posture

---

24 For a sensitive discussion of this journey, see Manfred Oeming and Konrad Schmid, *Job's Journey: Stations of Suffering*, CrStHB 7 (Winona Lake, IN: Eisenbrauns, 2015).

of chapter 3 reveals his short statements in chapters 1–2 to be but the beginning of the healing process.

The first poem in the book gifts its readers with a response that does not stop at silent acceptance and passive waiting. Against the terror of chapters 1–2, the simple words "Job opened his mouth" are a declaration and celebration of agency. Without Job's first step in the conversation, nothing will happen. He will not work through his pain, his supportive friends will not show their true face, and God will have no platform for a response. For those who, like Job, receive messages of indescribable loss and find themselves reborn into a dark world, Job's open mouth, his speaking against all odds, his imagination and questions and roaring offer an invitation to follow his example.

The poetry of Job 3 is an inspiration for what such a daring articulation might sound like. Leaving behind the abstractions of good and bad (2:10) and not concerned with theology or the problems of the world at large, Job's words are private and personal throughout: "I was born" (v. 3), "my mother's womb," "my eyes" (v. 10), "rest for me" (v. 13), "my sighing" (v. 24), "what I feared" (v. 25). Making this poem entirely his own and addressing nobody in particular allow for the necessary freedom of language and lament. Whether such words dwell on specific days and events, ask unanswerable questions, say aloud desperate and irrational wishes, or roar against outer and inner tensions, Job 3 embraces all such expression as a human response to a shattered world.

This license for speech is paired with a license for feeling and venting anger. The furious curses in verses 3–9 along with the frustration about "bitter living" (v. 20) and God's "hedging in" (v. 23) call for an authentic articulation of all emotions, in Job's day and in the world today.[25] As the words are spoken into empty space, such speech can confess every secret fear that now has come true and can call everything into question,

---

25 Alissa J. Nelson commends the work of Gerald West that documents how "reading the text of Job 3 in community with others infected with HIV/AIDS provides a traumatic and transformative experience wherein anger is manifested in the group;" *Power and Responsibility in Biblical Interpretation: Reading the Book of Job with Edward Said* (Sheffield: Equinox, 2012), 171–172; cf. Gerald West, "The Poetry of Job as a Resource for the Articulation of Embodied Lament in the Context of HIV and AIDS in South Africa," in *Lamentations in Ancient and Contemporary Contexts*, ed. N. C. Lee and C. Mandolfo (Atlanta, GA: SBL, 2008), 195–214.

including God's gift of life. For everyone who needs to articulate a shattered world, a poem like Job 3 offers language that speaks with unbridled abandon. But regardless of whether such intimate words are poetic or biblical, the fact that Job opened his mouth can give others the courage and creativity to open theirs.

The Work of World-Making

The language of Job 3 meets the real need of processing pain that, according to this biblical book at least, is satisfied neither by acceptance, silence, or company. But Job's words are not just an example of the expressive side that biblical poetry affords its readers. The imagery, perspective, and atmosphere of this chapter also raise awareness for the creative dimension of poetic compositions. The connection between poetry and creation is obvious in the Bible because many creation passages, such as Psalm 74 or Proverbs 8, are written in line-by-line format. Though somewhat obscured by the printing style of modern Bibles, the repetitions and balance of Genesis 1 likewise suggests a poetic composition. Biblical poetry, however, not only is the preferred mode for talking about creation but also is in itself creative. The joining together of the building blocks of words, phrases, and lines; the audible and visual appeal to the senses; the shaping of atmosphere and mood—all of these procedures imbue poetry with the special capacity of building worlds before the inner eye of their readers.[26] To witness these dynamics in a context of trauma and turmoil is not a unique side of Job 3, but can be observed also in passages like Isaiah 24, Joel 1, and Jeremiah 4.

> I look at the world—it has no form, no order!—
>   at the heavens, their light is gone.
> I look at the mountains—they are shaking!—
>   and all the hills are tossing to and fro.
> I look and notice that there are no people,
>   that all the birds of the sky have fled away.

Jeremiah 4:23–25

---

26 David Clines's reading of Isaiah 53 remains a worthwhile presentation of these dynamics: "The *way* in which language is event is by its creating of an alternative *world* and thereby destroying the universal validity of the conventional 'world;'" *I, We, He, and They: A Literary Approach to Isaiah 53*, JSOTSup 1 (Sheffield: JSOT Press, 1976), 54 (emphasis original).

These lines are no vision of the end times but a creative version of the world as it looked to the prophet in his day. The mountains were still standing, the sun still rising, but Jeremiah's words cut through the facade of such tranquility and fashion a world that truly reflects Judah's folly and God's withdrawal. Such visions of the world are at home primarily in the deep analysis of prophetic preaching and in the comforting visions of Jeremiah 30–33 and Isaiah 40–55,[27] but the same revelatory use of language is at work in Job 3.

For those for whom "the known, comforting old assumptive world is gone, and a new one must be constructed,"[28] the creative dimension of biblical poetry offers an avenue for just such a rebuilding exercise. Fashioning that world line by line and image by image is no naive exercise of make-believe but an honest expression that takes seriously the new, terrible reality. Those who have just buried their children will not see the world full of sunshine and birds. A life torn by loss and death can hardly be asked to inhabit the same space as the healthy and blessed people around it. The language of Job 3 embraces those who live in a world in which darkness is the defining element and offers vocabulary for speaking about the shadow that can cover everyday living. Job's curses on his birthday can help liberate those who share in his shattered life to speak such wishes aloud. His creative construction of the underworld likewise justifies the desire to inhabit a different world, a world free of crushed convictions and far away from the unpredictable ways of the God one once knew.

To follow Job into speaking a world into existence that is true to one's current reality is to join him on the path of authentic faith, as well as to embark with him on that long quest toward a better world. After all, the tension and turmoil in which Job 3 ends makes clear that the shadows and sighs are no place to live. "These new assumptions may seem valid, relatively apt descriptions of reality, but emotionally they are extremely unattractive."[29] At the early stage of anyone's journey from the old to the broken to the new world, the initial effort of creating a meaningful

---

27 "The very act of poetic speech establishes a new reality. Public speech, the articulation of alternative scenarios of reality, is one of the key acts of ministry among exiles;" Brueggemann, *Hopeful Imagination*, 95.

28 Janoff-Bulman, *Assumptions*, 71.

29 Janoff-Bulman, *Assumptions*, 94.

universe will likely look very dark. In the same way in which chapter 3 anticipates God's cosmic contemplation in chapters 38–41, this early, dark world will ideally change its form with the help of time and empathetic listeners. Yet even where life affords such hopeful company, the aspects of agency and articulation remain a key ingredient on the trek from darkness to dawn. Especially in a book that is so painfully aware of the problems of hearing suffering people on their own terms, Job's open mouth and the cathartic and creative use of Job's language are of the essence.

Living in Tension, Lost for Theology
Job's poetry normalizes unbridled, emotional outbursts in the face of the horrendous conflict between faith and experience. The book's language is honest in that it names the terrors of living in the dark rather than advocating quiet surrender. This particular quality of Job will resonate with anyone who is at a loss of words for articulating what has happened, what it feels like, and how self, world, and God may be understood.

Given how closely human life is defined in the Old Testament in relation to God, it is striking that the prologue's heavy focus on spiritual reality and divine justice is virtually absent from Job 3. The spotlight rests squarely on the speaker and on the immediate and intense expression of a shattered life.[30] Near its conclusion, however, the poem includes God after all—"Why does he give light to one who is troubled. . . . whom God has hedged in all about?" (vv. 20, 23)—and so the theological dimension of Job's pain cannot be left aside completely. These two verses in Job 3 are abstract questions rather than direct accusations, yet they draw God into the situation and sow the seeds for Job's confrontations later in the book. Especially chapters 9–10 exemplify this development, marking a key point on Job's journey and offering a fuller picture of the connection between the collapse of understanding oneself and the collapse of understanding God.

---

30 "For a book that is so dominated by intellectual issues of theodicy, it is amazing to find here not one strictly theological sentence, not a single question about the meaning of his suffering. . . . All this will come, in its time, but here we are invited to view the man Job in the violence of his grief. . . . With this speech before us we cannot overintellectualize the book, but must always be reading it as the drama of a human soul," David J. A. Clines, *Job 1–20*, WBC 17 (Dallas, TX: Word Books, 1989), 104.

I am blameless, I do not know myself,
I reject my life!
It is all the same—so I say: blameless or wicked, he makes
an end of them all!
If a disaster brings sudden death,
the despair of the innocent he would mock.
The earth is given into the hand of the wicked,
the faces of its judges he has covered.
If it is not him, who then is it?

Job 9:21–24

Hearing these words side-by-side with Job 3 is important because many readers who turn to this book for comfort will likely suffer silently from a breakdown of their theology. These verses from Job 9 join the Old Testament's embrace of personal emotions with an invitation to protest aloud against God.[31] The existential crisis of "I do not know myself" is tied up here with the confounding behavior of a God who ignores blamelessness, obstructs justice, and mocks the innocent. Earlier in Job 9, Job had used yet more direct words for God's responsibility. Rather than holding back the forces of chaos (see, e.g., Pss 46:2–3; 74:12–17), God "moves the mountains" and "shakes the earth from its place" (9:5–6)! It can be liberating to see that the book does not revert after chapter 3 to the stoic posture of chapters 1–2, but leans more strongly into accusing God.

So why did you bring me forth from the womb?
I could have passed away and no eye had ever seen me,
could have been as if I had not been, brought right from the womb
to the grave.
Are my days not but few?
So stop it, get away from me so that I might smile a bit
before I go without return to the land of darkness and deep shadow,
the land where twilight is like gloom,
deep shadow without order,
radiating like gloom.

Job 10:18–22

---

31 Bringing Job and Abraham into conversation, Richard Middleton highlights that protest rather than silent endurance is the Bible's preferred response to suffering; *Abraham's Silence: The Binding of Isaac, the Suffering of Job, and How to Talk Back to God* (Grand Rapids, MI: Baker Academics, 2021).

Job's longing for God to leave him alone breaks forth with equal vigor in 6:9 and 7:16 and recalls his alternative reality of Sheol in chapter 3. God's inexplicable attention has made his life so unliveable that any place far away from God would be pure bliss.

After the first outburst of Job 3 has passed by, passages like these are frequent and the book consistently and vigorously speaks at the intersection of tragedy and theology. To listen in on such protests against God can restore yet further the agency of those who, with Job 9:21, no longer know themselves because they no longer know God. The book normalizes such unrest, both in its emotional and its theological facets. It provides a language for protest, for verbalizing the disappointment and disillusionment of tragedy. This is one of Job's greatest gifts to his readers: that he walks with them from those old, assumptive worlds in which God could "give and take" to their actual world in which anything can be uttered, lamented, questioned, or seen for what it is, including one's theology.

Witnessing a Shattered World

The raw force of Job 3 and the sharp speech in Job 9–10 unleash a language for expressing tension and protest. Inasmuch as these poetic compositions grant to their readers this gift of words, the first response to Job's words too often is embarrassment, censure, and correction, both in the book and in its reception. The courageous action of opening one's mouth and shaking one's fist creates that crucial place where "survivors can get constructive feedback about the possibility of a benevolent, meaningful world."[32] But the responses of family, friends, and colleagues can also have the opposite effect. Everything that follows after Job 3 is a testimony to the significance of listening and of dialogue as well as to its manifold challenges. The book's readers continue to play the role of the observer, ever challenged to see the world through the eyes of their shattered fellow humans, ever wondering how they might respond in the place of Job's friends.

---

32 Janoff-Bulman, *Assumptions*, 142.

"Not a Sensible Person among You"

The question of how to receive Job's words is a major theme in the book. Although she is his first witness and the only family member to visit him in his crisis—everyone else appears only when he is restored (42:11)—Job's wife is routinely condemned. Her advice to give up and "curse God" might justify such dismissal, yet since Job himself abandons his pious acceptance just a chapter later, she might be the only person in the book who meets him with the honesty he deserves. She alone is willing to see the world as it actually is; she alone is brave enough to join Job in re-evaluating their dearly held assumptions.[33] The contrast to Job's three male friends could not be stronger. Their joint venture and silent presence in chapter 2 is a promising start, but the dialogues in chapters 4–27 fail in every respect. Eliphaz, Zophar, and Bildad democratize his suffering and do not hear it on its own terms (4:4–5), they are aghast that he would challenge their theology (8:8–10), and they can only interpret his tragedy along the categories of sin and judgment (11:6; 15:17–21; 22:4–5). The speeches get shorter and angrier, and, in the end, Zophar does not even take up his cue to speak and the conversation grinds to a halt.

Given how useless the three friends are in their response, it is striking how much space is granted to them. On one level, they are a sounding board for Job, allowing his character to emerge in all its evolving complexity. In view of their length and fervor, however, the frustrating dialogues serve primarily to confront the book's readers.[34] It is easy to chastise the trio without noticing how unsettling chapters 4–27 are for everyone who appreciates Job's initial response in chapters 1–2 or who shares the friends' convictions about divine sovereignty, sin, and

---

33 Her words can be translated as a call to give up his integrity or as approval ("you are blameless!") or as supporting his endurance ("Bless God and die"). "The text as it is, with its ambiguity, enables readers to explore different responses, and the way in which relationships are affected by trauma;" Hamley, "Patient Job, Angry Job," 89. See further Oeming and Schmid: "Job's wife becomes the one who voices the lament and thus proves to be a trusted companion;" *Job's Journey*, 34.

34 "The author uses Job to test one theological stance, just as he uses the friends to test another;" Michael V. Fox, "Job the Pious," *ZAW* 117 (2005), 359.

suffering. If Job's words are left standing as they are, if disaster actually strikes an innocent person of his caliber, surely anyone's assumptions about God might be shattered any day. In Job's own assessment, it is this unnerving conclusion that underlies his friends' unwillingness to receive his words ("You see my collapse and you are afraid!" 6:21).[35] Letting Job and those who share his fate express their emotions and listen nonjudgmentally to their view of the world and God is an important milestone on the path of their recovery, but this gift will come only from those who are honest enough to question their own assumptions or, more likely, who have had them shattered already.

If not with the outright blaming and aggression of Job's friends (cf. 18:1–3), the reception of Job's words has been marked by a tendency to suppress their emotional and theological provocation. In the *Testament of Job*, a rewritten version of the biblical book from the Second Temple period, Job explains to his children that God had informed him about Satan's attack and instructed him to "wrestle like an athlete and resist pain, sure of your reward" (1:22).[36] When his friends lament his loss, Job orders them to be silent and exclaims: "The whole world shall perish... but my throne is in the upper world" (7:35–36). The book's message is stated clear and simple: "Now my children, do you also show a firm heart in all the evil that happens to you" (6:31).[37] Such re-purposing of biblical stories was a common practice in its day and a quick comparison between Hebrews 11 and its Old Testament parallels reveals that the New Testament shares in this mode of interpretation. It is for this reason that James 5:7–11, the only passage that mentions Job by name,

---

35 "Victims are threatening to nonvictims, for they are a manifestation of a malevolent universe rather than a benevolent one... Survivors of extreme events are powerful reminders of human frailty;" Janoff-Bulman, *Assumptions*, 148.

36 All quotations come from Rudolf P. Spittler, "Testament of Job," in *Old Testament Pseudepigrapha*, vol. 1, ed. J. H. Charlesworth (Garden City, NY: Doubleday, 1983).

37 This version of Job is not easily compared with the original because it reads like a different story altogether: God's speech occupies but one sentence (10:9) and Job spends several chapters talking with his wife and daughters. Cf. Christopher Begg, "Comparing Characters: The Book of Job and the Testament of Job," in *The Book of Job*, ed. W. A. M. Beuken, BETL 114 (Leuven: Leuven University Press, 1994), 435–445.

speaks only of his faithfulness.[38] As in the *Testament of Job*, there is no protest, no raw emotion, but only the promise that all will work out for good if suffering is faced with endurance.

This particular angle to Job's grief continues in contemporary readings of Job, with bookshelves abounding with titles that celebrate Job's heroic endurance. For instance, the best-selling devotional commentary *Be Patient: Waiting on God in Difficult Times* reminds its readers that Job in chapter 3 "forgot the blessings that he and his family had enjoyed" and that "we live on *promises*, not explanations; so we shouldn't spend too much time asking God why."[39] Such efforts to rationalize Job's sharp words likely come from an impulse to provide biblical guidance for suffering believers, yet the superficial comfort and the dismissal of verbalizing one's pain can entrap Job's readers in the pious responses of chapters 1-2.[40] Even the smallest suggestion that patience is more biblical than protest, or that endurance triumphs over emotion, can quench all that Job offers to those who are "in turmoil" (3:26) and who do not know God or themselves anymore (9:21).

It is difficult to see how such a digestion of Job's poetry can resonate with readers who live under the cross of Jesus who himself suffered a severe shattering of his assumptions about divine presence and protection—"Why, why have you abandoned me?!"—and who are part of a community that routinely has had to integrate troubling new information into their assumptive worlds (e.g., Jer 21:1–5; Matt 11:3; Mark 8:32; Acts 1:6).[41] These texts and experiences are a testimony to the real need for language and listening, for letting Job 3 disrupt the safe worlds of its hearers.

---

38 For James 5 and Job, see Bruce Zuckermann, *Job the Silent: A Study in Historical Counterpoint* (Oxford: Oxford University Press, 1991), 13–15.

39 Warren W. Wiersbe, *Be Patient: Waiting on God in Difficult Times* (Colorado Springs, CO: David C. Cook, 1991), 25–26 (italics original).

40 "Implicit in these minimization responses is a failure to understand the shattered state of the victim's world and the overwhelming nature of the rebuilding process;" Janoff-Bulman, *Assumptions*, 158.

41 A modern example can be found in C. S. Lewis's *A Grief Observed* (London: Faber and Faber, 1961): "Not that I am (I think) in much danger of ceasing to believe in God. The real danger is of coming to believe such dreadful things about Him. The conclusion I dread is not 'So there's no God after all,' but 'So this is what God's really like. Deceive yourself no longer;'" 8.

Those who try to salvage Job's former integrity in the face of his curse
miss the point of the poetry. . . . There is another kind of integrity,
however, . . . one with which people could identify, one that would
express the fears, the anger, the hope, and the frustration of existential
experience. If the poet's paradigm is less faithful to God, it is more
faithful to human experience.[42]

Restoring Job's World

The painful conversations in chapters 4–27 demonstrate how difficult
it is to witness the collapsed world of a fellow human being. This in
itself is a worthwhile insight, but the book does not stop there. As with
the friends, God's conversation with Job in chapters 38–41 unfolds as
a dialogue, though this time Job is cast in the role of the respondent.
It may be tempting to put God into the role of a modern-day therapist
or appropriate God's approach as an inspired therapeutic manual. But
one plain observation about Job 38–42 troubles such applications right
away. God speaks one hundred and twenty-two verses and Job only
seven. This imbalanced exchange is not a healthy model for therapeutic listening, even less a biblical warrant for putting those who protest
against God into their place. For those who keep some critical distance,
however, the poetry in this final section of Job can yield a number of
clues for responding well to a shattered, assumptive world.

First of all, God's initiative and interaction acknowledge Job's turmoil and validate his unrelenting quest for meaning. God's long conversation with Job provides that important "firsthand evidence that
others can be good, that the client is worthy despite the traumatic experience."[43] As in Jeremiah and the Psalms, there is no indication that
God is offended by Job's fierce protest. God tolerates even the darkest
contours of Job's theology, yet this nonjudgmental listening must not be
misunderstood as uncritical agreement. God does not call Job a sinner,
but right at the start of chapter 38 Job is confronted for having spoken
"words without knowledge." This seems perhaps a harsh way to open

---

42 Rick D. Moore, "The Integrity of Job," *CBQ* 45 (1983), 31.

43 Janoff-Bulman, *Assumptions*, 162. God validates Job directly in 42:7—"you
have not spoken to me rightly, as my servant Job has"—though it is not clear
if this approval refers to his faith in chapters 1–2, his protest in chapters 3–32,
the rebuke of his friends, or his final response in 42:1–6.

the conversation, yet, as the topic of human limitation will resonate all through God's speech, it makes for an appropriate introduction. The poetry in chapters 38–39, by implication, will fill in this missing knowledge and it exercises this task in increments and by indirection.

> *Where were you when I laid the foundations of the earth?*
> *Do you comprehend the vast expanse of the earth?*
> *Where is the way of divided light, the east wind that is scattered upon the earth?*
> *Who can number the clouds with wisdom?*
> *Who has sent forth the wild donkey, who has loosened the bonds of the fierce ass?*
> *Do you give the horse its might, clothe its neck with a mane?*
> *Is it your understanding that makes the hawk soar?*

An extensive catalogue of rhetorical questions of this kind, God's oration does not ask for an answer but prompts Job and his readers with a "stern gentleness" to draw their own conclusions about God, the world, and themselves.[44] Contrary to Genesis 1, which builds up toward the creation of humanity, here the world and the animal kingdom stand complete on their own. God's cosmic tour remains silent about Job's situation and about human participation in general. The counterevidence of one person's shattered assumptions does not suffice to overthrow the good and intricate order that continues to exist apart from them.

This confrontation is not a strategy to minimize Job's pain or to say in a roundabout way that he does not matter. On the contrary, God's questions are gentle and interactional, and they honor Job's capacity of reflection. The sovereign lord of the world "invites him into his counsel, making him an intimate," meeting him on the same playing field of language that the frail human being had initiated in chapter 3.[45] God gradually exposes the beauty and detail of the world to question the foundations of Job's impossible world. Job is bid to behold the cosmic

---

44 Michael V. Fox, "Job 38 and God's Rhetoric," *Semeia* 19 (1981), 59. See also T. C. Ham, "The Gentle Voice of God in Job 38," *JBL* 132 (2013): 527–541.

45 Fox, "Job the Pious," 352. "Many images and metaphors that have been used earlier, not least in Job's agonized cries in chapter 3, are taken up in chapters 38–41;" Robert S. Fyall, *Now My Eyes Have Seen You: Images of Creation and Evil in the Book of Job*, NSBT 17 (Downers Grove, IL: InterVarsity Press, 2002), 26.

stage on which the morning stars sing (38:7), where mountain goats give birth in harsh conditions (39:3–4), where balance and grandeur reign.[46] As God's poem moves freely from luminaries to lightning, from snowfall to soaring eagles, perhaps a ray of light can break into the dark world that Job had extrapolated from his limited viewpoint.

The vast canvas of this cosmic contemplation is overwhelming and distracting—this certainly is not the kind of answer Job and his readers had expected—but for that very reason it is an effective strategy for "thought-stopping and cognitive restructuring."[47] Line by line, this rebuilt world takes shape and wraps up Job's life in the vast sphere of reality that his limited perspective would never allow him to see. The way toward a new and integrated view of self, world, and God lies open.

> To be properly human is to recognize that the world exists on its own terms. . . . In order to be truly human Job must be situated against the backdrop of creation as a whole. . . . The bigger picture is one in which the ordered and structured cosmos is not ordered and structured around the human enterprise, let alone Job's own life. There is at work here a more magnificent mind than the merely human.[48]

God's cosmic tour targets Job's dark cosmology but it does not simply demand a return to the shattered, assumptive world of Job 1:1–5. The expansive details about climate and creatures can easily obscure just how specifically the divine speeches respond to Job's personal and theological crisis. For this restless man who had preferred Sheol and feared that chaotic deity who shakes up the world (9:5–8), the poems in chapters 38–42 maximize God's maintenance of the cosmos. Shattering the assumptions of a neatly divided system of darkness and light, this vision of the world integrates even the most chaotic forces into God's kingdom.

---

46 "Yahweh has *recharacterized* creation for Job. . . . Yahweh's love embraces each creature's individuality and unique role within the wonderfully complex network of life. Yahweh has countered Job's chaos and curse of creation (ch. 3) with blessing and balance;" William P. Brown, *Character in Crisis: A Fresh Approach to the Wisdom Literature of the Old Testament* (Grand Rapids, MI: Eerdmans, 1996), 102 (italics original).

47 Janoff-Bulman, *Assumptions*, 164.

48 Thomas, *Vision of the Night*, 66.

Who shut in the sea with doors
when it came bursting forth from the womb,
when I made clouds its clothing
and darkness its swaddling band?

Job 38:8–9

Cast in the caring role of a parent, God embraces the raging chaos of the waters along with the earth's predatory animals (38:39–41), its ferocious and untamable beasts, and that endless host of carnivores whose "young suck blood" (39:30). The world is neither a rigid equation, nor is it darkness and mayhem. It is a complex web of chaos and structure in which the wonder of birth and the tragedy of windstorms coexist. The cosmology of chapters 38–39 strikes an authentic balance between the reliable goodness of God's world (e.g., light, rain) and its inherent violence and death. This honest and unbound version of human existence presents a more fruitful response than the strictly dualistic worldview of Job's friends.

> Excellent therapists provide us with methods for solving certain problems and engage us to consider not only new information but also old material in new and different ways. . . .Over time, these new appraisals and interpretations facilitate the integration of trauma-related thoughts, feelings, and images. The survivor's reconstructed assumptive world acknowledges the traumatic experience but is no longer wholly immersed in it.[49]

The response that is modelled in God's questions is a suggestive and stimulating effort to guide the troubled listeners to a new interpretation of their situation without ignoring the reality of chaos in their lives. Far from the avoidance or comparison that often mars human responses, Job 38–39 looks the magnitude of Job's suffering squarely in the face, a strategy that goes yet a level further in chapters 40–41.

The appearance of Behemoth and Leviathan in other biblical passages (e.g., Ps 74:14; Isa 27:1) and the wider ancient world suggests that these are not just two more animals, but symbols for chaos.[50] Spending

---

49 Janoff-Bulman, *Assumptions*, 164–165.
50 For a detailed discussion of the two beasts, see Ortlund, *Piercing Leviathan*, 119–144.

forty-three verses on the detailed descriptions of the strength and invincibility of these monsters seems like an odd way to comfort someone. But perhaps these closing statements from the whirlwind show that even God's language can come to its limits in the face of the unspeakable. Pushing onward the indirections of Job 38–49, the meticulous appraisal of Leviathan is a profound act of acknowledging and articulating Job's suffering without directly mentioning it. The force of iron hide, nostrils full of smoke, vapors, teeth, and fire—all of this grants a raw and real display of the unthinkable terror that can overthrow human life in God's world. The mythic image of Leviathan, a meaningful symbol in many contexts,[51] remains a useful therapeutic blueprint for all who cannot find the words to express the savage brutality that has hit them.

Seeing Things Too Wonderful

The question of how to respond to the language of a shattered world is central to Job, and readers today can find much inspiration in this biblical book, by both negative example and positive affirmation. For all that the divine speeches offer, however, Job's two brief replies to God in 40:3–5 and 42:1–6 indicate that the book is no foolproof recipe for recovery. Job responds initially with silence ("I will put my hand on my mouth," 41:4), yet the fact that God engages him with a second speech is a clear sign that the cosmic contemplation of chapters 38–39 was not intended to reduce Job to the pious surrender of chapters 1–2. God's patient rejoinder in chapters 40–41 elicits quite a different response— "Now my eyes see you"—that ends the conversation not with closed lips, but with a new vision.

This breakthrough elevates the transformative power of poetry. Job has not so much understood, but seen something about God in the Leviathan speech, something "too wonderful" (42:2–3), something that stirs up a small utterance that hints at closure and catharsis. "Therefore, I despise myself, and repent in dust and ashes." This statement, familiar from the most popular Bible translations (e.g., NRSV, ESV, NIV; "I abhor myself" KJV), can at best be heard as an expression of worship but Job's words also bristle with repression and defeat. Yet worse,

---

51 Cf. Angel, *Playing with Dragons*, 54–76.

some readers might understand them to say that self-loathing is part of recovery or that honest pursuits of God will end in humiliation. Apart from these pastoral problems, too quick an embrace of the traditional translation silences the profound ambiguity of Job's final statement. Does Job despise his life or his words? Does he repent, is he comforted, or has he changed his mind? Is he content on his ash heap or does "dust and ashes" refer as in Genesis 18:27 to human fragility?

That the particular Hebrew wording of 42:6 allows for all of these readings is in itself a meaningful message and laboring too hard for the proper reading might miss the point altogether.[52] Perhaps what is more important still is that Job rather than God is given the final word. An inspiring admission of therapeutic and theological limitations, this biblical book honors the human being and is content to leave questions open. In the place of a watertight solution and safe theology stands the speaking, suffering human being who must not be burdened with a call for clarity and catharsis. It is deeply hopeful to hear about Job's awareness of his limitations and about his new sight of God. But hearing his ambivalent, final words as a declaration of intellectual certainty, unshakeable faith, or emotional equilibrium expects too much of him and of anyone else still travelling on the long road of rebuilding their world.

Whatever any reader will hear in Job's second answer is, of course, a matter of what assumptions about God, humans, and suffering are brought to the text in the first place.[53] What all interpretations of Job 42:6 share, however, is the element of acceptance. Job has come to accept that his view of self, God, and world was limited to what he "has heard." The terrible reality of his own life and the kind imagination of the divine poems have opened his eyes to the unsettled reality of the human condition. Hearing Leviathan still roaring and roaming the earth, Job accepts "the possibility that catastrophe will disrupt ordinary

---

52 "It suggests strongly that the poet himself intended no explicit resolution;" William Morrow, "Consolation, Rejection, and Repentance in Job 42:6," *JBL* 105 (1986), 225.

53 For further discussion of Job 42:6 and other ambiguous passages in the book, see Eric Ortlund: "The Joban poet is skilfully unearthing the assumptions of the reader in his carefully worded text;" "Exegetical Difficulty and the Question of Theodicy in the Book of Job," *JESOT* 7 (2021), 111.

routine" and emerges from the collapse and recreation of his world "somewhat sadder, but considerably wiser."[54] Likely all readers of Job will have to start this journey at some point in their lives. Although the beginning and ending will look different each time, it is vital to see that Job would never have been able to open his eyes had he not first opened his mouth.

This poetic book ascribes to human language a central role for responding to shattered assumptions and for coming to terms with the real world and one's place and possibilities within it. As chapters 38–42 affirm, "one cannot wait until the world conforms to a better fantasy of it before one dare take the risk of living."[55] The book's epilogue suggests that such language can be the starting point for living courageously rather than cautiously. Job's forgiveness of his friends (42:10) and giving an inheritance to his daughters (42:15) shatter assumptions about justice, culture, and gender and witness to the unpredictable blessings that can take root even in this restless, raging world. Because Job opens his mouth, he sees with open eyes, and lives with open hands.

---

54 Janoff-Bulman, *Assumptions*, 175.
55 Thomas, *Vision of the Night*, 153.

CHAPTER 5

Caught in the Flow of Time
Qohelet's Poetry for Human Existence

O Lord, you have been our dwelling place,
generation after generation.
Before the mountains were born
and you brought forth earth and world,
from age to age,
you are God.
You turn humans to dust,
you say: 'Return, O children of Adam!'
For a thousand years in your eyes
are but a day gone by, a watch in the night.

All our days face your anger,
we finish our years like a sigh.
Our lifetime is seventy years,
with strength, eighty,
and what we treasure in them was toil and trouble.
It flashes by with haste
and we fade away.

Psalm 90:1–4, 9–10

With its feet firmly planted on the soil, the human condition is grounded in tangible ways in the material reality of the world. Marked off by the boundary line between water and land, every person stands on their own island of existence. But alongside these pockets of place, human life also inhabits a small space in the vast ocean of time. Though ultimately the more powerful force of life, the rushing current of days and years receives but a sliver of the attention that the material aspects of life claim. The reality of time remains in the background, silently exercising its control, and is often only seen when the world of things and space is shaken.

The trauma of Israel's collapse in the sixth century was one such moment. Before the Babylonian invasion, God's dwelling place was Mount Sinai and the sanctuary in Jerusalem (cf. Pss 26:8; 68:5) but now God dwells in a temple of time, in a spiritual home that is unshackled from geography and free from the human particulars of time, terror, and tragedy. The God of the land, the city, and the temple is now worshipped as the God of eternity. The placement at the head of book IV of the Psalter suggests that the opening lines of Psalm 90 respond to the laments of the shattered temple in book III (e.g., Pss 74:1–11; 79:1–13). Yet as the poem progresses, its theology becomes unsettling rather than comforting: short, quick, troubled, and with a definite ending, such is the human condition when penciled in on the eternal calendar of God.

The struggle with finitude is as old as humanity and remains a pressing issue in a world where the workday is divided across time zones and where hymns to productivity drown out the traditional narratives about life and death. The poetry of the Old Testament acknowledges that humans are bound by time, that the ticking clock is a real theological and psychological challenge. There is no better book than Ecclesiastes, the Bible's supreme blend of poetry and philosophy, to discover a biblical language for this experience and for articulating the human feelings, frustrations, and fears about time. It can be sobering to hear the grinding wheel of the seasons turn and turn and turn (Eccl 3), startling to see the sun set for the last time (Eccl 12). But at the end of the day, it can be profoundly comforting to recognize even amid these alarming sounds and visions the wisdom that Ecclesiastes offers for living well with time.

The Tyranny of Time

Not many aspects are so integral to human living as the topic of time. Neither physics nor philosophy, neither economics nor education, neither music nor sports can function without the measurement of temporal intervals. For an orchestra to harmonize at the composer's prescribed *andante* tempo, every instrument must play at 73 to 77 beats per minute. For athletes to compete, every lap-time must be measured against the others, every match performed in the same time span. But the fixation on the ticking clock goes much deeper than concerts and Olympic medals, touching on the foundational questions of origins and death. These limits of life and the unstoppable progression from one eon to the other are at the heart of research into entropy and quantum time,[1] but this is only the latest chapter in humanity's library on time. Already one of the first entries on these shelves, the *Epic of Gilgamesh* reveals a major concern with finitude.

> *But you, you toiled away, and what did you achieve?*
> *You exhausted yourself with ceaseless toil,*
> *you filled your sinews with sorrow,*
> *bringing forward the end of your days.*
> *Man is snapped off like a reed in a canebrake!*
> *The comely young man, the pretty young woman—*
> *all too soon in their prime Death abducts them.*[2]

The best use of time, the brevity of the human life span, the democracy of death—these ancient lines of poetry bring together some of the most challenging issues that have occupied humanity across the millennia.

Inasmuch as all people share these questions about life and death, every generation has had its own time and its own particular challenges. The first decades of the twenty-first century meet the world at a strange impasse. Advances in technology have reduced the hours required for basic daily maintenance, yet at the same time the competition and control of the digital realm leave many people severely overwhelmed to live their everyday life in only twenty-four hours.[3] From a psychological perspective, the human struggle with temporality is a relevant subject for many reasons. For instance, researchers may

---

1   See, e.g., Sean Carroll, *From Eternity to Here: The Quest for the Ultimate Theory of Time*, 2nd ed. (London: Oneworld Publications, 2011).

2   Andrew George, *The Epic of Gilgamesh: A New Translation* (London: Allen Lane, 1999), 86.

3   "The technologies we use to try to 'get on top of everything' always fail us, in the end, because they increase the size of the 'everything' of which we're trying to get on top;" Oliver Burkeman, *Four Thousand Weeks: Time Management for Mortals* (New York: Vintage, 2021), 47.

investigate the experience of time in different life stages or study the subjective experience of anxious or depressed patients who, according to psychologist Gioanna Mioni, "perceive time as passing faster or more slowly than do non-clinical subjects."[4] Alongside these studies about people's experience of time, the shape of contemporary society prompts the question of how people can cope with the limitless and overbearing claims on their time. Thomas Fuchs, a psychologist at the University of Heidelberg, links these impossible demands to a range of mental and social challenges.

> People who suffer from depression suffer under a slowing-down and an alienation of the time that they experience. . . But depression is not just an interruption of individual time. It may also be understood as an unhinging from the shared, social time, that is, as a mode of *desynchronisation*. The depressed person can no longer keep up with the progress of events, with expectations and deadlines. Depression can be a potential indicator for the excessive demands to which a high-speed society subjects its members. . . Depressive illnesses can be understood as reactions to the alienating reign of *linear time*.[5]

Fuchs sees this description of time to stand in marked contrast to premodern cultures where "traditions, rituals, and myths embed the present into a cycle of repeated past events," where the lives of individuals are not a "linear flight toward death" but a participation in the natural

---

4 See, e.g., William J. Friedman, "Developmental Perspectives on the Psychology of Time," in *Psychology of Time*, ed. Simon Grondin (Bingley: Emerald, 2008), 345–366. Giovanna Minoi et al., "Time Perception in Anxious and Depressed Patients: A Comparison between Time Reproduction and Time Production Tasks," *J Affect Disord* 196 (2016), 160. Ioannis Sargiannidis and colleagues arrive at a somewhat narrower conclusion: "In contrast to previous studies suggesting that unpleasant events induce a state during which the passage of time slows down, we found that anxiety is associated with temporal underestimation, i.e., that time flies;" "Anxiety Makes Time Pass Quicker while Fear Has No Effect," *Cognition & Emotion* 197 (2020), 11. See further Jingyuan Liu and Hong Li, "How Individuals Perceive Time in an Anxious State: The Mediating Effect of Attentional Bias," *Emotion* 20 (2020): 761–772.

5 Thomas Fuchs, "Chronopathologie der Überforderung: Zeitstrukturen und Psychische Krankheit," in *Das Überforderte Subjekt: Zeitdiagnosen einer beschleunigten Gesellschaft*, ed. Thomas Fuchs, Lukas Iwer, and Stefano Micali (Berlin: Suhrkamp, 2018), 52 (italics original). All translations of Fuchs's work are my own.

world.[6] The shift away from this way of life is commonly tied to economic and technological developments. Over time, modern societies came to live in triumphant independence from the world's natural pauses and progressions, eagerly pursuing higher rates of productivity outside of the constraints of clock and calendar. Its benefits notwithstanding, this invention of a timeless world takes its toll on human well-being. A purely linear timeline, for instance, can turn "every present moment essentially into a final opportunity," thereby creating pressures of regret and decision-making that entangle many people in "aimless ambition" and a "restless loss of the present."[7] The economy of linear time promises fulfilment farther down its narrow, rushing current, all the while leaving its frantic swimmers to wear themselves out in what is, in truth, an endless ocean where there is no arrival.

These dynamics can translate with detrimental consequence into the lived experience of individuals. Impossible demands for productivity and improvement provoke the shame of falling behind, which in turn is met by an ever higher rate of performance.[8] The increase of working hours and the nervous scurry to make the most of every moment can combine to an onset of burnout, anxiety, and depression that, in their extreme forms, rob their victims of time altogether.

> Depressed people do not get up on time, withdraw from social commitments, and live with a permanent feeling of staying behind and being excluded... [They] fall out of shared time, literally living in a different, thickly flowing time, while the linear time passes by around them.[9]

Underneath these personal tragedies lies a modern attitude that treats time as a commodity, as something that can be managed and controlled

---

6   Fuchs, "Zeitstrukturen," 60.

7   Fuchs, "Zeitstrukturen," 62–63.

8   "Once time is a resource to be used, you start to feel pressure, whether from external forces or from yourself, to use it well, and to berate yourself when you feel you've wasted it. . . . Soon, your sense of self-worth gets completely bound up with how you're using time;" Burkeman, *Four Thousand Weeks*, 24–25.

9   Fuchs, "Zeitstrukturen," 71–72. The tyranny of time can also contribute to rising levels of anxiety, which is always "infused with cultural templates, social influences, and material interests" that each in their own way can create anxious thoughts about the past, the present, and the future; Horwitz, *Anxiety: A Short History*, 4.

as a resource. This posture is reflected in common statements like "Do you have time this afternoon?" or "Let's make more time for this next week," as well as by the plethora of time-management apps. The lost battle against time, just like the curious phenomenon of FOMO ("fear of missing out"), emerges from the essential conflict between the illusion of time-control and the all-controlling power of time's arrow.[10] The current version of linear time runs too quickly, leaving behind everyone who no longer succeeds in "making up time," in synchronizing their limited capacity with the clockwork of an endless day.

Talking Time with Ecclesiastes

Pushed to new extremes in the contemporary context, the tension of competing ideas of time is not an invention of the digital age. Ancient societies did not blindly follow the weather but operated with a complex interplay between cyclical and linear time, between repetition and sequence.[11] The Hebrew poets and their ancient audiences knew nothing of the modern opposition between history and myth. Rather, the Old Testament presents an integrated view of worldtime that covers the whole range of regular seasons, personal moments, communal memories, and cultic participation in the past (cf. Deut 5:3) alongside episodes of sublime significance, such as the holy sabbath or primordial creation (*Urzeit*).[12] The cultural distance to this worldview

---

10 Burkemann speaks of "real psychological consequences... because our expectations are forever running up against the stubborn reality that time isn't in our possession and can't be brought under our control," *Four Thousand Weeks*, 118.

11 The schematic evolution from cyclical to linear time that is reflected in Fuchs's and many other studies stems from an overdrawn distinction between Hebrew and Greek thought. For a detailed analysis, see James Barr, *Biblical Words for Time*, SBT (London: SCM Press, 1962), 95–104, 139–142; Mark Brettler, "Cyclical and Teleological Time in the Hebrew Bible," in *Time and Temporality in the Ancient World*, ed. R. M. Rosen (Philadelphia, PA: University of Pennsylvania Museum, 2004), 111–128.

12 "Sacred history may be described as an attempt to overcome the dividing line of past and present, as an attempt *to see the past in the present tense*," Abraham Joshua Heschel, *God in Search of Man: A Philosophy of Judaism* (New York: Farrer, Straus and Giroux, 1955), 211–212 (emphasis original).

is immense, yet the contemporary struggle of "running out of time" and the ancient scriptures raise similar questions. How do humans talk about time? What does such language reveal about their attitudes and ambitions, their limitations and lifestyle? And what does it reflect about their view of self and the world? Thinking about these questions of articulation can be the starting point for cultivating a pace of life that steers clear of depressing timelessness and falling out of sync with healthy rhythms.

From Marcel Proust's *In Search of Lost Time* (1913–1927) to Michael Ende's children's story *Momo* (1973), the world of literature speaks of the real need of engaging in such contemplation and critique. The Old Testament poses no exception. The foundational struggles around mortality in Genesis 3–6 set the stage for a posture of time that can lament "times of trouble" (Ps 37:39), cry out in old age (Ps 71:9), and deplore the brevity of life (Pss 39:5; 89:47). That most of the attention to time unfolds in such short statements may create the impression that the Israelites had no abstract concept or reflections about time.[13] But already the complex horizons of Psalm 90—the times of God, mountains, and humans are shared but different—show that the library of Hebrew poetry offers a rich and relatable resource for speaking about temporality. This exercise of articulation is nowhere performed with more focus and nuance than in the language about time, times, and timing in Ecclesiastes.

If Job's misfortune shakes the pillars of the wisdom tradition, the perspective of Ecclesiastes threatens to collapse them altogether. Proverbs' parental pedagogy is largely absent; there are none of Job's dialogues or divine oracles; and all ideals of community and revelation are replaced by the voice of just one person. Qohelet, a figure clothed in Solomonic garb, rehearses his monologue as an exercise of personal observation that takes seriously the lessons learned from experience and emotion. This orientation puts Ecclesiastes in touch with the postmodern self, yet the book is very much at home in its own world. The first-person style takes its cue from the genre of ancient royal inscriptions ("I, Qohelet, was king over Israel in Jerusalem;" 1:12) that would

---

13 For a critical appraisal of these assumptions, see Mette Bundvad, *Time in the Book of Ecclesiastes,* OTM (Oxford: Oxford University Press, 2015), 24–43.

narrate accomplishments and preserve accolades for posterity.[14] However, the royal record of Ecclesiastes could not break more sharply with
such conventions. Qohelet speaks about his buildings, vineyards, feasts,
and wisdom only to tear it all down.

> *I turned my gaze to all the works which my hands had made,*
>   *to all the toil with which I toiled in making them.*
> *And look: It is all absurd, thoughts of wind,*
>   *no gain under the sun!*

Ecclesiastes 2:11

Statements like these have earned Ecclesiastes a grim reputation:
"Vanity of vanities! All is vanity!" This thesis frames the book (1:2;
12:8), suggesting that all its chapters deal with the futility of life; other
translations go yet further, having Qohelet declare that "everything is
meaningless" (NIV). Not many words have received so much attention as the Hebrew term *hebel,* which stands behind these translations.
Occurring thirty-eight times across the book's twelve chapters, this
particular word entangles every paragraph and sentence, and there,
exactly, lies the problem of interpreting what Qohelet has to say. The
vast range of occurrences means that *hebel* is not static, that a different passage requires a different English word. This flexibility of
word-meaning is just basic semantics, but in Ecclesiastes the variable
of *hebel* is itself an integral part of the message. Everything is *hebel*
because everything is subject to time and change, to the ambiguities
of life and language that can be interpreted now this way, now that.[15]
In chapter 2, for instance, Qohelet does not lament that work is meaningless but rather that the "person who will be after me" might be

---

14 Cf. Tremper Longman III, *Fictional Akkadian Autobiography: A Generic and
    Comparative Study* (Winona Lake, IN: Eisenbrauns, 1991).

15 "The word הבל [*hebel*], rather than being the key that unlocks 'the mean-
    ing' of Qohelet, is actually highly ambiguous and presents a gap of indeter-
    minacy which the reader is required to fill in in order to create meaning;"
    Doug Ingram, *Ambiguity in Ecclesiastes,* LHBOTS 431 (New York: T&T Clark,
    2006), 105. See also Samuel T. S. Goh, "The *Hebel* World, Its Ambiguities and
    Contradictions," *JSOT* 45 (2020): 198–216.

a fool and tarnish all his toil (vv. 18–21). The term *hebel* presents a useful symbol for this condition, a metaphor that applies the word's literal meaning of "vapor" or "breath" to the fleeting character of human accomplishments (e.g., Isa 57:13; Prov 21:6).[16] Like the mist that hovers for a while in the morning air, human existence is but a matter of time.

The Sea Is Not Full, the Ear Never Filled
Appreciating the complexity of *hebel* is a helpful safeguard against dismissing Qohelet's message from the start as overly negative. The pedagogy of Ecclesiastes is not as determined, not as dogmatic as to deserve such quick rejection. Especially the first two chapters are heavily interactive, including the reader by way of questions and descriptions as Qohelet plunges into his cross-examination of life.

> *What is the profit that remains for humans*
> *in all their toil that they toil under the sun?*
>
> Ecclesiastes 1:3

The honesty and openness of this question is a clear sign that Qohelet is not a nihilist but a person deeply committed to the search for meaning. He acknowledges that life is full of toil and trouble but he will not let such acceptance stand in the way of a thorough interrogation. Inasmuch as Qohelet's approach to wisdom is governed by his personal observations, his first line of inquiry stands firmly in the traditional arena of Israel's sages. Like Proverbs 8 and Job 38–41, Qohelet turns his eye in the book's prologue to the created order. But where these writers discover a beautiful network, the poet of Ecclesiastes sees a different world.

---

16 With inspiring poetic imagination, Daniel Fredericks understands *hebel* as an onomatopoeia: "It is *aspirated* initially with 'h' and continued by the *spirant* 'v' sound, thus spoken by the exhalation of breath that the word itself denotes. The pronunciation is itself a direct illustration of what the word means;" *Coping with Transience: Ecclesiastes on Brevity in Life*, BibSem 18 (Sheffield: JSOT Press, 1993), 12.

A generation is going, another is coming in,
and the earth is standing forever
and the sun rises and the sun comes in,
to its place, pressing on, there it is rising.
Going to the south and around to the north,
around and around the wind is going,
and on its rounds the wind is returning.
All rivers are going to the sea and the sea is not full,
to the place where the rivers are going
there they are returning to go.

Ecclesiastes 1:4–7

Everything in this poem is in motion. The verb "to go" (הלך) is repeated six times across just four verses, a new generation enters the scene, the sun hastens to its zenith, the wind blows round and round, and the rivers circle the earth. Confronted with all these moving parts and all this incredible energy, it is easy to miss the astounding fact that nothing gets accomplished in these poetic lines. For all its force, the wind just goes in circles; for all their travels, the rivers make no difference to the vast, blue eternity of the sea. Hebrew poetry typically unpacks its message by a gradual, forward-facing advancement, yet here the parallel phrases only manifest the reality of repetition and stagnation. Bound by relentless routine, the mighty sun and the strong rivers stay "there," in their place, ever rehearsing their scripted roles on the unchanging stage of the earth.

Similar to the worldview of Job 38–41 and Psalm 104, humans play but a small part in Qohelet's cosmology. The generations are mentioned first, yet they quickly fade into the crowd of all that is coming, going, rising, and returning in the world. The abundance of participle verbs highlights the continual and present nature of this circularity; it is a loop that nobody can leave, not even through death. The generations in verse 4 do not "come and go," but depart and become dust, the very matter of which the coming generation is made (cf. Gen 2:7; Eccl 3:20). The history of humanity "is nothing but an eternal dust-cycle" that knows neither endings nor epochs, that buries the significance of each hour under the faceless fabric of raw matter.[17] Qohelet's observations

---

17 Nili Samet, "Qohelet 1:4 and the Structure of the Book's Prologue," *ZAW* 126 (2014), 97–98. Ernest Becker finds yet more graphic words: "Creation is a

about the dust of every day opposes the dignity of the sixth day in Genesis 1, presenting humans not in charge of the world but as completely integrated into the natural realm and its frustrating economy of effort and effect.

> All words wear themselves out,
>   nobody can speak,
>   no eye is satisfied to see,
>   no ear filled from hearing.
> What has been will be,
>   what has been done will be done,
>   and there is no new thing under the sun.
> There may be something of which they say:
>   'Look at this! That is new!'
>   Already it has been for the eons
>   that were before us.
> There is no remembrance of the things before,
>   and even the things that will come later are not remembered
>   along with those that will come later still.

Ecclesiastes 1:8–11

Qohelet's poetry continues to engage its readers, including along its rhythms and repetition now also appeals ("Look at this!") and inclusive language ("before us"). Such efforts are needed given the controversial nature of his assertions. Despite all toil and trial, there is nothing new and no human activity—speaking, seeing, hearing, making—will ever arrive anywhere. All that was and is and will be is bound to trail off in the forgetful flow of time. Inventions, wars, leaders, and ideas—every specific, historical instance is but one in a long line of others.[18] Like the sea that is never full of the rivers, the ear will never be full of hearing

---

nightmare spectacular taking place on a planet that has been soaked for hundreds of millions of years in the blood of all its creatures. The soberest conclusion that we could make about what has actually been taking place on the planet for about three billion years is that it is being turned into a vast pit of fertilizer;" *The Denial of Death* (New York: Free Press, 1973), 283.

18 This statement can be read as a "realization of archetypes" (Michael V. Fox, *A Time to Tear Down and a Time to Build Up. A Rereading of Ecclesiastes* [Grand Rapids, MI: Eerdmans, 1999], 168–169) or against the fullness of history which sees ever-new people making the same, old experiences time and time again (Janowski, *Anthropologie*, 369).

another headline. So much energy, so much movement, yet what is remembered dwindles away under the distance of every new day.

That Qohelet's quest for meaning begins with bygone generations and frail memories indicates how closely his frustrations are tied up with the topic of time. The book's opening poem calls into question everything from progress to legacy, from certainty to impact, from memories to meaning. This systematic deconstruction highlights just how little remains, how human words and deeds share in the stagger-ing wastefulness of the elements. Worldtime and humantime are set side-by-side for this rhetoric of analogy, but the integration of creation and creatures is not total. Every generation and every sunrise enter the same stage (בוא, "come in," vv. 4–5), but only the mighty luminary has a lifetime subscription. The endless play of wind and water forms the backdrop against which every individual can see their finitude in sharp contours,[19] moving with open eyes and eager ears ever closer to the "land of forgetting" (Ps 88:12).

Time Is All, All Is Time

The first chapters of Ecclesiastes confront their readers with a number of startling claims but avoid the demand for silent compliance. Instead, Qohelet speaks as a companion, venting his honest frustrations before the reader and sharing his personal journey. His observations about the world lead right into an account of his earnest efforts to prove the cosmos wrong. Looking back at a series of experiments (1:12–2:23), Qohelet confesses that he employed all his royal privileges to leave a dent in the cruel cycle of life—but neither the mastery of wisdom, nor the excess of enjoyment, nor the excellence of wealth could break the power of time. The hours invested would pale in comparison with the end result, the next generation was always just around the corner to mar his accomplishments, and death would level everything anyways. The painful journey of chapters 1–2 is a case in point that the reality of time needs to be faced head-on, not with the hope of escaping from it but as a cathartic exercise of giving words to its experience.

---

19 "This is mortality: to move along a rectilinear line in a universe where every-thing, if it moves at all, moves in a circular order;" Hannah Arendt, *The Human Condition,* 2nd ed. (Chicago: University of Chicago Press, 1998), 19.

For everything there is a set time,
a time for every matter under heaven.
A time to conceive and a time to die,
a time to plant and a time to tear out what is planted.
A time to kill and a time to heal,
a time to tear apart and a time to build.
A time to weep and a time to laugh,
a time to mourn and a time to dance.
A time to throw stones and a time to gather stones,
a time to embrace and a time to stay far from embrace.
A time to seek and a time to let loose,
a time to hold on and a time to let go.
A time to tear and a time to sew,
a time to be silent and a time to speak.
A time to love and a time to hate,
a time of war and a time of peace.

Ecclesiastes 3:1–8

The art of Hebrew poetic composition is pressed into its most compact format in these lines. Across just seven verses, the word "time" (*ēt*) is repeated twenty-eight times, coupled in almost all verses with just one infinitive verb, yielding in Hebrew four words per line, eight words per verse. Exceptions to this formula appear in the first verse, the central verse, and the final verse that uses the nouns "war" and "peace" rather than the infinitive forms "to wage war" and "to make peace." But contrary to what this tight structure may suggest, Qohelet's poem is neither balanced nor ordered nor does it progress from A to Z. The time of birth makes a logical starting point, but the list as a whole is a fairly random assortment of human activities and experiences. The wisdom of Ecclesiastes 3 lies both on the surface of its words and deep underneath their meaning.

The extensive repetition of "time" is certainly the most obvious aspect of the poem. Its incessant presence establishes the fact that both the unique moments of life, such as conception or death, and the repeated events of planting, sowing, and building are all bound to the calendar. If there is a time for every thing, then time is everything: life's ever-present companion, the ticking clock determines the timing, duration, and sequence of all matters under heaven. The contrast that governs each parallel pair nuances this observation by breaking Time into different times. Each moment belongs to just one activity, that is, tearing cannot happen at the same time as sewing, nor weeping in the hour of laughter.

The back-and-forth motion across each line imbues each moment with its own significance but the poem never loses sight of the total time of human experience. For better and for worse, the deed of the day and the momentary grip of emotions are temporary. Those who enjoy a warm embrace today will need to keep their distance tomorrow; those who weep now will laugh again some other day. Like the rain, the rivers, and the wind, these rhythms speak of relief but also of risk. The pattern of time after time after time robs today's speakers of the illusion that silence will never be their lot and those dancing of the assumption that the day of mourning will not come around. Even the best of times will end; every perfect moment will be swallowed up by the next mundane hour.

This two-faced dimension of Qohelet's terse word pairs carries hope for tomorrow but also raises the uncomfortable question of whether the next day will indeed be better. Does weeping always turn to laughing? Can it not also sink into mourning and despair? That the duration and flow of the times cannot be predicted is troublesome enough, yet Qohelet's uneven transitions from positive to negative even undermine these categories themselves.[20] Letting go of things can be healthier than keeping them (v. 6), speaking can cause more pain than silence (v. 7), and mourning can be better than feasting and dancing (cf. 7:2!). These gaps and ambiguities are embedded within the highly structured frame of Ecclesiastes 3, creating an imprint of human living that speaks of regularity *and* uncertainty, that knows that life is no simple balance of good and bad days. Nothing about these times is self-evident, not least because many of them are outside of human control. Pulling out plants, throwing stones, and embracing another human being are things most people can do at any time, yet nobody decides the day of their birth or schedules the misfortunes of war, weeping, and silence.

---

20 "Positive and negative appear in no apparent sequence. . . . The pairs are not precisely complementary. Qohelet does not say, for example, 'to plant and to harvest' or 'to sew and to cut;'" Fox, *Rereading*, 193–194.

For all its straightforward structure and chanty veneer, the Bible's only poem about time vibrates with a tension between experience and evaluation, between decision and determination. The list of word pairs alone does not provide any clear guidance on how to live with the times. There is no clear progression from the "time to conceive" to the "time of peace," no criteria by which to determine that a certain time has arrived, no assurance about how long they will last.[21] The twenty-eight times cast all conceivable actions and sentiments into the same pool of time, drowning the thirst for perpetual harmony along with the illusions of control and accurate interpretation.[22] As with his cosmology in chapter 1, Qohelet does not pronounce these observations as a nihilistic manifesto, but as a relatable, realistic record of the human condition. This is what life under heaven is like—ordered, but without apparent logic; here and there under human control but altogether out of their hands; good and bad and good and bad, but also bad and worse or good and better. None of this means that humans are doomed to inactivity and failure. They *can* give birth, build, speak. But with verse 9, the question of "what profit remains for the workers?" cannot be avoided as all children, houses, and words are swept away anytime.

The times-poem can stand all on its own as an honest articulation of lived reality and as a concession to the limits of human endeavors. But Ecclesiastes 3 can also be read as a testimony to human possibilities. The poem's few words show the impressive range of actions and achievements, of emotional and relational grandeur all at once, proclaiming the richness of life that deserves to be celebrated even with the ominous ticking of time in the background. To see both sides and to endure their tension demands its own time. Perhaps it is this patient

---

21 Shawn P. White sees this as the primary meaning of "time" (עֵת) in Ecclesiastes: "Limited duration and effectiveness is the key feature of the use of עֵת here rather than the timing;" "'Why Were the Former Days Better Than These?': An Examination of Temporal Horizons in Ecclesiastes" (PhD diss; University of Edinburgh, 2013), 35.

22 "In the experiences of the world in which people find themselves nothing of absolute validity can be affirmed. What is experienced on any given occasion has always shown itself to be in some way conditioned and relative;" Gerhard von Rad, *Wisdom in Israel,* trans. James D. Martin (London: SCM Press, 1972), 139.

exercise that can carry the reader to the resting place where the poem stops: a time of peace. Too often, however, Ecclesiastes's timely word about the human condition is lost to short-lived contemplation or the age-old debates around free will and predetermination. The generic statement of verse 1 demands no such reading,[23] neither will verses 10–17 eradicate the complexities of time and timing.

> I saw the business that God has given to the children of Adam to pursue:
>   everything he has made for its right time,
>   eternity he has also given into their hearts
>   without people being able to find out the work
>   that God has made from beginning to end.

> Ecclesiastes 3:10–11

In sharp contrast to the times-poem, here only God acts, "making" (×2) and "giving" (×2) time to humans. Underneath all their building, weeping, and sewing lies a deep dimension of "eternity" ('lām), of God's work unfolding across all time. Everything that God makes is forever; humans can neither add to it nor reduce it (v. 14).

This statement resonates with other wisdom passages that speak about divine determination. But as in Proverbs 16:9—"The human mind plans its path and the Lord establishes its step"—there is no good reason for putting divine and human action in absolute opposition in Ecclesiastes. God does not ordain or orchestrate every laugh and tear but creates the circumstances, the occasions for when comic relief or grief is the right thing to do. Side-by-side with firm elevations of God's foresight and authority (e.g., Eccl 6:10), the human condition remains marked by agency and responsibility (5:1–5; 7:16–17; 11:1–10).[24] Qohelet's words may be read as a reversal of Proverbs 16:9 in which God plans all paths and humans decide when to take their first step. Human living in time has more to do with decision-making

---

23 The Hebrew word zĕmān, which is parallel to 'ēt in verse 1, is no special theological word (i.e., it is never used in connection with God). It describes events that recur, like the festival of Purim (Esth 9:27; 31), as well as events that are unique and not entirely in one's hand, such as Nehemiah's time of returning from Jerusalem (Neh 2:6).

24 For further discussion, see Nili Samet, "How Deterministic Is Qohelet? A New Reading of the Appendix the Catalogue of Times," ZAW 131 (2019): 577–591.

than with fatalism, leaving humans in that challenging place of having no access to the divine masterplan yet needing to determine if today is the day for that overdue embrace, if now is the right moment to be quiet.

My Personal Apocalypse
Qohelet's observations about toil and time occupy much of the book's opening chapters and lay a foundation for later statements (e.g., "To every matter there is a time," 8:6). He discovers wisdom in the unpredictabilities of life ("better is the end of something than its beginning," 7:8), yet at times the realism of the prologue and the times-poem drops to new depths of helplessness.

> *I turned and I saw under the sun*
> *that the race is not won by the swift,*
> *nor the battle by the mighty,*
> *the wise do not get bread*
> *neither the learned riches,*
> *or the knowledgable favour*
> *for time and tragedy will meet them all.*
> *For nobody knows their time:*
> *like fish pulled up in an evil net,*
> *like birds caught in a trap*
> *so are the children of Adam ensnared at an evil time*
> *which falls on them suddenly.*
>
> Ecclesiastes 9:11–12

This poem visualizes the injustice and personal tragedies that come with time. Taking its place alongside the cosmic analogies and terse word pairs of chapters 1 and 3, the poetry of Ecclesiastes 9 majors in similes. Imagery involving animals, nets, and traps is typically reserved for the wicked as they chase the righteous (e.g., Pss 10:9; 140:5) or fall prey to their own devices (e.g., Job 18:9–10; Ps 9:15), yet here all such ethical divides are irrelevant. The mighty, the wise, the righteous—everyone alike will be met by time, that ultimate and undying foe. All must submit to the final authority of death, time's alter ego, whose victory is sure but always again surprising, sudden, and shattering.

Perhaps because of its unspeakable terror, the grim fact of mortality has inspired the Hebrew poets to pen some of their most creative and imaginative texts. The author of Isaiah 14 scripts a theatrical scene in the underworld; the writer of Psalm 49 pictures death as a shepherd who safely guides his sheep to Sheol; Habakkuk 2 envisions the grave as a greedy mouth. Qohelet's final poem is no less graphic in its portrayal of human endings and so it is unfortunate that most Bible translations do not print this poetic vision in versed layout. The look of the passage on the page is important, not just for tracking its repetitions and structure but also for keeping in mind that it speaks with that lavish poetic voice that locates the meaning of a text above and beyond the words that it uses.

> So think of your creator in the days of your youth
>   before the bad days come and the years arrive
>   of which you say: "There is nothing in them that I enjoy,"
>   before sun and light grow dark,
>   along with moon and stars,
>   and the clouds return after the rain,
>   on the day when the guards of the house tremble,
>   the men of might are bent over,
>   the grinders cease for they are few,
>   and those who look through windows grow dark,
>   doors are shut in the street,
>   the sound of the mill is low,
>   the bird rises to sing
>   but all the singers of song are bowed low,
>   even what is on high they fear and the terrors along the way,
>   the almond tree will blossom,
>   the locust carry heavy burdens,
>   the caper-fruits burst open,
>   but mortals are going to their eternal home,
>   and the mourners go round and round in the street,
>   when the silver cord is snapped, the golden bowl shattered,
>   the jug cracked at the spring, and the wheel smashed at the well,
>   and the dust returns to the earth just as it was,
>   and the breath returns to God who gave it.

Ecclesiastes 12:1–7

The entire passage takes its cue from the personal call in verse 1. Qohelet shifts his attention from himself to the creator, drawing a circle back to the prologue while also tipping his hat to the tradition that views wisdom as a word to the young. Introduced already in 11:9–10, the relationship of sage/student or parent/child is familiar from Proverbs, but here as everywhere the concession to convention is colored by Qohelet's sharp turns and deconstructive language. In contrast to his fellow sages, he embraces a thoroughly positive view of youth—"O youth, enjoy yourself in your youth!" (11:9; cf. 4:13–16)—but in familiar fashion immediately turns around and casts the looming shadow of "the bad days" over life's first chapters.

The uninterrupted flow of words in chapter 12 lends a sobering realism to the unstoppable force of years and seasons. All six verses read in Hebrew as one massive sentence, adding image to image, turning sounds to silence, light to darkness, delight to dust. The verses bleed into each other, leaving no pause for questions or objections, rolling all details into one overwhelming vision of aging and dying. This avalanche of cosmic, social, and bodily descriptions weaves a range of separate domains into one compact fabric. The lights in the sky "grow dark," so do the faces in the windows (חשך in vv. 2–3); the clouds return, as does the breath of humans (שוב in vv. 2, 7); God shall be remembered, but the singers fear what is on high (v. 5). These connections and contrasts create an atmosphere of diminishment, deterioration, and decay, but the message of the poem is not that simple, not that monochrome.

As in Qohelet's first poem, the temporal horizons of people and planet once again stand at odds. The rising of the singing bird jars with the singers bowed low. The springtime renewal of trees and insects heightens the permanent end of mortal humans. All people will go to their eternal home; the world will go on being home to countless more. As a daring strategy to impart this hard truth to his readers, Qohelet takes recourse to the cosmic imagery of world-endings and maps it onto the mundane, everyday event of death. The poem lays hold of the symbolism of the darkened sun that is familiar from prophetic visions of God's cosmic judgment (e.g., Isa 13:10; Joel 3:15) and employs it to paint the small personal end of one human life with the thickest brushstrokes possible.[25] The lack of light, the dominion of silence, the shattering of

---

25 Other elements, such as the birds and the broken pottery, also make a symbolic contribution to this "terrifying vision of the tenebrous end-time, a vision of death;" C. L. Seow, "Qohelet's Eschatological Poem," *JBL* 118 (1999), 221.

human strength and society, the crack and snap of every human-made object—all of these items convey together the weight of death, engulfing their young listener in a terrible scene of their own finitude.

This way of speaking poses a notable counterpoint to the rhetoric that dominates chapters 1–11. Its preference for empirical treatments and emotional outbursts notwithstanding, Ecclesiastes knows of the capacity of poetry to create an atmosphere and to appeal to the imagination. Qohelet dreams a nightmare of a dark sky that no longer enjoys the cycles of the sun. He conjures a gloomy landscape where mighty men jump nervously at the slamming of doors, where no human sings, where the clouds rush back after the rain. These strange details have been interpreted literally as a funeral scene or as the change of seasons but also with full allegorical abandon. The grinders stand for lost teeth, the darkened onlookers for failing eyesight, the fading song for deafness. Both reading strategies suit parts of the poem,[26] but when pushed to the extreme they make the appeal to the senses too concrete, the scope too narrow.

All preoccupation with precision may miss the drama of death that unfolds line by line. Each sight and sound is familiar on its own, but they amass in this kaleidoscopic fabric to a vision that is palpable, that cannot be avoided. "We see our own death, and Qohelet will not let us turn away."[27] Revelation and confrontation join forces in the wake of the imperative that opens the poem. The old sage knows firsthand the quick path that descends from youthful joy to the world of silence, but he also knows that this bitter reality cannot be communicated with facts or charts. It needs to be seen, heard, felt, and feared.

A Biblical Language for the Tyranny of Time

When compared to many other books in the Old Testament, Ecclesiastes possesses all the characteristics that should make for easy reading.

---

26 While the NLT fully embraces the allegory, the NJPS records it in footnotes. Robert Gordis at first agrees with the "moving 'Allegory of Old Age' [that] practically all commentators have recognized from the Talmud to our day," but then identifies several features that "are best taken literally and not figuratively;" *Koheleth: The Man and His World. A Study of Ecclesiastes,* 3rd ed. (New York: Schocken Books, 1968), 338–339.

27 Fox, *Rereading,* 349.

With its twelve chapters, it is relatively short and compact, it requires but little knowledge of ancient history and geography, and its first-person speech is informal and accessible. That Qohelet's words have been such a challenge for readers across the centuries has to do, therefore, largely with its content and perspective. The scant interest in "life above the sun" might be a hurdle for readers who look beyond this life,[28] yet the book's contribution lies precisely in this perspective. No other biblical writer is so unabashedly concerned with the actual experience of human existence. Qohelet offers a wealth of words that captures that reality, that speaks to and for anyone who looks like him at the world with confusion and questions. The tyranny of time, the fear of forgetting, and the dilemma of decisions and death take pride of place in the book's language about the human condition, a language that is the first step toward a new attitude toward the ticking clock.

Lamenting the Sunset

One of the most profound gifts that the Hebrew poets bestow upon their readers is the extensive lament tradition of their day. Compositions like the Psalms, Jeremiah, Job, and Lamentations challenge spiritual triumphalism and emotional repression alike, leaving no doubt that all of life's troubles can be brought before a listening God. Such pleas for help emerge from situations of conflict, illness, and guilt, but they can also be the result and the direct response to God's inscrutable ways and absence (see, e.g., Ps 10:1; Jer 12:1–2; Lam 5:19–22). But for all the diversity and depth of these texts, Israel's poets rarely lament the basics of life, the very structures of space and time that God has established. The speaker of Psalm 39 comes close enough.

---

28 Qohelet consistently keeps God in his focus (e.g., 1:13; 2:24; 5:1–6; 7:1–14; 12:13–14) and the emphasis on life "under the sun" simply highlights "the broad applicability of his observations;" Fox, *Rereading*, 165. Although Easter Sunday makes a profound difference for how Christians think about mortality, they continue to live "in the world" (John 13:1; 17:11). Like Jesus, who worked in the confines of time (Mark 1:35–39) and faced its limitations (Matt 24:36; John 7:6), they must navigate the tension of "making the most of the time" (Eph 5:16; Col 4:5) while coping with lost opportunities and difficult decisions. For reflections on time and Christian living, see James K. A. Smith, *How to Inhabit Time: Understanding the Past, Facing the Future, Living Faithfully Now* (Grand Rapids, MI: Brazos Press, 2022), which is structured around a range of passages from Ecclesiastes.

Let me know, O Lord, my end,
 and the measure of my days, what will it be?
 I know that I am passing away.
See, you have made my days but a hand-breadth wide,
 my lifespan is like nothing before you!
Surely, all are a vapor,
 all mortals who are standing strong.

           Psalm 39:5–6

The psalmist holds God accountable for human transience, but this confrontation is quickly paired with a confession of sin (vv. 9–12; see also Pss 90:8–12; 144:4). On the contrary, Ecclesiastes's statements about God and time are uninterested in questions of guilt and culprits. The book is content to express the unspeakable pain of the fleeting day, to lend language to the lamentable reality of *hebel* that befalls every single person. Qohelet's first poem captures the world's stagnation, the bondage of humans, and the waste of energy and effort. By joining worldtime and humantime, the prologue displays the sheer magnitude of time's arrow: the turning wheel of generations and seasons is a force that is too strong to be stopped.

This motion adds a tragic tint to every moment because not a single one of them will remain or return. Every unique day will be swallowed up by the marching minutes and be lost forever. The sun is not bothered by its mindless repetition, the winds not disappointed by their eternal circles. But for humans who are gifted with creativity, ambition, and memory, the passing years accumulate a personal record of loss and grief. Since there is no limit to what can be seen, heard, or spoken, there will be no arrival, no ultimate satisfaction and, in the long run, no remembering. On the vast canvas of cosmic clockwork, even the greatest achievements will be forgotten and all doctrines of progress grow tired when life walks in circles. All of the typical topics of lament, such as opposition, illness, or divine absence, carry within the painful striving for time and the fear of finitude. But even just on its own, losing time, day by day, is a profoundly unhappy part of the human condition.

For mortal beings whose very bodies and minds testify to this loss, the tyranny of time needs some kind of response. Steering clear of distraction, escapism, and surrender, the practice of lament makes concrete the struggle felt within, it speaks aloud about the pain of today, and it gives voice to the actual experience of living in this world. Ecclesiastes 1 models this practice by performing a counter-liturgy to the celebration of God's wonderful world that often dominates the spheres of preaching, devotion, and music. Imbued with the same canonical authority as Genesis 1 and Psalm 8, Qohelet's poetry about wasted winds and weary words normalizes the human struggle with time as a cosmic reality. Heaving with that same *hebel*-breath, the times-poem in chapter 3 offers a rhythmic contemplation of the ultimate truth that every moment comes and goes, that humans are powerless before the flow of time, that time is all and all is time.[29] The longer the poem runs, the more the pain of impermanence gains momentum and the complexity of decision-making shows its face. There are no re-runs of yesterday, no guarantees for a better tomorrow, and no access to the divine masterplan behind this ebb and flow. Such helplessness deserves recognition and recital.

Ecclesiastes embraces all those finite beings who are haunted by their bygone youth, who cannot cope with their calendar, and whose daily living falls short of the staggering expectations of world and self. Driven to make the most of every moment, mere mortals all too often collide with the reality that the poetry of Qohelet articulated long ago and that the chronopathology of Thomas Fuchs involves so prominently in mental struggles. As one of the available therapeutic responses, Fuchs suggests a re-positioning toward the tyranny of time. A healthy posture toward schedules and seasons will learn to see the twisted timescale of its surroundings in all its impossible and exhausting shades. But it will also allow itself to take a step back and to feel the sadness of each sunset.

---

29 "Eternality is the string upon which the alternate beads of human activity are strung. To use Qoheleth's metaphor, the poem breathes rhythmically with metrical inhaling and exhaling. A time for this, a time for that. Inhale, exhale; inhale, exhale. The cadence of polarity and opposition. The poem's very structure expresses the 'breathing' of life, breathing not the air, but breathing experiences and their opposites in and out of reality;" Fredericks, *Transcience*, 27–28.

One of the goals amid an obsessively optimistic culture of universal communication and consumption may be the cultivation of an attitude of *melancholy*, a culture of slowing-down, of remembering, yes, even of grief which, by its nature, works against depression.[30]

The language of Ecclesiastes speaks as a reasonable and realistic companion in support of such an attitude. Its poetry is rich with imagery, atmosphere, and emotion, cultivating a posture of grief that can liberate its readers to feel the loss of time. Beyond that, the stirring scenery in chapter 12 invites a lament about the terror of death, about that tyrant who shuts every door and silences every song. That Ecclesiastes ends by putting such weight on final endings promotes an honest look at life that has little patience for the repression of death.[31] There must be a response to those days without pleasure, to the lost hours of mindless labor, to the decay of every precious product made by human hands. In Qohelet's view, this plain fact of life should be met with lament and grief and with an honest sadness. After all, "the heart of the wise is in the house of mourning" (7:4).

Arriving in Time

Qohelet's poetry brings to light what is arguably one of the most constant and critical issues of being human. The moon and sea are not anxious about their finitude, neither do the animals who know their time of migration (Jer 8:7) and their season for birthing (Job 39:1) struggle with the calendar. Blessed and cursed with the ability to reflect and respond, human beings have to deal with their consciousness of time. The expressive response of lament that Qohelet models is one of the first steps on that journey, but any conductor who schedules a liturgy of loss must contend with the possibility of resistance from the choir.

We recoil from the notion that this is it—that *this* life, with all its flaws and inescapable vulnerabilities, its extreme brevity, and our limited influence over how it unfolds, is the only one we'll get a shot at. Instead, we mentally fight against the way things are.[32]

---

30 "Zeitstrukturen," 75 (italics original).

31 On the various ways in which death has been symbolized and rationalized, see Becker, *Denial of Death*, 11–24.

32 Burkeman, *Four Thousand Weeks*, 29–30 (italics original). As the philosopher Blaise Pascal (born 1623) noted, the resistance to the flow of time may also

Similar to the illusions about a stable world and every posture that has been shattered by despair and trauma, much of the human struggle with time is rooted in a conviction of invincibility. Fuchs lists a number of assumptions that attend the onset of burnout and depression. For instance, "if I labor hard enough, there will be a reward" or "my life is one steady ascent and my energy insatiable."[33] The pedagogy of Ecclesiastes is acutely aware of the hold of these beliefs. Rather than plainly calling for acceptance or chastising its readers, the book models a gentle journey of time-awareness.

Proceeding in opposite fashion to Job's process, Qohelet begins with the impersonal and impartial showcase of the created order. There can be little disagreement with his poetic snapshot of the aimless cosmos, no opposition from anyone who has felt the untiring wind on their skin and stood at the shoreline of the vast ocean. One look out the window, one more fall and spring season—the drama of loss, decay, and death is always on stage. The poetic appeal to the senses in Ecclesiastes's first and last chapters engineers a self-guided tour that invites its participants to make their own observations and come to their own terms for time.[34] For all his provocation, Qohelet really is a gentle tour guide who knows that art speaks louder than arguments and that real learning relies on agency and autonomy.

Nevertheless, arriving in time is a complicated affair. In order to derail any premature disagreement, Ecclesiastes pursues a rhetoric from below. The character of Qohelet is presented as the ideal candidate for cracking life's code and yet even he comes up short. His deep frustration— "I hated life!" (2:17)—can create solidarity and the combination of

---

be a tragic coping mechanism: "The fact is that the present usually hurts. We thrust it out of sight because it distresses us, and if we find it enjoyable, we are sorry to see it slip away.... The present is never our end. The past and present are our means, the future alone our end. Thus we never actually live, but hope to live, and since we are always planning how to be happy, it is inevitable that we should never be so;" *Pensées*, rev. ed., trans. A. J. Krailsheimer (London: Penguin Books, 1995), 13.

33 "Zeitstrukturen," 70.

34 On the place of the imagination and emotion in Qohelet's pedagogy, see Anne W. Stewart, "The Poetry of Wisdom and Imagination: Intellectual Contributions of *Wisdom in Israel*," in *Gerhard von Rad and the Study of Wisdom Literature*, ed. Timothy J. Sandoval and Bernd U. Schipper, AIL 46 (Atlanta, GA: SBL Press, 2022), 185–210.

transparency and life experience lends a humble authority to his voice
even in the face of its controversial observations. The demands of good
decision-making, for instance, are ultimately quite frustrating, yet
with a poet who has lived through the ups and downs of his own poem
perhaps its message can be accepted. Qohelet does not tone down the
contradictions of life. To the contrary, each case study of *hebel* labors
to show its readers the absurd, twisted, and transient flavor of reality.
Addressing everyone who stands between the time to be born and the
time to die, the book's language of time is an empathic companion on
the uncomfortable trail of time.

Living in Time, Today

In Ecclesiastes and other Hebrew poetry, the language of time is a complex interweaving of divine, cosmic, and human times, full of the tension between repetition and finitude, between responsibility and veiled
horizons. The ways in which humans may respond to these chronicles
of existence is just as complex and certainly not a straightforward journey from lament to acceptance to well-being. The second half of Psalm
90 demonstrates how conflicted the posture toward time can become.
Whereas verse 12 arrives at a place of compliance—"How to number
our days, that make known to us, let us get a wise heart!"—the grief-
struck demands that follow break sharply with this attitude.

> Turn it around, O Lord!
>   How much longer?
>   Have compassion with your servants!
> Satisfy us in the morning with your steadfast love,
>   and we will sing and be glad all of our days!
> Grant us joy for the days when you have afflicted us,
>   for the years when we saw evil.

Psalm 90:13–15

For a poem that begins with such lofty speech about God's eternal character, this shift of tone is stunning. The call for God to "turn it around"
reverses the earlier concession to finitude ("you turn humans to dust,"
שׁוּב, in vv. 3, 12), the question "How much longer?" laments the burden

of impossible endurance (e.g., Pss 6:4; 13:1–2; 74:10), and the accusation about affliction and evil appeal for a redeeming of time itself. Speaking in the context of Israel's exile,[35] Psalm 90 lowers its head before God's higher ground of time (cf. Isa 40:8). While it holds that gesture, the poem raises up its fists against both God's timing and trial. Ecclesiastes provides the language, license, and inspiration for such conflicted practice while also affirming that it is possible to live well with time rather than toil against it or succumb to the tight corners of its currents.

Retracing the Circle of Life

Any first encounter with Ecclesiastes's poetry is perhaps more likely to produce resistance than revelation, more prone to breed confusion than clarity. But it lies in the very nature of wisdom literature to reserve its fruits for those who read again, ponder, and read once more.[36] Returning to the prologue, the recognition that human words are weary and that neither seeing nor hearing will ever exhaust the endless potential of a lifetime can be as limiting as it can be liberating. No longer is every conversation burdened with the weight that it matters; no longer need every sermon or public speech bring about real change. To release one's spoken words into this freedom is not irresponsible but a natural consequence of the *hebel*-quality of all things. There is no predictable correlation between effort and outcome, neither in the course of rivers nor in human rhetoric, investment, or planning (cf. 11:2–6). Qohelet breaks down all claims to mastery and shifts the focus to the beauty of speech and sound and to the plain enjoyment of conversation. His poem also delivers the human heart from the illusion that the right speaker or the right listener will redeem it from its mundane existence. Like the rivers, human words can bubble forth without the burden of making the

---

35 Cf. Klaus Seybold, "Zu den Zeitvorstellungen in Psalm 90," *TZ* 53 (1997), 104–107.

36 As von Rad observes for Ecclesiastes 3: "It is a question, in the first instance, of the experience of limitation which is imposed on human energies. People can do nothing but yield to this fact. . . . they are not, however, prevented from reflecting on it; they can go further and even attempt to derive some profit from it and to perceive in it some kind of mysterious order;" *Wisdom*, 139.

sea overflow. Like the wind, human work can flow step by step without frantically rushing to change the world.

To embrace their share in the rhythms of the earth affords mortal creatures with an opportunity to ground themselves in the real world. The incapacity to break free from the cycle of life condemns planet and people to routine, yet the same dynamic can also have a healthy leveling effect. If the mountains and the sun achieve so little despite all their strength, why expect a seismic shift at the hands of a fragile human being? What claim to significance can any short life make on the vast timeline of the cosmos? The subtle integration that unfolds across Qohelet's first poem elevates mundane, day-to-day existence to the status of cosmic norm. Whether this wholesome anthropology is heard in a culture where kings and priests tower above the people or in a culture where the unattainable lifestyle of celebrities is exalted above everyone else, Qohelet's realism keeps both feet firmly on the earth's unchanging ground.[37] Humans are not called to out-compete creation or to live as gods on earth. Limits deserve to be lamented, but they can also pave the road for an arrival at oneself and at one's time. Without first seeing the absurdity of life for what it is, the human condition likely will resemble an uphill struggle toward significance and each mediocre moment will be dismissed as a failure.

To combat such profound misinterpretations, Ecclesiastes describes the world as a magnificent orchestration in which each participant plays at their own time signature and yet all keep time together in that beautiful, endless song of life. This great fugue is propelled forward by arpeggio and reprise, by counterpoint and dissonance, and neither the divine composer nor the wise listener is much bothered that the *da capo* in the score does not yet stand with an *ad fine*. To the contrary, as long as God, humans, animals, and earth listen to one another's melodies, the cycles will continue, the music will play

---

37 Burkeman describes this reorientation as "cosmic insignificance therapy" that delivers to its recipients "an invitation to face the truth about your irrelevance in the grand scheme of things.... dropping back from godlike fantasies of cosmic significance into the experience of life as it concretely, finitely—and often enough, marvellously—really is;" *Four Thousand Weeks*, 213.

on, and many more will join the choir and deepen the harmonies.[38] There is a time for quiet retuning, for being alone and listening to one's own rhythms and rests. But there is also a time for standing at rivers that have been winding their ways for centuries, a time for walking under the bright blossoms of spring, and a time for sitting in a meadow bristling with the vibrant sound of grasshoppers and bees. The human journey through time is enriched by every crossover with the circles of its fellow travelers. A life lived well in time, says Qohelet, cannot keep its eyes narrowed on its own path and listen only to its own music but needs to look left and right and listen up. Living in time will always be a challenge but it will be all the harder if one's own clock is heard ticking loudest.

Believing in the Moment

Discerning a healthy balance between the limiting and liberating contours of Qohelet's digestion of time is but one of Ecclesiastes's many contradictions. Wisdom will cause much vexation (1:18) but it also "lights up the face" (8:1); all accomplishments will thin out over time, yet humans should work hard at their tasks (9:10); death makes an end even to the best efforts yet it can also be a place of rest (4:1–3; 6:1–6).[39] Rather than awaiting resolution, these criss-cross trajectories unmask the absurdities of life and make exception the norm. Their dialogical mechanics of limiting and leveling lay the foundation for Qohelet's search for meaning. When all grand structures and certainties have collapsed, goodness can be found where it truly resides: in the simple moments of everyday living.

---

38 "The author displays an understanding of the cyclical character of life, from planetary elements, to the weather, to human life and death and there is an appreciation of the circularity of the process;" Katharine J. Dell, "The Cycle of Life in Ecclesiastes," *VT* 59 (2009), 189.

39 In a daring antidote to the dramatic portrayal of chapter 12, Qoheleth concludes in 7:1 that "the day of death is better than the day of birth." On the book's ambivalent attitude toward death, see James L. Crenshaw, "The Shadow of Death in Qoheleth," in *Israelite Wisdom: Theological and Literary Essays in Honor of Samuel Terrien*, ed. John G. Gammie et al. (Missoula, MT: Scholars Press, 1978), 205–216.

There is nothing better for mortals
  but that they would eat and drink
  and see the good life in their toil.
    For this, too, I saw
    is from the hand of God.

Ecclesiastes 2:24

I know that there is nothing better for them
  than to be glad and to do good in their life.
  But even when anyone eats and drinks
  and sees the good in all their toil,
    that is a gift from God.

Ecclesiastes 3:12–13

Go, eat your food with joy,
  and drink your wine with a good heart,
    for God is already pleased with your work. . . .
Take to heart the life with the woman you love,
  all the days of your hebel *life*
    which God has given you under the sun,
  all the days of your hebel *life.*
For that is your portion in life, in your toil.

Ecclesiastes 9:7–9

Placed in proximity to the book's most corrosive *hebel*-statements, these good words advocate a view of time that embraces the present and shuns the broader perspective of schedules, lifetime, and eternity. The impossible horizon of lasting significance is replaced by a midday meal; the inflated demands on actions and accomplishments is substituted for an evening drink. Qohelet does not bid his readers to a banquet or an open bar, but to a table that is decorated with the simplest pattern of sustenance. Pulling up a chair to such goodness requires the tough surrender of certainty and ambition but in exchange one may participate in the true grandeur of human existence: a simple moment, a shared meal.

Even such joyful minimalism, however, will not resolve the frustrations of the human condition. Even in simplicity, life is still *hebel* (twice in 9:9) and the temptation of idolizing joy and escaping into excess always lingers in the human heart (cf. 2:1–2). Once again, the path toward life's joy and the liberation from hurry lies along the embrace of limits. "Pleasure is pleasant, and that is the end of the story."[40] One of the ways in which Qohelet directs his readers toward this posture is to remind them that even the best that life has to offer is enmeshed in the larger cycles of nature's sustainability and divine grace. Wheat has to grow; grapes have to ripen. The enjoyment of the earth's bounty is no reward but a gift from God. Like the manna in the desert and the daily bread in the Lord's Prayer, everything that is given to humanity speaks of God's generosity.

Yet, the relentless repetition of picking up morsels in the desert and thanking God for a set table shows that even the life of faith is not immune to the grip of *hebel*. Commitments get old, receptivity becomes routine, gratefulness grows stale. But perhaps Qohelet's focus on the moment can infuse these divine gifts with a new sweetness. Repetition can dull the essence of anything but it simply is part of life, including all exercises of devotion. Arriving in this reality may lighten the burden of spiritual pressure and embrace instead that

> ultimate insight is the outcome of *moments* when we are stirred beyond words, of instants of wonder, awe, praise, fear, trembling and radical amazement. . . . It is at the climax of such moments that we attain the certainty that life has meaning, that time is more than evanescence, that beyond all being there is someone who cares.[41]

Such wise words may be received as a theological version of Qohelet's minimalism because they share its balance of limitation and liberation. To live with the God of time is not something that can be mastered or controlled. Certainty and insight stir in the heart unprompted, they arrive from without, and they cannot bear the burden that is placed on them because they, too, are subject to time's arrow. "The immediate

---

40 Fox, *Rereading*, 123. "What chance brings one's way should be enjoyed to the fullest—but without any sense of claim upon it. All that one can bring to the situation is receptivity;" Carol A. Newsom, "Positive Psychology and Ancient Israelite Wisdom," in *The Bible and the Pursuit of Happiness: What the Old and New Testaments Teach Us about the Good Life*, ed. Brent A. Strawn (Oxford: Oxford University Press, 2012), 133.

41 Heschel, *God in Search*, 131 (italics original).

certainty that we attain in moments of insight does not retain its intensity after the moments are gone."[42]

Ecclesiastes's language for time articulates an authentic way of life that accepts, laments, and embraces the strange condition of the human experience. This particular kind of life recognizes God's gifts of food, drink, revelation, and wisdom for what they are: brief moments of relief and reassurance that are true and good even as they already are passing away. Living in time is always a life that trusts in yet another such moment.

Finding Rhythm, Losing Time

The life-affirming statements that punctuate Ecclesiastes are formative for the human posture toward time but they can also speak a word of healing to everyone who has, in Fuchs's words, "fallen out of shared time." Inasmuch as depression may be understood as a pervasive loss of feeling and connection, Fuchs proposes that "one of the most important strategies is the rhythmitisation of life."[43] With its sequences and cycles, Ecclesiastes can inspire a way of living that avoids the "empty succession of linear time" that Fuchs has encountered in the plight of his patients. Qohelet's poetic voice still today challenges any version of the tyranny of time that would push even the most basic human needs to the edge of the calendar. There must be a time to heal, a time to laugh, and a time of peace. That such dissent comes from a self-critical king adds a political edge to Ecclesiastes's wisdom, which is perhaps especially important to hear amid the complex intersection of economics and human well-being that marks many societies today.

> What is really needed is a resistance against the de-rhythmitisation of life that spills over from the inherent dynamic of a capitalist economy to all areas of society. . . . If "money is time," then there is no intrinsic resistance in the economic system, no element of deceleration. . . . [What is needed] is an attitude towards life that remembers the past and the victims of progress, that sees in the natural world an

---

42 Heschel, *God in Search*, 132.

43 Fuchs, "Zeitstrukturen," 74. Whereas the DSM-V defines depression broadly as "the presence of sad, empty, or irritable mood" (p. 155), Swinton offers a thicker description: "Depression is not an absence of happiness. Nor is it the presence of sadness. It is an antifeeling that results in an ongoing struggle to find and hold on to joy," *Finding Jesus in the Storm*, 84.

alternative realm in need of protection, that remains cautious about all ideas of acceleration and is skeptical about the euphoria of progress, all the while avoiding cultural pessimism and hostility of progress.[44]

This difficult balance between resistance and cultural participation vibrates with the same tension that marks Qohelet's contradictions. Making an effort of living well in time will be a struggle and have its fair share of compromise and disappointment. The present day will still suffer from tomorrow's schedule and the cultural narratives of productivity will be hard to shake off. The pursuit of a healthy posture toward time is worth every minute, but in the end, even the best take on time will not escape the *hebel*-condition of human life which, absurdly, sees mastery and misery as two sides of the same coin. "For in much wisdom is much vexation, and who increases knowledge, increases pain" (Eccl 1:18).

Qohelet's observations are an enduring inspiration, but not because of their therapeutic or political orientation, and not even because of their honesty and spiritual insight. Each of these dimensions is precious, yet they all draw their energy from the one aspect that makes Ecclesiastes's concept of time so profound. The importance of rhythms surfaces everywhere in the Old Testament, be that in the days of Genesis 1 and the plethora of religious festivals. Yet only Ecclesiastes—and especially the times-poem in chapter 3—articulates a thorough "humanising of the perception of time."

> No longer is it the seasonal cycle of nature, the festivals of the cultus, nor yet the movement of the heavenly bodies that controls the passage and awareness of time. Rather time is first and foremost characterised by the lifespan of each individual. . . . The passage of time is perceived as a series of life-opportunities to which each human being responds freely and creatively according to the needs and dictates of the moment.[45]

This anthropology of time, this concern for the actual experience of everyday living, appears to some extent in the sabbath day that ordains

---

44 Fuchs, "Zeitstrukturen," 74–75.

45 R. E. Clements, *Wisdom in Theology*, Didsbury Lectures (Carlisle: Paternoster Press, 1992), 50–51.

rest for the whole household, including all foreign workers and animals (Exod 20:9; cf. Mark 6:27). This pattern of deceleration can keep the pace of contemporary society in check,[46] yet Ecclesiastes 3 goes a step further. Neither in explicit contrast to the demands of the labor market nor as a conscious *imitatio dei*, this poem defines time solely in relation to human living. Time is what people make of it, how they fill it with their most mundane activities, with planting, laughing, and dancing. Qohelet stops the clock and allows his companion humans to live in their own time and to be present today without any concern about a larger calendar on which their hours are scripted.

As an antidote to all the frustrations, lost years, and the bad days that will come, the ideal living with time is to forget, just once in a while, about time altogether. Such moments are rare but real, and they are found in just the place where Qohelet arrives in his search for meaning: seated at the table of simple pleasures, warmed by the company of others (4:7–12), absorbed in creative work without any regard for its outcome (9:10; 11:6).[47] All of this is transient, none of it is meaningless. These are the moments in which humans can turn their back on the vast, turbulent ocean of things and space and step into "that realm of time where the goal is not to have but to be, not to own but to give, not to control but to share, not to subdue but to be in accord."[48]

---

46 Cf. Walter Brueggemann, *Sabbath as Resistance: Saying No to the Culture of Now* (Louisville, KY: Westminster John Knox, 2014).

47 "In an age of instrumentalisation, the hobbyist is a subversive: he insists that some things are worth doing for themselves alone, despite offering no pay-offs in terms of productivity or profit. . . . To pursue an activity in which you have no hope of becoming exceptional is to put aside, for a while, the anxious need to 'use time well;'" Burkeman, *Four Thousand Weeks*, 158–159.

48 Abraham Joshua Heschel, *The Sabbath* (New York: Farrar, Straus and Giroux, 1951), 3.

CHAPTER 6

Wise Words for the Weary
Speaking with Agur about the Good Life

Is not wisdom calling?
Is not understanding lifting its voice?
At the top of the hills, on the road, between the paths,
she takes her stance.
Besides the gates, before the city, at the entrance of the doorway,
she shouts aloud:
'To you, O people, I call,
my voice goes to all human beings!

The Lord begot me at the beginning of his ways,
the first of his works from that ancient time. . . .
I remained faithfully by the Lord's side,
I was pure delight, day by day, dancing before him at all time,
dancing through the living realm of his earth, delighting with
humankind!
Now, O children, listen to me:
Happy are those who keep my ways.
Listen to instruction and become wise—do not spurn it!
Happy is everyone who listens to me. . . .
For all who find me find life
and find favor with the Lord.'

Proverbs 8:1–4, 22, 30–35

The land on which humans tread is unstable, the horizon heavy with dark clouds, and the current of time too fast. Yet, the sun still rises and treasures still wash up at the shore. The vast sea of the human condition bears many pearls that, amid the ebb and flow of the dark waters, cross the shoreline as heralds of good news. The weary people who hold them in their hands can know, if only for a while, that life is good, that life is worth it. Deep insights of this kind demand to be treasured because they are flushed quickly enough out of the human hand by tomorrow's waves. The Hebrew poets leave no doubt about the precarious nature of the good life, penning more laments than psalms of praise, expressing more questions and frustration than epiphanies. The land of wonder and wisdom that Job and Ecclesiastes envision swims easily out of view in the verbose darkness of their utterances. But that does not make it utopian. The Bible's vast reservoir of verse is an enduring testimony to the human condition with all its uncertainty and trouble, but its authors did not set out to erect a monument to tragedy.[1] Qohelet enjoys his dinner, the Psalms open with the line "Happy is the person," and even Job gets to spend many decades with his family, before and after the tragedy. Fulfilment, joy, the good life. The Hebrew poets have much to say about such things.

The poem of Proverbs 8 joins this conversation and holds nothing back. Wisdom, personified as a woman, cries out to the reader and takes her stance. In the open, where all can hear her voice and watch her twirl, she celebrates her heritage as God's companion in creation, a force as essential as the limits of the sea (v. 29), older than hills and fields and sky. Such pedigree puts Lady Wisdom into her own cosmic category, yet she is not looking for adoration. Her defining characteristic is joyful abandon, her deepest desire the sharing of her splendor. To find her is to find life itself (v. 35). But this ancient voice does not beckon her readers with an easy message. The tension between pearls and perils, the limits of insight, and the ambiguity of experience and expression make the quest for the good life a complex adventure.

For all the frustrating as well as for all the fascinating shades of being human, a language is needed that is as deep as time itself. Among those who have learned that language are the Hebrew sages who stand behind Proverbs. One of them, a mysterious man named Agur, concludes this

---

1 For these and other case studies, see Brent D. Strawn, ed., *The Bible and the Pursuit of Happiness: What the Old and New Testaments Teach Us about the Good Life* (Oxford: Oxford University Press, 2006).

book on a personal note that may offer a blueprint for how to articulate loss and limits and how to discover wonder and well-being. Agur
and the wisdom tradition for which he speaks bubble with ideas and
intricacy, wading through the long stream of human thought about the
good life that is as old as Lady Wisdom's joyous dance at creation and
that still trickles through today's bookshelves.

Positive Psychology in Wisdom's World

Similar to the Old Testament poets who turn every so often to the
brighter side of life, a group of psychologists found their own happy
place amid the tragedies of their daily routine. From its first days, psychology had been concerned with alleviating mental, emotional, and
personality challenges, yet as psychologist Martin Seligman observes,
"people want more than just correct their weaknesses. They want lives
imbued with meaning and not just fidget until they die."[2] A leading
figure in a wave of research that cultivates well-being rather than
reacts to its absence,[3] Seligman aims to push beyond subjective sen-
sations by focusing on positive emotions, character traits, and institutions. This approach is holistic and takes a long view at the good life
but it is burdened with choices. Tossing and turning between parental
expectations, cultural norms, and personal dispositions and dreams,
even just the successful identification of one's ideal set of traits can be
overwhelming.

Aware of this struggle, Seligman and his colleague Christopher
Peterson have compared around two hundred virtue codes from various cultures. They arrived at the stunning conclusion that nearly

---

2 *Authentic Happiness: Using the New Positive Psychology to Realize Your Potential for Lasting Fulfillment* (New York: The Free Press, 2002), 9.

3 See, e.g., Christopher Peterson, *A Primer in Positive Psychology* (Oxford:
Oxford University Press, 2006); Samuel S. Franklin, *The Psychology of Hap-
piness: A Good Human Life* (Cambridge: Cambridge University Press, 2010);
Susan A. David, Ilona Boniwell, and Amanda C. Ayers, eds., *The Oxford
Handbook of Happiness* (Oxford: Oxford University Press, 2013). The search
for human happiness, of course, is not as new as Seligman's title might suggest.
From Aristotle to Voltaire, from Locke to Maslow, the topic has been central to
human reflections on life; cf. Darrin M. McMahon, *Happiness: A History* (New
York: Grove Press, 2006).

all of them endorse the same set of core traits, namely, wisdom and knowledge, courage, love and humanity, justice, temperance, spirituality and transcendence.[4] Most of these six traits are outward-facing. Learning requires engagement with the world, justice and love focus their attention on other people, and spirituality reaches beyond the self altogether. While such curiosity and outreach may promise endless excitement, Seligman affirms the long-held notion of a set range of happiness. Whether people win the lottery or crash their car, in a short time both billionaires and survivors report similar levels of positive emotions as before the life-altering events.[5] Such extreme examples speak for the genetics of happiness—"half of your score on happiness tests is accounted for by the score of your biological parents"[6]—yet the limits of joy are also set by the nature of joy itself. No matter how exuberant, achievements and pleasure bring no lasting satisfaction because they demand in their wake yet greater joys for reaching the top of the emotional range.

The reality check of set range and hedonic treadmill shows that pushing the boundaries of bliss will disappoint, that moderation and restraint are key to living well. But there are several strategies to ensure a permanent residency in the upper range of that margin. Seligman's first advice is an active awareness of the differences of past, present, and future emotions. Whether through gratitude and forgiveness, the challenge of negative beliefs ("our reflexive explanations are usually distortions"),[7] the savoring of pleasure, or the gratification of "flow,"[8] each human being has a considerable influence over cultivating good experiences in their lives. This responsibility extends to discovering one's

---

4 A fuller discussion of these traits is available in their co-authored *Character Strengths and Virtues: A Handbook and Classification* (Oxford: Oxford University Press, 2004).

5 "When positive and negative events happen, there is a temporary burst of mood in the right direction. But usually over a short time, mood settles back into its set range;" *Happiness*, 83.

6 *Happiness*, 59.

7 *Happiness*, 112.

8 This concept was first described by Mihaly Csikszentmihalyi, *Finding Flow: The Psychology of Engagement with Everyday Life* (New York: Basic Books, 1997), and may be experienced whenever challenging, creative exercises, be that work, play, or sports, absorb one's attention to the point of a loss of self-awareness and time.

"Signature Strengths," the character traits that will nurture the six core virtues. For instance, wisdom is cultivated with creativity, curiosity, and perspective; transcendence with gratitude, hope, and humor. The daily integration of these strengths in work, love, and parenting can transform a pleasant life into a good life. Using one's strengths "in the service of something larger than you are,"[9] such as religion or philanthropy, may in turn transform a good life into a meaningful life.

Seligman's work, though not without its fair share of criticism,[10] has been brought into conversation with many fields within the humanities, including pastoral counselling and biblical interpretation. Biblical scholar Carol Newsom's essay "Positive Psychology and Ancient Israelite Wisdom" is part of this dialogue and has tested out Proverbs as a possible match for Seligman's observations. Proverbs' portrayal of wisdom has, in Newsom's view, some affinities with the good life. Wisdom is an antidote to wickedness and death, a tree of life (Prov 3:18; 11:30; 13:12; 15:4), and a pathway to "length of days, years of life, and peace" (Prov 3:2).

Moreover, similar to Seligman's holistic approach, "Proverbs is primarily focused on the satisfactions that come from the nexus that connects disciplined and virtuous character, diligent work, and the rewards these will bring (6:6–11; 12:11)."[11] In contrast to Ecclesiastes where time and toil press every good thing into small, hedonic pockets, Lady Wisdom offers a transformation that goes beyond positive emotions. She shares herself as the link between creator and creatures, teaching all her children that "knowing wisdom is to root oneself in the creative forces and orderly structures that give rise to the generativity of the world."[12] Discovering the good life is an exercise that requires a look beyond the

---

9 *Happiness*, 283.

10 For some economic and methodological concerns, see Barbara Ehrenreich, *Smile or Die: How Positive Thinking Fooled America and the World* (London: Granta Books, 2010). Other points of contention are Seligman's reliance on self-reporting questionnaires and the lack of attention to cultural complexity and social justice; cf. Mary Clark Moschella, "Positive Psychology as a Resource for Pastoral Theology and Care: A Preliminary Assessment," *J Pastor Theol* 21 (2011): 1–16.

11 "Israelite Wisdom," in *The Bible and the Pursuit of Happiness, 123-124*. See also Brown, *Character in Crisis*, 22–49.

12 "Israelite Wisdom," 127.

confines of one's island of living and language. There is a world out there, and its rhythms, rules, and riches call for attention.

Newsom's reflections demonstrate that reading the Bible with positive psychology bears much potential but they also show that the vast distance to ancient Israelite culture needs to be kept in view. On the one hand, the cosmological dimensions that Newsom highlights call for commitment and participation. On the other hand, they resist the modern gospel of human betterment. The Hebrew poets demand certain behaviors (e.g., Prov 3:9–12), yet their compositions are no "self-improvement book."[13] Lady Wisdom is not the voice of reason within or an eight-step program. She is a divine gift, a cosmic force who dances and speaks where and when she wishes. There is a balance—and more often a tension—between human activity and human dependence on a transformation that comes from without. In the words of Job 28, people may dig and search as much as they can, but wisdom will remain "hidden from the eyes of all living" and only "God understands her way" (vv. 21, 23).

Wisdom is hard won and not without competition. Lady Wisdom is all too aware of the human disposition to ignore her speech ("do not spurn it!" Prov 8:33) and the parental voice of Proverbs 1–9 has much to say about the lures of folly and the temptation to define the good life without concern for the world at large. Whereas these complexities receive but a modicum of attention in *Authentic Happiness*,[14] positive psychology's hope to inspire human well-being resonates deeply with Proverbs. Naturally, Seligman's modern methods of statistics and experiments are nowhere to be found in this book's quest for the good life. Agur and his fellow sages pursue instead a pedagogy of poetic puzzles, images, and parables showing that the articulation, the playfulness, and the exchange of human words play a key role for discovering how humans may live well.

---

13 Seligman describes *Authentic Happiness* in this way on page 140.

14 "The acquisition of wisdom is thus depicted as something that does not come easily to an individual and that is acquired only through resisting one's natural inclinations to seek immediate pleasure;" Newsom, "Israelite Wisdom," 123. Especially the positive institutions in *Authentic Happiness* look at the world through somewhat rose-tinted glasses, presuming that everyone is privileged to choose parenthood, satisfying work, and a romantic relationship. Moreover, it is worth considering that triumph over life's difficulties is no guarantee for positive living. As Moschella points out, "it is often in the middle of pain, sin, and suffering that the awareness of the goodness of life or of God dawns;" "Resource," 12.

Proverbs' Winding Way to Wisdom

In comparison to the skepticism of Job and Ecclesiastes, Proverbs seems to take a far more level-headed approach to life and to communicating its reflections on the human condition. Its wisdom does not grow out of personal crisis or theological dilemma but is passed down by father and mother and rooted in the "fear of the Lord" (1:7). The division between the parental speeches in chapters 1–9 and the catalogue of pithy sayings in chapters 10–29 promotes easy access and application.[15] The promises and warnings in the first part foster a willingness to learn wisdom, the second part presents that wisdom verse by verse, proverb by proverb.

> *My child, if you accept my words*
> *treasure my commandments,*
> *bring your ear to listen to wisdom*
> *stretch your heart to understanding,*
> *and if you call out for insight and raise your voice for understanding,*
> *if you seek it like silver and search for it like treasures*
> *then you will understand the fear of the Lord*
> *and the knowledge of God you will find.*
> *For the Lord gives wisdom,*
> *from his mouth come knowledge and understanding.*
>
> Proverbs 2:1–6

> *Listen, my child, and accept my words,*
> *and you will have many years of life.*
> *In the way of wisdom, I have taught you,*
> *I have led you in straight paths.*
> *When you walk, your step will not be hindered,*
> *when you run, you will not stumble.*
> *Hold fast to discipline, do not let go!*
> *Guard it, for it is your life.*
>
> Proverbs 4:10–13

These passages can read like a formulaic transaction between submission and success, yet Proverbs is not as simplistic as it might seem. In

---

15 Proverbs has the appearance of a manual, yet the specific setting in which it may have been used is hard to pin down (e.g., family, court, schools); cf. Katharine J. Dell, *The Book of Proverbs in Social and Theological Context* (Cambridge: Cambridge University Press, 2006).

the first passage, for instance, the listener is called to value their parents' input, to make a serious effort on their own ("listen, call, seek!"), and to receive insight from on high. None of these by itself is a feasible way to live—the wisdom of one generation may simply not apply to the next,[16] deep insights cannot be forced, and God is not an instant problem-solver—yet neither do the three work easily together. The benefits of wisdom are compelling, but the actual process of becoming wise is a complex tangle of respect, responsibility, and revelation.

Even though Proverbs elevates the third of these items above the others (cf. "fear of the Lord" in 1:7; 9:10; 19:23; 31:30, etc.), the book remains keenly attuned to the complicated reality of earthly life. The mundane issues that occupy chapters 10–29 (e.g., money, friendship) lend to this part of the Old Testament a markedly human and secular character. There is, for instance, nothing intrinsically spiritual about the insight that "truthful speech is established forever, but a deceitful tongue lasts but a moment" (12:19). This quality of Proverbs raises the question of authority that, along with the theological prologue in 1:1–7 and the voice of revelation in chapter 8,[17] finds an answer in the literary shape of chapters 10–29. This random assortment of proverbs has frustrated early and contemporary readers alike,[18] yet it is precisely through this lack of system and sequence that the complexity of reality and wisdom are mirrored. At one time, the short life of lies will be learned through personal experience; at another time, the confession that "lips of deceit are an abomination to the Lord"

---

16 For instance, the warning against the temptations of the "strange woman" (Prov 2:16–19) is no universal truth about women or foreigners but remains wholly embedded in the conventions of patriarchy and purity of its day; cf. Claudia V. Camp, *Wise, Strange and Holy: The Strange Woman and the Making of the Bible,* JSOTSup 320 (Sheffield: Sheffield Academic Press, 2009).

17 Cf. Eugene Ulrich, "From Literature to Scripture: Reflections on the Growth of a Text's Authoritativeness," *DSD* 10 (2003): 13–14. The contrast between secular and spiritual should not be pushed too far: "For Israel there was only one world of experience. . . . The experiences of the world were for her always divine experiences as well, and the experiences of God were for her experiences of the world;" von Rad, *Wisdom,* 61–62.

18 The preference to topical organization of later wisdom books, such as *Ben Sira,* and of the countless contemporary titles that present Proverbs' perspective on parenting, friendship, money, etc. is a familiar solution to the book's perceived disarray.

(12:22) will shape one's way with words. By blurring distinctions and creating overlap, the literary universe of Proverbs replicates the messy day-to-day world and affirms the active cooperation of God, community, and self.

This resistance to order goes yet deeper. The sheer number of sayings in chapters 10–29 takes the dynamics of parallelism to a new level by asking their readers to read each of them side-by-side with the others.[19] What results from such holistic reading is a first-hand encounter with the complex universe in which human life unfolds. Patterns will emerge and familiarity will grow as one looks at this literary snow globe. But every so often the peaceful landscape must be turned upside down to reveal new reflections of reality. Wealth is a divine blessing, but the wicked are often rich (18:23; 22:7); poverty can be a good thing (15:16; 17:1); even the righteous fall (24:16). Proverbs is neither naive nor simplistic, nor does it promise a perfect life.[20] Instead, it offers a good life, a life that promotes curiosity and authenticity and that does not fear alternatives and new evidence.

The Hebrew sages value open communication more than closure, receive an open hand more readily than a fist of absolute truth slammed on the table. They join in Lady Wisdom's delight of the world and seek to cultivate an openness to life, a real investment of thought, time, and reflection. This educational agenda is at work in all proverbs whose exceptional terseness and complex parallel patterns demand prolonged observation and contemplation.

> *There is a straight way before someone,*
> *but at its end are ways of death.*

Proverbs 14:12

---

19 "To avoid overstating truth or teaching half-truths through isolated proverbs, sages call on their disciples to learn all of them (22:18);" Bruce K. Waltke, *The Book of Proverbs. Chapters 1–15*, NICOT (Grand Rapids, MI: Eerdmans, 2004), 39. For instance, the well-known adage "Dedicate a youth according to what his way dictates, and even when he is old he will not depart from it" in 22:6 is but "a single component of truth that must be fit together with other elements of truth in order to approximate the more comprehensive, confused pattern of real life" (p. 38).

20 Cf. Peter T. H. Hatton, *Contradiction in the Book of Proverbs: The Deep Waters of Counsel*, SOTSMS (Hampshire: Ashgate, 2008).

These two lines combine a neutral, positive statement with a rather dismal assertion. A "straight" life is usually a sign of piety (3:6; 11:5), laudably lived by those who withstand temptation and folly (9:15; 15:21). Does the second line suggest that even such conduct is not safe? Or does it warn the reader that straight ways end, that good choices must be made again and again? Or is there perhaps a hint here that perception and reality can be fundamentally at odds in life's walk? The relationship between these paths is far from clear but that is exactly the point. Offering true yet open and partial impressions of life, the sayings in the book "not only transmit packets of truth, they also *train* the reader in a mode of thinking: identifying behaviors and associating them with their consequences. In other words, they train the reader to think like a sage."[21]

From these poetic microcosms to the endless conversation of all proverbs, from the parental rhetoric to the flamboyant lyrics of Lady Wisdom, Proverbs' school of wisdom runs on a curriculum of language and literary patterns. The first lesson of all who attend this school must concentrate on its way with words and the wide spectrum with which the sages would answer the tormented cry "Where shall wisdom be found?" of Job 28. Language matters not just for expressing frustration and pain but also for discovering the good life. Proverbs' witty realism embraces both dimensions, yet there is no chapter that holds them in such precarious and personal balance as Agur's turbulent utterances in chapter 30.

Agur's Wisdom for the Weary

Agur is perhaps the most obscure of all Hebrew sages. In view of the narratives in 1 Kings and the attribution in Proverbs 1:1, 10:1, and 25:1, Solomon would have been a more accessible and familiar candidate. Despite these connections, Solomon never speaks for himself

---

21 Michael V. Fox, "The Rhetoric of Disjointed Proverbs," *JSOT* 29 (2004), 177 (emphasis original). The book's Hebrew name *mišlê* (from the verb *māšal*, "to be like") is programmatic for the comparison of lines A and B in each proverb that, as Fox's study shows, is not always straightforward. See further J. G. Williams, "The Power of Form: A Study of Biblical Proverbs," *Semeia* 17 (1980): 35–58.

in Proverbs and nothing in the book is explicitly tied to his biography.[22] All proverbs, all words in chapters 1–9, and even the warnings of King Lemuel's unnamed mother (31:1–9) are spoken by a faceless, anonymous voice. Only Agur speaks as a named individual. Only Agur reflects on human life in first-person speech. The inclusion of Agur's rumination near the end of Proverbs is no mere afterthought, but assigns him the honor of retrospection and evaluation. As soon as Agur opens his mouth, however, it becomes clear that he is far from asserting any kind supreme standing.

> *The words of Agur, son of Yaqeh,*
> *an oracle, an utterance of a man:*
> *"I am weary, God, I am weary, God,*
> *I am spent!*
> *For I am too stupid to be human,*
> *I do not have human understanding.*
> *I have not learned any wisdom,*
> *nor have I known the knowledge of the Holy One."*

Proverbs 30:1–3

The opening lines of Proverbs 30 are troubled by many questions about translation and interpretation.[23] Agur's father provides little orientation. Even if Agur's name is symbolic, the options range from "I wander" to "I am afraid," neither of which elucidates his poem. Moreover, the terms "oracle" (המשא) and "utterance" (נאם) are technical terms for prophetic speech,[24] but what follows are hardly words of divine authority. The verbatim repetition ("I am weary, God, I am weary, God")

22 The preface of chapters 1–9, the plurality of "the wise" (22:17), and the mention of "the men of Hezekiah" who transmitted Solomon's proverbs in chapters 25–28 suggest that Proverbs is the result of a long process of compilation. Solomon's way of life, in any case, raises serious concerns about his qualifications as a wise teacher (cf. 1 Kgs 11:9–13).

23 For instance, instead of "an oracle" (*hammaśāʾ*), one could translate "from Massa," which is a northern Arabic tribe (cf. Gen 25:14; 1 Chr 1:30). For a review of proposals, see Eva Stromberg Krantz, "'A Man Not Supported by God': On Some Crucial Words in Proverbs XXX 1," *VT* 46 (1996): 548–553, and Hans-Friedemann Richter, "Hielt Agur sich für den Dümmsten aller Menschen?," *ZAW* 113 (2001): 419–421.

24 Notably, נאם (*něʾum*) appears only twice elsewhere with human subjects (Balaam in Num 24; David in 2 Sam 23). For the intersection of genres, see

elevates Agur's frailty, which moves in the third line toward surrender ("I am spent" or "I am consumed, eaten up"). Negative builds upon negative, and though the poem starts with addressing God, it ends at a defeated distance from the Divine.

The shambles of these verses compact to a strange inversion of all that one might expect at the end of a book that promotes wisdom training and the maturing of character. Here is a human being whose deepest pain is to have fallen short of being human, an esteemed speaker at a loss for words, a resourceful person who labored at becoming wise and failed. Agur will share many penetrating insights in Proverbs 30, yet this is where he begins: a vulnerable admission of failure, weakness, and disappointment.

Agur's raw self-assessment must not be bypassed too quickly. For the pursuit of the good life, Agur's words question the dogma of self-improvement and undermine the mastery of wisdom. This is not where the wise parents had hoped their child to arrive (cf. 22:6), not the life that Lady Wisdom had promised, not the traits of a positive character![25] Yet these confessions of human helplessness and this emotional frankness play a crucial part in the process toward human flourishing particularly because they are so unusual and provocative. The wisdom quest was a royal prerogative in the ancient world and even though Agur is not lifted into the ranks of Solomon, Hezekiah, and Lemuel, his authoritative oracle of failure is a self-critical stab at power. The inclusion of his words in Proverbs makes it likely that he was an educated and privileged member of his society, yet without any pretense he declares that even the most esteemed seekers will wear themselves out.

Along with Lemuel's mother and the "mighty woman" of Proverbs 31,[26] Agur has the final word in Proverbs and he uses this stage

---

Markus Saur, "Prophetie, Weisheit und Gebet. Überlegungen zu den Worten Agurs in Prov 30, 1–9," *ZAW* 126 (2014): 573–576.

25 These verses do not exemplify the "rotten-to-the-core" doctrine of human depravity against which Seligman's psychology pushes with such fervor (cf. *Authentic Happiness*, 10). Like the prayer of Psalm 73:22 ("I am stupid... I was a beast towards you"), Agur's negative view of self is but a snapshot on the human journey. It is a lament, not a verdict.

26 The final chapters of Proverbs resonate with the tendency toward gender balance of chapters 1–9, which give a stage to father *and* mother as well as to Lady Wisdom (cf. 1:20–33; 4:1–9; 8:1–36; 7:1–27). Agur's challenge to conventional wisdom also resonates with 31:10–31 that effectively moves wisdom

to humanize rather than to glorify the experience of life and learning. In a gesture of defeat, he throws up his hands in the air because there, precisely, hangs the ceiling of the human condition.

> *Who has gone up to heaven and come down again?*
> *Who has gathered wind in the hollow of their hands?*
> *Who has wrapped up water in a garment?*
> *Who has set up all the ends of the earth?*
> *What is that person's name, what the name of their child?*
> *If you know!*
>
> Proverbs 30:4

The cosmic interrogation undermines all claims to dynastic grandeur ("the name of their child"),[27] yet Agur's quick-fire queries are no embittered taunt against royal power. Heard in tandem with his own "I do not know" in verse 3, the final "If you know!" makes the gentle assertion that each and every human being shares in his limitations.

Agur's life and language push back against a naive approach to the wisdom enterprise, yet they also challenge "those who speak about God as if he were familiar to them and the subject had no difficulties."[28] Seligman advocates the annual practice of "weighing up your life" in which he takes stock of his current experience of work, love, and health.[29] Agur's self-portrayal in verses 1–4 may be understood as a similar practice, albeit not with the intention to see trends or potential, but

---

to the domestic realm. This text, however, must be read with care as it confines the good life of the "mighty woman" to a place of limited power and promotes neither leisure activities nor any influence outside of the culturally defined domain. Cf. L. Juliana Claassens, "The Woman of Substance and Human Flourishing: Proverbs 31:10–31 and Martha Nussbaum's Capabilities Approach," *JFSR* 32 (2016): 5–19.

27 "A wisdom text has, for public consumption, been turned into an anti-wisdom text. All values implicit in the king's celestial encounter with the gods has been eradicated;" Nick Wyatt, *Myths of Power: A Study of Royal Myth and Ideology in Ugaritic and Biblical Tradition*, UBL (Münster: Ugarit-Verlag, 1996), 319.

28 William McKane, *Proverbs: A New Approach*, OTL (Philadelphia, PA: Westminster Press, 1970), 647. This emphasis on the gulf between creature and creator resonates with the rest of Proverbs, which never speaks about knowing God, or equates wisdom with God, or makes any promises about God's presence.

29 *Authentic Happiness*, 95–96.

as the pure catharsis of putting words to everything that weighs down life's enjoyment and goodness. Being human, growing in understanding, knowing God: Agur stretches out his hand to everyone who like him has not much to show in these areas. The universal limits that he exposes pull humanity's head out of the clouds and plant each human foot firmly on the ground of reality because it is only there that any reflection about well-being and meaningful living will make any sense.

The Good Life, Nevertheless!

The scope of interpretations of verses 1–4 is a sign of a challenging text but also a telling commentary on how Agur's words have landed with their readers. Perhaps verse 3 reads "I have not learned wisdom, *but* I know the knowledge of the Holy One," perhaps Agur is a radical skeptic, perhaps he is a supreme model of pious humility.[30] That each of these readings can be upheld is a stellar example of Proverbs' resistance to closure. The parents and Lady Wisdom locate understanding in the home, the heart, the heavens; the proverbial universe of chapters 10–29 asserts and affirms only to nuance and negate. The good life is a complex affair, so much is clear before Agur opens his mouth. But just how frustrating, humiliating, and isolating this quest can be remains hidden until his languishing lines appear on the page.

Agur adds a note of humanity to all readings that hear only discipline and divine authority in Proverbs. His words are a testimony to the human need to articulate life and limits as they actually unfold. Speaking such words can be healing, reduce pressure, and create companionship. As in Agur's poetic composition, it can be the beginning rather than the end on the road to the good life, the discovery of possibility rather than the despair of limits.

> *Every word of God is refined,*
> *he is a shield to those who take refuge in him.*
> *Do not add to his words,*
> *lest he reprove you and you turn out to be a liar.*

Proverbs 30:5–6

---

30 For Agur's middle ground, see Rick D. Moore, "A Home for the Alien: Worldly Wisdom and Covenantal Confession in Proverbs 30:1–9," *ZAW* 106 (1994): 96–107.

The shift from Agur's declaration of defeat to these conservative words is so severe that one may question whether they come from the same speaker.[31] As Proverbs 30 continues, this composite impression grows. Short poems about social justice alternate with teaching about wise speech and comparisons between animals and humans. Whether authored or arranged by an editor, the sequence of the words of Agur requires above all contemplation and a search for connections. The high view of divine speech (vv. 5–6), for instance, takes its lead from God's inaccessibility (v. 4). Since wisdom is hard to get and God hard to know, the human journey depends on revelation. But even such commitment to traditional theology is not without human participation.[32] Agur and his fellow humans cannot ascend to heaven but they can "take refuge" in the right places and trust in what they have received rather than try to push the boundaries.

This embrace of orthodoxy must be heard in the wake of Agur's outburst in verses 1–4. Honest expressions of doubt and weakness can all too often be perceived as a dead-end of faith and are at times eyed with suspicion by speaker and listener alike. Agur's personal example shows that this must not be so. Crisis and comprehension, weariness and worship, confusion and commitment—neither element in these unlikely pairs must cancel out the other. Such wisdom is aware of the tensions of living and advocates the good life, nevertheless. Agur's outburst is but a part of that life. Yet without the occasional release of such resignation and without the ever-new assent to the limits of being human, it is doubtful that the other parts will survive.

What is championed here is, in the end, the combined wisdom of the weary words of Agur and the refined words of God. These two voices speak together not in a spirit of competition, of adding or of lying, but

---

31 Leo Perdue, for instance, hears in verses 5–6 a "religious sage" rebuking Agur's cynicism; *Proverbs*, IBC (Louisville, KY: John Knox Press, 2000), 259. The overlap between these verses and other texts (e.g., Ps 18:30; Deut 4:2) also deserves some attention (cf. McKane, *Proverbs*, 648). Saur is among the exegetes who resist the "resolution of tensions" and favors reading Proverbs 30 as a dialogue or collage; "Überlegungen," 573.

32 "We see here a decisive shift from wisdom tradition to covenantal canon, from investigation of nature to revelation in history. . . . Vital truth is seen finally to be a matter not of human search but of divine disclosure. Yet it is nevertheless disclosure that demands something;" Moore, "Worldly Wisdom," 100–101.

as a wholesome expression of the human condition. The good life that is born from accepting one's limits along with God's gifts is on display in the next verses.

> Two things I ask of you,
>   do not withhold them from me while I live.
> Falsehood and lying word remove from me,
>   neither poverty nor riches give to me,
>   let me receive just the bread that is my portion,
>   so that I will not be filled up and renounce and say:
>   'Who is the Lord?'
>   and so that I will not go poor and steal
>   and profane the name of my God.
>
> Proverbs 30:7–9

Agur's posture toward life gets increasingly more personal and practical. That the focus remains initially on the topic of positive speech creates a seamless transition (cf. כזב, "lying" in vv. 6, 8), but the perspective shifts from the realm of revelation to the horizontal plain of human relationship.[33] The good life of Proverbs 30 lies beyond the individual. While Agur is happy to build his house on this traditional pillar of wisdom learning, he also erects a few on his own. His request about lying resonates with his fellow sages (e.g., Prov 6:19; 14:15; 19:5), but his petition for a median standard of living has no equal in the Old Testament.[34] What began as a weary confession about human limitations now morphs into their warm approval. Agur arrives in that same happy place that Seligman's observations about hereditary happiness, the set range of emotions, and the hedonic treadmill have brought into view: the broad and blessed margin between excess and want.

There is a humble contentment in Agur's daily bread that is perhaps only tasteful to those who have reached the point of weariness, who were once consumed by their own efforts. Qohelet warns of the exhaustion of study (Eccl 12:12), yet Agur's "two things" plead for moderation in the

---

33 Translations commonly round up verse 9—"and deny *you*" (NRSV; ESV; NLT) or "and disown *you*" (NIV)—though there is no personal pronoun in the Hebrew text. Since none of Agur's requests are outside of human reach, both God and a fellow human can be in view (see the direct address in v. 6).

34 See R. N. Whybray, *Wealth and Poverty in the Book of Proverbs*, JSOTSup 99 (Sheffield: JSOT Press, 1990), 80.

domains of speech and possession. That a positive character is built on
the reliability of what is spoken and what is heard is a familiar tenet. But
no matter how well-selected one's company might be, the highs and lows
of life might still breed hubris and blasphemy that show their ugly face
first of all in how humans use language. Agur's concern with word and
wealth lies ultimately with honoring God, yet the malleable condition of
the human heart is a hurdle just as much for the pursuit of a good life.[35]
Initially, Agur had no choice but to accept his limits of learning and life
(v. 7 reads literally "before I die"). Now he treasures restraint and medioc-
rity as a sure foundation for his personal, social, and spiritual well-being.

The Wonderful World of Wisdom

As the loose flow of reflection continues, the next vignette elaborates on
the havoc that speech can create. Slandering servants before their master
(v. 10), cursing father and mother (v. 11), and the blindness to one's corruption (vv. 12–13) are all negative examples of a life that pushes beyond
its limits. But ultimately, it is people whose "teeth are swords and jaws
are knives to devour the needy from the earth" (v. 14) who confirm the
need for treating Agur's "two things" as one and the same thing.[36]

At this point in the poem, Agur's untethered contemplation has
traveled from his emotional self-assessment to an impossible journey
to heaven and from his daily bread to mouths full of knives. Authentic
insight about the good life can be found in many places. The remainder
of Proverbs 30 adds to this kaleidoscope of comprehension yet another
viewpoint, namely, the animal kingdom and the forces of the cosmos.
The second half of the chapter is built almost exclusively around the
formula "x/x + 1" that appears in many places in the Old Testament and
other ancient texts.

> One thing God has spoken,
> two things are what I have heard. (Ps 62:12)

---

35 "Divine intervention is balanced with human responsibility here in a way that
    takes the empirical conditions of human life seriously. . . . [Agur] continues to
    depend upon the practical insights of wisdom in facing the prospects of every-
    day life;" Moore, "Worldly Wisdom," 102.

36 "Thus his two prayers have the same goal: to be kept free from temptation;"
    Michael V. Fox, Proverbs 10–31, AB 18B (New Haven, CT: Yale University
    Press, 2009), 859.

In two days he will make us alive,
*   on the third day he will raise us up. (Hos 6:2)*

In six moments of distress he will deliver you,
*   in seven he will not let disaster reach you. (Job 5:19)*

Sometimes these parallel structures simply provide a framework for descriptions; at other times, the thought of line A (x) advances to a climax in line B (x+1).[37] Agur utilizes the conventional poetic device for both ends and for many other purposes beside.

The leech has two daughters: 'Give! Give!'
Three things there are that are not satisfied,
*   four that never say 'Enough!'*
*   Sheol and the barren womb,*
*   a land that is not satiated with water,*
*   and a fire that does not say: 'Enough!'*

Proverbs 30:15–16

The sudden appearance of toddler leeches and a speaking fire is baffling, yet even this excess of parataxis bears its moments of insight.[38] The parasites, for instance, hold the mirror up to the humans who curse their parents (v. 11) and the boundless consumption of grave and ground echoes the cannibalistic greed of the razor-mouthed villains (v. 14). These pictorial parallels include human beings in the gluttony of the world and take a stab at all claims to cosmic exceptionalism ("Who has gone up to heaven?"). But there is something in Agur's mathematics that does not add up. Earth, fire, and Sheol are non-human and outside of human control, but the barren womb is notoriously near the bone. It breaks the pretense of four equals and one can only wonder why Agur

---

37 For examples and discussion, see W. M. W. Roth, *Numerical Sayings in the Old Testament: A Form-Critical Study,* VTSup 13 (Leiden: Brill, 1965). This poetic device is not restricted to the Bible; cf. Ariel-Ram Pasternak and Shamir Yona, "Numerical Sayings in the Literatures of the Ancient Near East, in the Bible, in the Book of Ben-Sira and in Rabbinic Literature," *RRJ* 19 (2016): 202–244.

38 For an argument for high-level editorial skills in the second half of the chapter, see Andrew E. Steinmann, "Three Things. Four Things. Seven Things: The Coherence of Proverbs 30:11–33 and the Unity of Proverbs 30," *HS* 42 (2001): 59–66.

has included it. Is the human desire for offspring a form of greed? Are people consumed with the drive to expand their species and improve their social rank?[39] Or is it the sad affinity between death and barrenness that is in view?

However one may understand the three items and then the fourth, the connection to the destroyers of the surrounding verses highlights the human participation in the power dynamics of the world. These verses are no appraisal or plain lesson but a revelation of the fierce forces with which human existence must grapple and amid which health, joy, and contentment must be found. Studying the leech and kindling the raging flames, humanity can discover itself as a part of the everyday drama of life and death, limit and excess, desire and disappointment. Agur's next poem infuses such contemplation of the common good with a sense of wonder.

> *Three things are too wonderful for me,*
> *four I do not comprehend:*
>> *The way of an eagle in the skies,*
>> *the way of a snake upon a rock,*
>> *the way of a boat in the midst of the sea,*
>> *and the way of a man with a young woman.*

Proverbs 30:18–19

Though unified by the repetition of "the way," the emphasis rests here clearly on the fourth item and on the quandary of comprehension. Agur's admission raises yet another objection to the traditional wisdom model and especially to its royal contours. Adam's naming of the animals (Gen 2:20), Solomon's lectures on trees and animals (1 Kgs 5:13), and the private zoos of Mesopotamian monarchs all reflect the ancient ideology of the king as the ruler of the universe.[40] Agur's words shake

---

39 McKane interprets all items that surround the woman's womb as "metaphors of her appetite for sexual intercourse, for the fierce urge to remove the reproach of her barrenness;" *Proverbs*, 656. Fox sees no such hierarchy between the four items: "Barrenness, personified like the other devoureres, craves *nonexistence*. . . . The world, even nature itself, is full of unappeasable desires. . . . This voraciousness is not inherently wicked; it is just the way things are;" *Proverbs 10–31*, 868 (emphasis original).

40 The Assyrian ruler Assurbanipal II, for instance, collected a wide range of animals: "I formed herds of wild bulls, elephants, lions, ostriches, male monkeys,

up the claim to dominion that the Bible extends to all humans (cf. Gen
1:26). Not domestication, analysis, or understanding is his response,
but wonder. As in the previous saying, the movement from three to four
does not ask for answers or lessons in biology but for contemplation
and questions. Why would the snake choose the more difficult ground?
How do the boat and the bird keep their head up amid their stormy
surroundings? How long will each traveler need to complete their way,
what is their destination, and is it worth the effort?

The more observations the terse triplet sparks, the sharper the link
between animal and human behavior will come into focus. The way of
love can be just as rocky and random as other terrestrial trajectories, just
as mysterious as other combinations of energy and endurance, just as
smooth and traceless as a bird in the air. Only time will tell whether those
who pursue that way are as competent in navigating their path as their
fellow explorers of ground, sky, and water. The way of the young man may
fail because of his poor time management, his lack of interest in the long
haul, or as Agur's fifth way in verse 20 suggests, because his companion
sails off after he has finally reached the shore. "Such is the way of the
adulteress: she eats, wipes her mouth, and says: 'I have done no wrong.'"

Birds, boats, and boulders are common sights and the pursuit of love
likewise is a familiar experience, thankfully, no longer only for young
men. All four items are everyday appearances but Agur's addition of
bird plus snake plus boat plus lover prompts his readers to look closer
and to discover how obscure, how awe-inspiring, and how mystifying
their ways truly are.[41] That Agur's words develop from "too stupid" to
"too wonderful" suggests that the same reality can be seen with different eyes, that something as mundane as a bird in flight may reveal the
limits and also the longings of the human heart. To join the created
realm rather than stand above it, to learn but be contented with what

---

female monkeys, wild asses, deer, *aialu*-deer, female bears, panthers, *senkurru*,
beasts of mountain and plain, all of them in my city Calah. I displayed them
to all the people of my land;" A. Kirk Grayson, *Assyrian Rulers of the Early
First Millennium BC I (1114–859 BC)*, RIMA 2 (Toronto: University of Toronto
Press, 1991), 226.

41 "Maybe that's the point. Perhaps some proverbs are meant simply to evoke
wonder. Period. Things are wonderful, indeed 'too wonderful,' because they
take us into the realm of the unknown;" William P. Brown, "Wisdom's Wonder: Proverbs, Paideia, and Play," *CovQ* (Aug/Nov, 2010), 16.

remains unknown, to wonder at the world rather than master it—this is the peaceable wisdom of a life lived with open eyes.

Continuing his school of observation, Agur shares in verses 21–23 and 29–31 two further reflections on threes and fours. Both poems advocate a stable ordering of society. The earth shakes when a slave becomes king (v. 21); the mighty lion and the king with his army are keeping good step (v. 31).[42] Such traditional assertions stand strangely alongside Agur's low view of human heroism and this dissonance becomes even stronger when the poem in verses 24–28 is read with them.

> Four there are who are small in the world,
>   but they are the wisest of the wise:
> The ants are a people not strong,
>   but they make preparation in the summer for their food.
> The badgers are a people not mighty,
>   but they set up their house on the rocks.
> The locusts have no king,
>   but they all go out divided in companies.
> The lizard you may catch by hand,
>   but it is found in the king's palace.
>
>   Proverbs 30:24–28

In contrast to the previous numerical poems and the blatant judgment of Proverbs 6:6 ("Go to the ant, O lazy fellow, study her ways and get wise!"), this set includes no movement from three to four, no contrast or climax, no mixing of humans and animals, and no member who does not belong. The small master-sages are simply listed, one by one, each with their limitations and powers. All four species are furtive and fidgety, yet all are described in terms of mastery and warfare.

Set against the grain of the rigid social strata in the surrounding verses, this poem reveals an alternative take on life. No king is needed when everyone marches together, any lack of power can be compensated by proper planning, those who cultivate ingenuity and persistence can build even on difficult ground, and even the most powerful places

---

42 Raymond C. Van Leeuwen sees here a "serious sociopolitical statement, one that promotes a royal hierarchical view of society;" "Proverbs 30:21–23 and the Biblical World Upside Down," *JBL* 105 (1986), 602.

are open to those who play to their strengths.[43] The wisdom of these four unlikely teachers is surprising and practical, imaginative and communal. But it also warns all who tower above these small champions that first impressions can deceive and that the accepted hierarchies are not the only way to live well and successfully. The ant has a lesson not just for lazy people but also for the powerful elite.

Low-Pressure Living

The words of Agur readily break up into separate poems, each with its own perspective, appeal, and application. Yet the wheel of wisdom turns best only when Proverbs 30 is read as a whole and with a warm embrace of its parataxis, its loose flow of connections, contrasts, and chasms. Neither the healing transition from weariness to wonder nor the tension between divine distance and God's word, neither the two-sided posture to human limitations nor the unease with political structures calls for resolution. To the contrary, it is precisely the messiness and short attention span of Proverbs 30 that map the road to the wise, good life. Self-reflection, revelation, social observation, wonder, and nature walks—all of these together yield understanding. Ignoring any one of these avenues or prioritizing one over the others will create blind spots and press reality into a narrow box. Agur's final words warn against such an approach to life.

> *If you have been foolish enough to exalt yourself*
> *if you pondered destruction,*
> *put your hand on your mouth!*
> *For pressing milk brings forth butter,*
> *and pressing the nose brings forth blood,*
> *and pressing anger brings forth conflict.*

Proverbs 30:32–33

As cautionary words against self-exultation appear in the Old Testament primarily in royal contexts (cf. 1 Kgs 1:5; Ezek 17:14; Dan 11:14), the political realm, once again, is near the surface. Here and throughout his words, Agur's vision of life sees no problem with power as long as those who wield it stay humbly in touch with their humanity and

---

43 Agur's critical nod toward kingship emerges in yet stronger contours in conversation with Proverbs 28–29, which are aimed at aspiring leaders; cf. Christine Roy Yoder, "On the Threshold of Kingship: A Study of Agur (Proverbs 30)," *Int* 63 (2009): 254–263.

take an active role in the good life of others.[44] The threefold object lesson of undue "pressing" (מיץ) speaks against the misuse of force but it also marks a meaningful conclusion to the chapter as a whole. Grounded in Agur's tired testimony and his contented place between excess and deprivation, Proverbs 30 identifies the lifestyle of the leech ("Give! Give!") as a sure path to unhappiness. Pressing the issue too far, striving too hard, demanding too much certainty, and taking oneself too seriously will breed a language that nobody should hear—"Put your hand on your mouth!"—and that will not give life to others. The cultivation of a positive character flows instead from an honest commitment to limitations, a real investment in the spiritual and social realm, and an unbounded amazement of being human in this world.

Agur's juxtaposition of the many facets of life imagines a kind of existence that knows of its own crises, has learned to live between confusion and confession, and remains open, nevertheless, to hearing God's word and learning from ants and lizards. Such a life is not all positive or always fulfilling. It is not perfect and it is certainly not easy. It is, however, a good life because it is realistic in its reach, liberated in its limits, and engaged in its environment. For some people, the calm and simple day-to-day exercise of being human might suffice to call such a life not merely good but meaningful. For others, it may be the occasional discovery of wonder amid unending waves of weariness that will infuse their life with meaning. And then there are again others for whom meaning can only ever be found in something and in someone beyond themselves.[45]

---

44 "The deepest satisfaction comes from understanding oneself as embedded not only within but as an active and constructive part *of* a moral order. This is what it means that wisdom 'gives life;'" Newsom, "Israelite Wisdom," 133 (emphasis original). The link between such participation and the good life is a sporadic element in Seligman's *Happiness*, which keeps its eye even in the areas of marriage, parenting, and work firmly on the "abundant gratification" of the individual (p. 185).

45 Seligman's understanding of the meaningful life that unfolds "in the service of something larger" resonates with Victor Frankl's thoughts about "the self-transcendence of human existence:" "Being human always points, and is directed, to something, or someone, other than oneself—be it a meaning to fulfill or another human being to encounter. The more one forgets themselves—by giving themselves to a cause to serve or another person to love—the more human they are;" *Man's Search for Meaning*, trans. Ilse Lasch (Boston, MA: Beacon Press, 2006).

Agur's language about life has enough space for them all and offers words to all who, like him, need to express the reality of their personal life without holding back the sharp tones of disappointment and the high notes of delight. These intimate dimensions of Agur's poem are valuable and hospitable, but Proverbs 30 travels beyond the small island of a happy self. Agur's eyes reach beyond the shoreline and scan the horizon for a glimpse of companion creatures and creator. His poetic abandon and open arms model a life that knows its wisdom and meaning to be out there with the ant and the Almighty, with the freedom of the eagle and the fellowship of every living being.

The Good Life of Language

Agur's stunning compilation of perspectives is fully in keeping with the open posture of Proverbs. He does not break away from the easy and straight path; he does not abandon the tradition or tweak its cosmology. None of his challenges to power structures or his tension between creed and confusion are revolutionary attitudes. What sets Agur's poem apart from Proverbs 1–29 is rather its intimate style, its personal concession to being "too stupid," and his discovery of things "too wonderful." In this respect, Agur is fully at home with the other wisdom books that likewise reveal a conspicuous preference for articulating their reflections in the form of extensive, personal memoirs. Job's agony and open eyes, Qohelet's frustration and joy, Agur's failure and wonder—the first-person speeches of these individuals are authentic and accessible, allowing their readers to make them their own words. The speaking "I" that shares its struggles and insights is inviting but it has its limits. Agur, Job, and Qohelet are, after all, male characters who speak from a distant world and whose lives cannot be accessed or imitated. Yet, across this divide, their words—as much as the words of Lady Wisdom, Proverbs' mothers, and Job's wife—awaken their hearers to the shared human need for language. In the public sphere and in personal reflection, human beings need words for living in this world with all that is difficult, with all that is good.

The human condition is no lake where the boundaries remain the same from year to year but a river that curves and flattens, that rushes and deepens. What the Hebrew poets bequeath upon their hearers are no universal truths about being human but a deep dive into the particular waters of their day. Agur and the other sages call their readers to attend closely to their strokes and circles, their sentences and questions. Watching the Hebrew poets swim so comfortably in the elements of life and language can encourage those who would rather not test the waters to wade into the current on their own. This peculiar practice of imitation and independence lies at the heart of the wisdom tradition that was alive and active well before the Hebrew sages and that did not cease to bubble forth after Job, Qohelet, and Agur.[46] Ben Sira, one of the many sages who joined their ranks toward the end of the first millennium BCE, captured these dynamics in a beautiful poem that has drunk deeply from Lady Wisdom's chalice and freely passes it on to other weary humans.

> *The first human did not fully know wisdom,*
> *and neither will the last one search her out.*
> *For her thought is vaster than the sea,*
> *and her counsel deeper than the great abyss.*
> *As for me, I was like a brook from a river,*
> *like a channel going out to a garden.*
> *I said: 'I will water my garden,'*
> *And see, my brook became a river,*
> *and my river became the sea!*
> *I will give instructions shining like the light,*
> *I will make them clear from far away.*
> *I will yet again pour forth teaching like prophecy*
> *and leave it to future generations.*
> *See, I have not toiled for myself alone,*
> *but for all who search for wisdom.*

Ben Sira 24:28–34

Vaster than the sea, the wealth of wisdom will never be exhausted by any human being. Even so, from the first to the last, people will search for the best way to think, speak, and act in this world. Ben Sira is all

---

46 See, e.g., Richard J. Clifford, ed., *Wisdom Literature in Israel and Mesopotamia*, SymS 36 (Atlanta, GA: SBL Press, 2007); John G. Gammie and Leo G. Perdue, eds., *The Sage in Israel and the Ancient Near East* (Winona Lake, IN: Eisenbrauns, 1990); James H. Charlesworth and Michael A. Daise, eds., *Light in a Spotless Mirror: Reflections on Wisdom Traditions in Judaism and Early Christianity*, Faith and Scholarship Colloquies (Harrisburg, PA: Trinity Press, 2003); Mariam Kamell Kovalishyn, "Wisdom in the New Testament" in *Oxford Handbook of Wisdom and the Bible*, ed. Will Kynes (Oxford: Oxford University Press, 2021), 173–186.

too aware of this larger story in which he participates, knowing that
he is but a "brook from a river" and not the river itself. But as he goes
about his business of nurturing his small circle of influence, his garden,
something astounding happens. His trickle of human words becomes
a river that becomes one with the oceanic pool of Lady Wisdom. Like
the words of Agur that speak alongside every refined word of God, so
Ben Sira speaks in tandem with wisdom's voice. This joint venture is
no competition, no acclaim to greatness or originality. What is offered
here is a commitment to tradition, to the joy of receiving and passing
on, to the speaking of old words into new situations: "See, I have not
toiled for myself alone."

Ben Sira's regard for the wisdom of old and his concern for all
future generations is a testimony to the life of language and its place in
the quest for the good life. Returning to the rich reservoir of Hebrew
poetry, Ben Sira's work finds authentic expressions of being human in
the proverbs, riddles, and images of his ancestors.[47] He stands firmly in
the current that has reached him from the ancient sea of wisdom. But
as he takes from its waters and nurtures his garden, a surprising spring
of water bubbles up that is old and new at the same time. The strange
blend of imitation and independence brings words to the human ear
that can speak anew of the good life, that can articulate in unpredictable ways what it means to live well on this earth. The wisdom of Proverbs, Agur, and Ben Sira goes to show that something can be said and
must be said about the human experience. Then and now, each sage and
speaker needs to know their own garden and their own toolshed, yet
they all draw their water from the same vast sea of words and wisdom.

That there is such language for things too wonderful, for "thought
vaster than the sea," is itself a sign that life is good. As with the terrors of

---

47 "The writer knows the Bible so well that he expresses his thoughts in the
    phraseology of previous biblical books; his work becomes, as it were, a mosaic
    of biblical terms and images;" Roland E. Murphy, *The Tree of Life: An Explora-
    tion of Biblical Wisdom Literature,* 2nd ed. (New York: Doubleday, 1996), 67.
    This recourse to the Hebrew scriptures is a defining mark of Second Temple
    Jewish literature, including the New Testament: "By even a conservative esti-
    mate, at least 70% of the Jesus tradition is in the form of some sort of Wisdom
    utterance such as an aphorism, riddle, or parable;" Ben Witherington, *Jesus the
    Sage: The Pilgrimage of Wisdom* (Minneapolis, MN: Augsburg Fortress, 1994),
    155–156.

storm, despair, and loneliness, the language of Hebrew poetry embraces all who search for meaning and can help them to put the experience of being human into words. Agur's field trips and Ben Sira's gardening are an inspiration to imitate such speech. But the mysteries and wonders that they discover also show that there is much of life—the good and the wonderful as much as the painful and the worrisome—that no human being will ever be able to say. Words can do a lot of things, yet pressing them too hard will only bring forth a small world.

EPILOGUE

Feet buried in the warm sand and one hand at the brow to block out the sun, the human journey across the sea of life needs every so often to stop and squint back over the path it has trodden. Seasoned travelers know that such moments of pause are rare and that all sense of arrival is an illusion. They understand that everything they have learned about being human so far has not exhausted this staggering, spectacular experience. The Hebrew poets appear to have been these kinds of people. Free of claims to clarity or closure, their snapshots of the human condition are as intense as they are incomplete. Much more can be said and has been said by the other writers who inhabit the Bible.[1] But for this moment, the poets's words must suffice, not only because time is rare but also because life often remains too difficult still to say more about the unspeakable reality of anxieties, loneliness, and despair. Hebrew poetry offers no compact solution to life's troubles. The treasures that these ancient texts hold rest in their words, their images, their raw and real perspectives, their wounds and wonders. The poets have taken the plunge and have seen how cold and dark, how confusing and weighty life can be. Yet they have returned to dry land and have carried up from the depths a language that is honest and hard and that breaks past the limits of the safe life on land.

Creative Words, Creating Worlds

From its first to its final verses, the Bible stands as a massive testimony to the power of language. God's spoken word organizes the world into a liveable shape and the story that unfolds from Genesis 1 onward can

---

1 "We cannot merely interrogate the Old Testament for some fixed and finished portrayal of the human. Rather, we need to hear it in its own terms, and this means listening sympathetically to its many tones," McConville, *Being Human in God's World*, 9.

be sketched along a handful of other pivotal scenes of divine address. Abraham's call to leave home, Moses's reception of the law, and David's royal covenant are watershed moments in the biblical narrative. Each is initiated by God but none of them is a monologue. The key figures of the Old Testament speak with God and their questions, doubts, and concerns alert their readers to the active role that human words play in the drama of this planet. But the Bible's story must not be reduced to these memorable moments of revelation and leadership; the exercise of speaking and the depths of dialogue are also at the heart of each and every small life. The stage of Old Testament narratives is filled with unnamed speakers who change the course of history,[2] yet the spoken word carries just as much power in the poetic books.

The obstacles to human flourishing that the Psalms, Jeremiah, Job, and Qohelet face are not as concrete and not as easily expressed as the wars, droughts, and violence that appear in biblical narratives. The anxieties of life are vague, the experience of loneliness is uncanny, the grip of despair and depression stifles final forms of expression. The ticking clock is loud enough, yet the years run like grains of sand through the human hand. Across the poetic books, the human condition is marked by substantial, severe sufferings that are all the worse because of their slippery surfaces, round corners, and irregular shapes.

The gravity of these speechless scenarios is reflected in the radical responses that they evoke. Appealing to the cosmic drama of chaos, reaching down to the underworld, and shattering cultural norms, the voices of the Hebrew poets must leave behind all conventional diction to express the inarticulable. The lonely psalmist who conjures up images of shadow and death, the crushed prophet who confronts God, the open mouth of Job, the passionate explosions of Qohelet and Agur—all speakers break the silence that engulfs the most painful parts of the human experience. Wherever the familiar phrases and comforts fall short, wherever theology and wisdom no longer suffice, a new language must be born to navigate the rough seas of existence.

---

2 See, e.g., my "The Servants of Saul: 'Minor' Characters and Royal Commentary in 1 Samuel 9–31," *JSOT* 40 (2015): 179–200, or Gina Hens-Piazza's *The Supporting Cast of the Bible: Reading on Behalf of the Multitude* (Minneapolis, MN: Lexington/Fortress Academic, 2020).

Yet despite all their extreme force, the words of the Hebrew poets are never destructive. Neither the anxious storm nor the prophetic woes aim to overthrow the tradition in which they arise. The foundational commitments to God's control and care are not left behind. To the contrary, when the waters rise and the world crumbles, these tenets become more important than ever because life provides a license, for the very first time, to question them, to rail against their limits, to demand an answer. Hebrew poetry is a lexicon, a liturgy that can be rehearsed, but it is much more than that. These biblical passages model a mode of speaking, a mindset that sees no conflict between dependence and daring initiative, that can hold its ground in the tension of creed and crisis. Like the new language for loneliness, despair, and time's tyranny, this mode is a remarkable manifesto of human artistry and agency. Job's construction of an alternative world far from God, Jeremiah's divine reflections in Lady Jerusalem's mirror, and Ecclesiastes's horrors of the pointless world are so challenging because they are so creative. The Old Testament imbues human language with the power to articulate life on earth in all its depth and darkness. But these compositions also declare that human words can create worlds, that they can claim new land, that they can trace the shoreline anew whenever they meet it way too far inland.

For a story that starts with a divine monologue, the Bible's countless creaturely conversations and outcries plant the human species firmly on the soil of God's earth. Hebrew poetic compositions do not always follow the script of Psalm 46 or Job where God enters the stage in the final act and speaks a mighty word of comfort or resolution. Even in these texts, the community and the open-eyed sufferer receive the honor of the final word and lend to the biblical landscape a startling human authority. The Bible's poems have not survived because of their quasi-magical properties or because their first readers considered them as infallible revelation. Alongside other factors, such as liturgical use, these passages owe much of their afterlife to the character of their speakers. What the blameless track record adds to Job's anguished lines, for instance, is provided in Jeremiah and Ecclesiastes by the gravitas of royal, prophetic, and scribal command. The same dynamics surface in Moses's association with Psalm 90 and the Solomonic flair of the wisdom books.

Against all appearance, however, the passages that bear these venerable names have not built their legacies on lineage any more than the nameless poetry of the Psalms. Instead, the appeal and authority of these scriptures is consistently based on their speakers' loss, pain, failure, and frailty. These voices do not articulate the unspeakable pockets of the human condition because they had the resources to escape from them but because their lives demanded such expressions. They were heard, gathered, treasured, translated, and passed on because of countless other lives who made the same demand. They spoke and continue to speak for all who are likewise stranded on an inarticulable island with nothing more, with nothing less, than their words.

Being Human

Reading the poetry of the Old Testament is no easy task. Each passage is a gateway to a strange world, clad in literary conventions and cosmic horizons that are distant and hard to capture. But this is only part of the problem. First readers and seasoned students of scripture alike must face the sharp and unsparing nature of the documents in front of them. The Old Testament contains glorious pockets of cosmic stability and stories of human hospitality and care; it is rich with divine words of comfort and promises of restoration. But in the broad sweep of all its chapters and verses, the portrayal of the human condition tilts toward tension, conflict, and struggle. The Eden project collapses onto itself the moment all actors are on the stage; nearly all key characters in the ensuing drama get pulled into the spiral of self-interest, intrigue, and hurt. Every joyous song is followed by a lament and even the most popular passages of hope stand with one leg in the realm of tragedy.

The historical reality of Jerusalem's vast collapse can in many ways account for this bleak vision of humanity, as can ancient Israel's manifold internal and external struggles. Turning to this context is illuminating. Yet the historical task must not reduce the outlook of the Hebrew poets to the margin of those extreme situations in the past. The character of the biblical texts and the emergence of the canon hardly allow for such a narrow window. The extensive efforts of editing and expanding as much as the labors of translation and preservation are a strong sign that these scriptures were widely embraced as a meaningful picture of the human condition that speaks well beyond its first occasion.[3] Living with some degree of anxiety, being alone in the world, encountering hopeless situations, discovering the real world underneath the ruins of one's assumptions, losing the battle against time, and being worn out by the search for wisdom—nobody is exempt from these experiences altogether even if some people may suffer them in their most extreme forms. They are not a mark of defeat and weakness, not a sign of insufficient faith. What the Hebrew poets have expressed in their words is the shared reality of what it means to be human.

This observation is somber but it must not be mistaken for a pessimistic, defeatist attitude. The zest for human existence that exudes from the words of Qohelet and Lady Wisdom makes ample space for celebrating life, as do the praise of the Psalms and Job's open eyes. None of these positive statements, however, make a fundamental difference to the struggling story of human living. The Hebrew poets know that now and then, life is good, even unspeakably good. But such knowledge will not resolve the tension or tip the scales. Even the most positive texts in the Bible attest to the complexity and chaos of life. This perhaps is the most difficult truth, namely, that

> the human condition is such that pain and effort are not just symptoms which can be removed without changing life itself; they are rather the modes in which life itself, together with the necessity to which it is bound, makes itself felt. For mortals, the 'easy life of the gods' would be a lifeless life.[4]

To face the reality of life alone, to despair of events that are beyond one's control, and to look with open eyes at the transient nature of each moment are not problems that can be solved. As unpleasant as they are and as grave as they can become, these experiences are so deeply ingrained in the exercise of being human that their absence would yield a different mode of being altogether.

---

3 "Suffering, and survival of it, was written into the Bible. This helps explain why these scriptures survived into the present when many other ancients texts did not. . . . Experiences of suffering can teach forms of wisdom that transcend their original contexts;" Carr, *Holy Resilience*, 5.

4 Hannah Arendt, *The Human Condition*, 120.

In a painful and perplexing paradox, getting in touch with the aspects that often defy life is to take a step closer toward understanding life and, one can hope, toward living with more grace toward oneself and others.[5] Life is what it is and it will not be bent into some ideal shape. This is the sad but wise insight that reflects with such irresistible light from Job's open eyes, that rings forth from the song of the lonely bird and the sharp sounds of Qohelet's snapped silver cord and shattered golden bowl.

Embracing Humanity

The daring realism of the Hebrew poets is a hard lesson. Any craving for security, any advertisement for "your best life now," and any dogmatic grip on what the Bible should and should not say makes this lesson yet harder. As if aware of the obstacles to its own message, the school of Hebrew poetry runs a curriculum of empathy. Its esteemed resident authors write tangled scripts that are true to the confusing experience of life. Keynote speakers such as Jeremiah, Job, and Qohelet stammer through their lectures on subjects that are difficult to articulate. From the individual voices of Psalms 69, 88, and 102 to Agur's stupidity, from Lady Jerusalem's desperate acceptance to Qohelet's hatred of life, the pedagogy of Hebrew poetry relies on first-person speeches that are as honest as possible about the human condition. The aim is to be authentic rather than authoritarian, to speak as a companion human rather than as an expert who has reached some higher level of existence. This posture suggests that the ultimate concern of the Bible's raw portrayal of the human condition is thoroughly therapeutic. This mode of being-with is a valuable pastoral exercise which, in the words of Henri Nouwen, pursues

the careful and sensitive articulation of what is happening in the community so that those who listen can say: 'You say what I suspected, you express what I vaguely felt, you bring to the fore what I fearfully kept in the back of my mind. Yes, yes—you say who we are, you recognise our condition.'[6]

---

5 As Lynch observes, anyone who aspires to care for struggling people "must leave their own ideal society. They must have faced and conquered their own scandal at the human condition;" *Images of Hope*, 55–56.
6 Nouwen, *Wounded Healer*, 39.

That Hebrew poetry does not hold back about the dark and difficult sides of being human is a gesture of grace. It is a selfless step toward another human being, a vulnerable opening of one life to another. Eager to guide and sustain their fellow travelers, the poets of these ancient texts take the first step onto new land and freely share the hard-won wealth that they have dug up in its rocky soil. They do not seek to alienate their readers but beckon them to arrive, maybe for the first time, on that weather-torn and restless common ground of life.

The poetic, pastoral craft of this welcome demands a sensitive way with words. Treading the precarious line between disillusionment and hospitality, the Hebrew poets know that their compositions need to be personal as well as indirect. Evoking shades of despair rather than painting life against a black background, hinting at the contrasts between worldtime and humantime, and letting images speak for themselves, they include their readers as active participants on the journey back to land. They honor human agency and responsibility. Their words are an invitation to articulate, acknowledge, and accept the reality of life because only this practice will stop their readers' impossible attempts to swim farther than breath and current will ever allow. Qohelet's contradictions and Agur's contented portion embrace the limits of living rather than kicking harder and harder against them. If life is seen for what it is—chaotic, lonesome, and far too quick—all the good pockets of rest, company, and hope can likewise be seen for what they are. A community can be a haven of calm, loneliness can be a place of creativity, the endless cycle of life can reduce the burden of significance. Despair can open eyes to the many things that one can control; shattered assumptions can start a breakaway from narrow horizons. These aspects of being human deserve to be celebrated yet none of them will redeem life on earth. None of them will eradicate pain and difficulty from being an essential part of the human condition.

The honest words of the Hebrew poets accept humanity for what it is, but they are so much more than that. As Lamentations 2 and Psalm 46 turn their gaze to the sea, as Psalm 102 lifts its eyes to that solitary bird, and as Qohelet feels the same old wind on his skin and smells fresh almond blossoms, they remind their companion humans of the vast world that surrounds each painful life. The grass, the ants, and all other beings carry out their short and demanding parts on the cosmic stage, which, as Job and Agur know so well, is indeed too wonderful to comprehend. For all the inherent trouble of the human condition, there is a whole world of communion and comfort out there.

All Hebrew poetry agrees on this point, yet the horizon is cast farther still to include the creator who takes responsibility for the shoreline, accepts the anguished rage that mere mortals hurl toward the skies, and imagines with the hopelessly entrapped that new day when Jeremiah's field will bear its first harvest. God's voice, gifts, and perspective meet the human condition with empathy and understanding, ever eager to open the eyes of struggling people so that they may see the horizon beyond their small islands and may know that the shaky ground of today is not hidden from the caring gaze of the maker of life. God is not ignorant or indifferent to the human condition. God embraces humanity by being with the people of this world, in deed, in person, in word. This is good news, for as long as there is speech at the shoreline, as long as there are conversations in the storm, the human journey will go on.

Bibliography

Abernethy, Andrew T. "'Mountains Moved into the Sea': The Western Reception of Psalm 46:1 and 3 [45:1 and 3 LXX] from the Septuagint to Luther." *JTS* 70 (2019): 523–545.

Ackerman, H. C. "Saul: A Psychotherapeutic Analysis." *Anglican Theological Review* 3 (1920): 114–124.

Alter, Robert. *The Art of Biblical Narrative*. New York: Basic Books, 1981.

———. *The Art of Biblical Poetry*. New York: Basic Books, 1985.

American Psychiatric Association. *Diagnostic and Statistical Manual of Mental Disorders*. 5th ed. Arlington, VA: American Psychiatric Association, 2013.

Anderson, G. Oscar. "Loneliness among Adults." https://www.aarp.org/research/topics/life/info-2014/loneliness_2010.html.

Angel, Andrew R. *Chaos and the Son of Man: The Hebrew* Chaoskampf *Tradition in the Period 515 BCE to 200 CE*. LSTS 60. London: T&T Clark, 2006.

———. *Playing with Dragons: Living with Suffering and God*. Eugene, OR: Cascade Books, 2014.

"Anxiety Disorder: Facts & Statistics." https://adaa.org/understanding-anxiety/facts-statistics.

Arendt, Hannah. *The Human Condition*. 2nd ed. Chicago: University of Chicago Press, 1998.

Ash, Christopher. *Job*. Preaching the Word. Downers Grove, IL: Crossway, 2014.

Austin, Steve. *Hiding in the Pews: Shining Light on Mental Illness in the Church.* Minneapolis, MN: Fortress Press, 2021.

Ayali-Darshan, Noga. *The Storm-God and the Sea: The Origin, Versions, and Diffusion of a Myth throughout the Ancient Near East.* Translated by Liat Keren. ORA 37. Tübingen: Mohr Siebeck, 2020.

Bailey, Jeanne. "From Hopelessness to Despair." Pages 135–152 in *Hopelessness: Developmental, Cultural, and Clinical Realms.* Edited by Salman Akthar and Mary Kay O'Neil. London: Karnac, 2015.

Bang, Ki-Min. "A Missing Key to Understanding Psalm 46: Revisiting the Chaoskampf." *CBW* 37 (2017): 68–89.

Barr, James. *Biblical Words for Time.* London: SCM Press, 1962.

Barré, Michael L. "'Wandering About' as a Topos of Depression in Ancient Near Eastern Literature and in the Bible." *JNES* 60 (2001): 177–187.

Barstad, Hans M. *A Way in the Wilderness: The" Second Exodus" in the Message of Second Isaiah.* JSSM 12. Manchester: University of Manchester Press, 1989.

Batsleer, Janet and James Duggan. *Young and Lonely: The Social Conditions of Loneliness.* Bristol: Policy Press, 2021.

Becker, Ernest. *The Denial of Death.* New York: Free Press, 1973.

Begg, Christopher. "Comparing Characters: The Book of Job and the Testament of Job." Pages 435–445 in *The Book of Job.* Edited by W. A. M. Beuken. BETL 114. Leuven: Leuven University Press, 1994.

Berlin, Adele. *The Dynamics of Biblical Parallelism.* Revised and expanded. Grand Rapids, MI: Eerdmans, 2008.

Betjeman, John. *Collected Poems.* London: John Murray, 2001.

Bier, Miriam J. *"Perhaps There Is Hope": Reading Lamentations as a Polyphony of Pain, Penitence, and Protest.* LHBOTS 603. London: T&T Clark, 2015.

Bingaman, Kirk A. "A Pastoral Theological Approach to the New Anxiety." *Pastoral Psychol* 59 (2010): 659–670.

———. "Caring for the Anxious: A Postmodern Approach." *JSMH* 10 (2007): 3–17.

Blyth, Caroline. "'I Am Alone with My Sickness': Voicing the Experience of HIV- and Aids-Related Stigma through Psalm 88." *Colloq* 44 (2012): 149–162.

Bonhöffer, Dietrich. *Gemeinsames Leben.* Gütersloh: Gütersloher Verlagshaus, 2006.

Bower, Bruce. "'Deaths of Despair' Are Rising. It's Time to Define Despair." https://www.sciencenews.org/article/deaths-of-despair-depression-mental-health-covid-19-pandemic.

Bowler, Kate. *No Cure for Being Human*. London: Rider, 2021.

Bozak, Barbara A. *Life Anew: A Literary-Theological Study of Jer. 30–31*. AnBib 122. Rome: Editrice Pontificio Istituto Biblico, 1991.

Brettler, Mark Zvi. "Cyclical and Teleological Time in the Hebrew Bible." Pages 111–128 in *Time and Temporality in the Ancient World*. Edited by R. M. Rosen. Philadelphia, PA: University of Pennsylvania Museum, 2004.

———. "Images of Yhwh the Warrior in Psalms." *Semeia* 61 (1993): 135–165.

———, Peter Enns, and Daniel J. Harrington. *The Bible and the Believer: How to Read the Bible Critically & Religiously*. Oxford: Oxford University Press, 2015.

Brewer, Judson. "We've Got Anxiety All Wrong." *PT* (July/Aug 2021): 30–33.

Bringle, Mary L. *Despair: Sickness or Sin? Hopelessness and Healing in the Christian Life*. Nashville, TN: Abingdon Press, 1990.

Brown, William P. *Character in Crisis: A Fresh Approach to the Wisdom Literature of the Old Testament*. Grand Rapids, MI: Eerdmans, 1996.

———. *Seeing the Psalms: A Theology of Metaphor*. Louisville, KY: Westminster John Knox Press, 2002.

———. "Wisdom's Wonder: Proverbs, Paideia, and Play." *CovQ* (Aug/Nov, 2010): 13–24.

Broyles, Craig C. "The Psalms and Cult Symbolism: The Case of the Cherubim-Ark." Pages 139–158 in *Interpreting the Psalms: Issues and Approaches*. Edited by David Firth and Philip S. Johnston. Downers Grove, IL: IVP Academic, 2005.

Brueggemann, Walter. *Hopeful Imagination: Prophetic Voices in Exile*. Philadelphia, PA: Fortress Press, 1986.

———. *Sabbath as Resistance: Saying No to the Culture of Now*. Louisville, KY: Westminster John Knox, 2014.

"Bulletin: Families and Households in the UK: 2021." https://www.ons.gov.uk/peoplepopulationandcommunity/birthsdeathsandmarriages/families/bulletins/familiesandhouseholds/2021.

Bundvad, Mette. *Time in the Book of Ecclesiastes*. OTM. Oxford: Oxford University Press, 2015.

Burkeman, Oliver. *Four Thousand Weeks: Time Management for Mortals.* New York: Vintage, 2021.

Caballero, Lara E. et al. "Are Loneliness and Social Isolation Associated with Cognitive Decline?" *Int J Geriatr Psy* 34 (2019): 1613–1622.

Cacioppo, John, James. H. Fowler, and Nicholas A. Christakis. "Alone in the Crowd: The Structure and Spread of Loneliness in a Large Social Network." *J Pers Soc Psychol* 97 (2009): 977–991.

Camp, Claudia V. *Wise, Strange and Holy: The Strange Woman and the Making of the Bible.* JSOTSup 320. Sheffield: Sheffield Academic Press, 2009.

Cantz, Paul, and Kalman Kaplan. "Biblical Narratives for Positive Psychology and Suicide Prevention: An Evidence-Supported Approach." *MHRC* 20 (2017): 654–678.

Carr, David M. *Holy Resilience: The Bible's Traumatic Origins.* New Haven, CT: Yale University Press, 2014.

Carroll, Sean. *From Eternity to Here: The Quest for the Ultimate Theory of Time.* 2nd ed. London: Oneworld Publications, 2011.

Case, Anne, and Angus Deaton. *Deaths of Despair and the Future of Capitalism.* Princeton, NJ: Princeton University Press, 2020.

Charles, J. Daryl, ed. *Reading Genesis 1–2: An Evangelical Conversation.* Peabody, MA: Hendrickson, 2013.

Charlesworth, James H., and Michael A. Daise, eds. *Light in a Spotless Mirror: Reflections on Wisdom Traditions in Judaism and Early Christianity.* Faith and Scholarship Colloquies. Harrisburg, PA: Trinity Press, 2003.

Charry, Ellen T. *Psalms 1–50: Sighs and Songs of Israel.* BTCB. Grand Rapids, MI: Brazos Press, 2015.

Christenson, Randall. "Parallels between Depression and Lament." *JPCC* 61 (2007): 299–308.

Claassens, L. Juliana. "Jeremiah: The Traumatized Prophet." Pages 358–373 in *The Oxford Handbook of Jeremiah.* Edited by Louis Stulman and Edward Silver. Oxford: Oxford University Press, 2022.

———. "Preaching the Pentateuch: Reading Jeremiah's Sermons through the Lens of Cultural Trauma." *Scriptura* 116 (2017): 27–37.

———. "The Woman of Substance and Human Flourishing: Proverbs 31:10–31 and Martha Nussbaum's Capabilities Approach." *JFSR* 32 (2016): 5–19.

Clark, Jayne V. "Struggling through Singleness." *JBC* 29 (2015): 7–18.

Clements, R. E. *Wisdom in Theology.* Didsbury Lectures. Carlisle: Paternoster Press, 1992.

Clifford, Richard, ed. *Wisdom Literature in Israel and Mesopotamia*. SymS 36. Atlanta, GA: SBL Press, 2007.

Clines, David J. A. *I, We, He, and They: A Literary Approach to Isaiah 53*. JSOTSup 1. Sheffield: JSOT Press, 1983.

———. *Job 1–20*. WBC 17. Dallas, TX: Word Books, 1989.

Cohen, Shaye S. *From the Maccabees to the Mishnah*. 2nd ed. Louisville, KY: Westminster John Knox Press, 2014.

Coleman, Monica. *Bipolar Faith: A Black Woman's Journey with Depression and Faith*. Minneapolis, MN: Fortress Press, 2016.

Collins, Adela Yarbro. *The Combat Myth in the Book of Revelation*. HBR 9. Missoula, MI: Scholars Press, 1976.

Colwell, John E. *Why Have You Forsaken Me? A Personal Reflection on the Experience of Desolation*. Eugene, OR: Cascade, 2012.

Cook, Christopher C. H., and Isabelle Hamley, eds. *The Bible and Mental Health: Towards a Biblical Theology of Mental Health*. Norfolk: SCM Press, 2020.

Copeland, William et al. "Associations of Despair with Suicidality and Substance Misuse among Young Adults." *JAMA Netw Open*. 3 (2020): e208627. doi:10.1001/jamanetworkopen.2020.8627.

Crenshaw, James L. "The Shadow of Death in Qoheleth." Pages 205–216 in *Israelite Wisdom: Theological and Literary Essays in Honor of Samuel Terrien*. Edited by John G. Gammie et al. Missoula, MT: Scholars Press, 1978.

Csikszentmihalyi, Mihaly. *Finding Flow: The Psychology of Engagement with Everyday Life*. New York: Basic Books, 1997.

Culley, Robert C. "Psalm 102: A Complaint with a Difference." *Semeia* 62 (1993): 19–35.

Dames, Nicholas. "The New Fiction of Solitude." *The Atlantic* (Apr 2016): 92–101.

David, Susan A., Ilona Boniwell, and Amanda C. Ayers, eds. *The Oxford Handbook of Happiness*. Oxford: Oxford University Press, 2013.

Davies, Mark G. "Solitude and Loneliness: An Integrative Model." *JPT* 24 (1996): 3–12.

Day, John. *Yahweh and the Gods and Goddesses of Canaan*. JSOTSup 265. London: Sheffield Academic Press, 2002.

Dell, Katharine J. *Shaking a Fist at God: Struggling with the Mystery of Undeserved Suffering*. Chicago, IL: Triumph Books, 1997.

————. *The Book of Proverbs in Social and Theological Context*. Cambridge: Cambridge University Press, 2006.

————. "The Cycle of Life in Ecclesiastes." *VT* 59 (2009): 181–189.

————. "The Use of Animal Imagery in the Psalms and Wisdom Literature of Ancient Israel." *SJT* 53 (2000): 275–291.

Dickinson, Emily. "There Is No Frigate Like a Book." Page 83 in *Emily Dickinson: Selected Poems*. Selected by J. M. Dent. London: Phoenix, 2010.

Edmondson, Donald et al. "From Shattered Assumptions to Weakened Worldviews: Trauma Symptoms Signal Anxiety Buffer Disruption." *J Loss Trauma* 16 (2011): 358–385.

Ehrenreich, Barbara. *Smile or Die: How Positive Thinking Fooled America and the World*. London: Granta Books, 2010.

Ellens, J. Harold, and Wayne G. Rollins, eds. *Psychology and the Bible: A New Way to Read the Scriptures*. 4 volumes. Westport, CT: Greenwood-Praeger, 2004.

Ellis, Albert. *How to Control Your Anxiety before It Controls You*. London: Robinson, 2019.

Fauconnier, Gilles, and Max Turner. *The Way We Think: Conceptual Blending and the Mind's Hidden Complexities*. New York: BasicBooks, 2002.

Firth, David G. "Anxiety: Some Perspectives from the Old Testament." Pages 96–104 in *The Bible and Mental Health: Towards a Biblical Theology of Mental Health*. Edited by Christopher C. H. Cook and Isabelle Hamley. Norfolk: SCM Press, 2020.

————. "Reading Psalm 46 in Its Canonical Context: An Initial Exploration in Harmonies Consonant and Dissonant." *BBR* 30 (2020): 22–40.

Fischer, Alexander. *Tod und Jenseits im Alten Orient und im Alten Testament: Eine Reise durch Antike Vorstellungs- und Textwelten*. SKI.NF 7. Leipzig: Evangelische Verlagsanstalt, 2014.

Fishbane, Michael. "Jeremiah IV 23–26 and Job III 3–13: A Recovered Use of the Creation Patterns." *VT* 21 (1971): 151–167.

Fløysvik, Ingvar. *When God Becomes My Enemy: The Theology of the Complaint Psalms*. Concordia Academic Press, 1997.

Foreman, Benjamin A. *Animal Metaphors and the People of Israel in the Book of Jeremiah*. FRLANT 238. Göttingen: Vandenhoeck & Ruprecht, 2011.

Fox, Michael V. *A Time to Tear Down and a Time to Build Up. A Rereading of Ecclesiastes*. Grand Rapids, MI: Eerdmans, 1999.

————. "Job 38 and God's Rhetoric." *Semeia* 19 (1981): 53–61.

———. "Job the Pious." *ZAW* 117 (2005): 351–366.

———. *Proverbs 10–31*. AB 18B. New Haven: Yale University Press, 2009.

———. "The Rhetoric of Disjointed Proverbs." *JSOT* 29 (2004): 165–177.

———. "The Rhetoric of Ezekiel's Vision of the Valley of the Bones." *HUCA* 51 (1980): 1–15.

Fuchs, Thomas. "Chronopathologie der Überforderung: Zeitstrukturen und Psychische Krankheit." Pages 52–79 in *Das Überforderte Subjekt: Zeitdiagnosen einer beschleunigten Gesellschaft*. Edited by Thomas Fuchs, Lukas Iwer, and Stefano Micali. Berlin: Suhrkamp, 2018.

Franklin, Samuel S. *The Psychology of Happiness: A Good Human Life*. Cambridge: Cambridge University Press, 2010.

Frankl, Victor. *Man's Search for Meaning*. Translated by Ilse Lasch. Boston, MA: Beacon Press, 2006.

Fretheim, Terence E. *Jeremiah*. SHBC. Macon, GA: Smith & Helwys, 2002.

Friedman, William J. "Developmental Perspectives on the Psychology of Time." Pages 345–366 in *Psychology of Time*. Edited by Simon Grondin. Bingley: Emerald, 2008.

Fromm, Erich. *The Fear of Freedom*. London: Routledge, 1960.

Fromm-Reichmann, Frieda. "Loneliness." *Psychiatry* 22 (1959): 1–15.

Fyall, Robert S. *Now My Eyes Have Seen You: Images of Creation and Evil in the Book of Job*. NSBT 17. Downers Grove, IL: InterVarsity Press, 2002.

Gammie, John G. and Leo G. Perdue, eds. *The Sage in Israel and the Ancient Near East*. Winona Lake, IN: Eisenbrauns, 1990.

George, Andrew. *The Epic of Gilgamesh: A New Translation*. London: Allen Lane, 1999.

Gerstenberger, Erhard. *Leviticus: A Commentary*. OTL. Louisville, KY: Westminster John Knox, 1996.

Goh, Samuel T. S. "The *Hebel* World, Its Ambiguities and Contradictions." *JSOT* 45 (2020): 198–216.

Goldingay, John. *Psalms. Volume 2: Psalms 42–89*. BCOT. Grand Rapids, MI: Baker Academic, 2007.

Goodman, Peter William. "Waters That Witness: How the Bible's Rivers Help Convey Its Message." *BTB* 53 (2023): 42–56.

Gordis, Robert. *Koheleth: The Man and His World. A Study of Ecclesiastes*. 3rd ed. New York: Schocken Books, 1968.

Graybill, Rhiannon. "'Hear and Give Ear!': The Soundscape of Jeremiah." *JSOT* 40 (2016): 467–490.

Grayson, Kirk A. *Assyrian Rulers of the Early First Millennium BC I (1114–859 BC)*. RIMA 2. Toronto: University of Toronto Press, 1991.

Greene-McCreight, Kathryn. *Darkness Is My Only Companion: A Christian Response to Mental Illness*. Revised and expanded. Grand Rapids: Brazos Press, 2015.

Griffin, J. *The Lonely Society?* London: Mental Health Foundation, 2010.

Groenewald, Alphonso. "Mythology, Poetry and Theology." *HTS* 62 (2006): 909–924.

Grossmann, Konrad. "Macht und Ohnmacht. Von der Schwierigkeit, das eigene Leben zu beeinflussen." *Systemische Notizen 19* (2006): 4–11.

Gruber, Mayer I. "Fear, Anxiety and Reverence in Akkadian, Biblical Hebrew and Other North-West Semitic Languages." *VT* 15 (1990): 411–422.

Hammoud, R. et al. "Lonely in a Crowd: Investigating the Association between Overcrowding and Loneliness Using Smartphone Technologies," *Sci. Rep.* 11 (2021). Article number 24134.

Ham, T. C. "The Gentle Voice of God in Job 38." *JBL* 132 (2013): 527–541.

Hatton, Peter T. H. *Contradiction in the Book of Proverbs: The Deep Waters of Counsel*. SOTSMS. Hampshire: Ashgate, 2008.

Hawkley, Louise C., and John T. Cacioppo. "Loneliness Matters: A Theoretical and Empirical Review of Consequences and Mechanisms." *Ann Beh* 40 (2010): 218–227.

Havergal, Frances Ridley. *Under the Surface*. 3rd ed. London: J. Nisbet, 1876.

Hens-Piazza, Gina. *The Supporting Cast of the Bible: Reading on Behalf of the Multitude*. Lexington/Fortress Academic, 2020.

Heschel, Abraham Joshua. *God in Search of Man: A Philosophy of Judaism*. New York: Farrer, Straus and Giroux, 1955.

———. *The Sabbath*. New York: Farrar, Straus and Giroux, 1951.

Hildebrandt, Samuel. "Are God's 'Good Plans' Not Good Enough? The Place and Significance of Jer 29:15 in Jeremiah's Letter to the Exiles." *JSOT* 45 (2021): 561–575.

———. "'I Am a Lonely Bird:' Psalm 102 and the Psychology of Loneliness." *BTB* 56 (2023): 68–76.

———. *Interpreting Quoted Speech in Prophetic Literature: A Study of Jeremiah 2.1–3.5*. VTSup 174. Leiden: Brill, 2017.

———. "'I Sat Alone:' The Language of Loneliness in the Hebrew Bible." *ZAW* 133 (2021): 512–525.

————. "Quoting the Words of God: Language and Theology in Jeremiah 4.10 and 32.25." Pages 130–144 in *From Words to Meaning: Studies on Old Testament Language and Theology for David J. Reimer*. Edited by Samuel Hildebrandt, Kurtis Peters, and Eric N. Ortlund. HBM 100. Sheffield: Sheffield Phoenix Press, 2021.

————. "The Servants of Saul: 'Minor' Characters and Royal Commentary in 1 Samuel 9–31." *JSOT* 40 (2015): 179–200.

————. "Whose Voice Is Heard? Speaker Ambiguity in the Psalms." *CBQ* 82 (2020): 197–213.

————. "When Words Become Too Violent: Silence as a Form of Nonviolent Resistance in the Book of Jeremiah." *BibInt* 29 (2021): 187–205.

————. ""Woe Is Me!": The Book of Jeremiah and the Language of Despair." *JBL* 139 (2020): 479–497.

Hillers, D. R. "The Reaction to Bad News." *ZAW* 77 (1965): 86–90.

Hogue, David A. "Sometimes It Causes Me to Tremble: Fear, Faith, and the Human Brain." *Pastoral Psychol* 63 (2014): 659–671.

Holwell, Eve. "Literary Depictions of Hopelessness: A Short Story, a Novel, and a Poem." Pages 85–105 in *Hopelessness: Developmental, Cultural, and Clinical Realms*. Edited by Salman Akthar and Mary Kay O'Neil. London: Karnac, 2015.

Horwitz, Allen V. *Anxiety: A Short History*. Baltimore, MY: John Hopkins University Press, 2013.

Houston, James M. "Exploring the Continent of Loneliness." *Crux* 46 (2010): 2–13.

Hsu, Shih-Wei, and Jaume Llop Raduá, eds. *The Expression of Emotions in Ancient Egypt and Mesopotamia*. CHANE 116. Leiden: Brill, 2021.

Human, Dirk J., ed. *Psalms and Mythology*. LHBOTS 462. New York: T&T Clark, 2007.

Ingram, Doug. *Ambiguity in Ecclesiastes*. LHBOTS 431. New York: T&T Clark, 2006.

Jacobson, Rolf A., and Karl N. Jacobson. *Invitation to the Psalms: A Reader's Guide for Discovery and Engagement*. Grand Rapids, MI: Baker Academic, 2013.

————. "Many Are Saying:" The Function of Direct Discourse in the Hebrew Psalter. JSOTSup 397. London: T&T Clark, 2004.

Janoff-Bulman, Ronnie. *Shattered Assumptions: Towards a New Psychology of Trauma*. New York: Free Press, 1992.

Janowski, Bernd. *Anthropologie des Alten Testaments: Grundfragen, Kontexte, Themenfelder.* Tübingen: Mohr Siebeck, 2019.

———. *Arguing with God: A Theological Anthropology of the Psalms.* Translated by Armin Siedlecki. Louisville, KY: Westminster John Knox, 2013.

———. "Das Erschöpfte Selbst: Zur Semantik der Depression in den Psalmen und im Ijobbuch." Pages 77–125 in *Das Hörende Herz.* BThAT 6. Göttingen: Vandenhoeck & Ruprecht, 2018.

Jingyuan, Liu, and Hong Li. "How Individuals Perceive Time in an Anxious State: The Mediating Effect of Attentional Bias." *Emotion* 20 (2020): 761–772.

Joyce, Paul. "Lamentations and the Grief Process: A Psychological Reading." *BibInt* 1 (1993): 304–320.

Johnston, Philip. *Shades of Sheol: Death and Afterlife in the Old Testament.* Leicester: Apollos, 2002.

———. "The Psalms and Distress." Pages 63–84 in *Interpreting the Psalms: Issues and Approaches.* Edited by David G. Firth and Philip S. Johnston. Downers Grove, IL: InterVarsity Press, 2006.

Jung, C. G. *Answers to Job.* Translated by R. F. C. Hull. Cleveland, OH: Meridian Books, 1960.

Kaiser, Barbara Bakke. *Reading Prophetic Poetry: Parallelism, Voice, and Design.* Eugene, OR: Pickwick, 2019.

Katz, Robert L. "A Psychoanalytic Comment on Job 3:25." *HUCA* 29 (1958): 377–382.

Kettler, Christian D. *The God Who Rejoices: Joy, Despair, and the Vicarious Humanity of Christ.* Eugene, OR: Cascade, 2010.

Kierkegaard, Søren. *Spiritual Writings: Gift, Creation, Love. Selections from the Upbuilding Discourses.* Translated by George Pattison. New York: Harper Perennial, 2010.

Kille, D. Andrew. "Psychology and the Bible: Three Worlds of the Text," *Pastoral Psychol* 51 (2002): 125–134.

Kline, Peter. "Imaging Nothing: Kierkegaard and the *Imago Dei.*" *ATR* 100 (2018): 697–719.

Knowles, Michael. *Jeremiah in Matthew's Gospel: The Rejected-Prophet Motif in Matthean Redaction.* JSNTSup 68. Sheffield: Sheffield Academic Press, 1993.

Koehler, Ludwig, and Walter Baumgartner. *The Hebrew & Aramaic Lexicon of the Old Testament.* Translated by M. E. J. Richardson. Leiden: Brill, 1994.

Kovalishyn, Mariam Kamell. "Wisdom in the New Testament." Pages 173–186 in *Oxford Handbook of Wisdom and the Bible.* Edited by Will Kynes. Oxford: Oxford University Press, 2021.

Krantz, Eva Stromberg. "'A Man Not Supported by God': On Some Crucial Words in Proverbs XXX 1." *VT* 46 (1996): 548–553.

Kraus, Hans-Joachim. *Psalms 1–59: A Commentary.* CC. Minneapolis: Augsburg Publishing House, 1988.

Kruger, Paul A. "Emotions in the Hebrew Bible: A Few Observations on Prospects and Challenges." *OTE* 28 (2015): 395–420.

Kübler-Ross, Elisabeth. *On Death and Dying.* New York: Macmillan, 1969.

Kugel, James. *The Idea of Biblical Poetry: Parallelism and Its History.* New Haven, CT: Yale University Press, 1981.

Laing, Olivia. *The Lonely City: Adventures in the Art of Being Alone.* Edinburgh: Canongate Books, 2016.

Lasater, Philip Michael. "'The Emotions' in Biblical Anthropology? A Genealogy and Case Study With ירא." *HTR* 110 (2017): 520–540.

Levenson, Jon D. *Creation and the Persistence of Evil: The Jewish Drama of Divine Omnipotence.* Princeton, NJ: Princeton University Press, 1994.

———. *Sinai & Zion: An Entry into the Jewish Bible.* New Voices in Biblical Studies. New York: HarperSanFransisco, 1985.

Levinson, Hanne Løland. *The Death Wish in the Hebrew Bible.* SOTSMS. Cambridge: Cambridge University Press, 2021.

Lewis, C. S. *A Grief Observed.* London: Faber and Faber, 1961.

Lewis, Marshall H. *Viktor Frankl and the Book of Job: A Search for Meaning.* Eugene, OR: Pickwick, 2019.

Linafelt, Tod. "Why Is There Poetry in the Book of Job?" *JBL* 140 (2021): 683–701.

Lindström, Fredrik. *Suffering and Sin: Interpretations of Illness in the Individual Complaint Psalms.* Stockholm: Almqvist & Wiksell, 1994.

"Loneliness—What Characteristics and Circumstances Are Associated with Feeling Lonely?" https://www.ons.gov.uk/peoplepopulationandcommunity/wellbeing/articles/lonelinesswhatcharacteristicsandcircumstancesareassociatedwithfeelinglonely/2018-04-10#which-factors-independently-affect-loneliness.

Longman III, Tremper. *Fictional Akkadian Autobiography: A Generic and Comparative Study*. Winona Lake, IN: Eisenbrauns, 1991.

Lufkin, Bryan. "The Rise of Japan's 'Super Solo' Culture." https://www.bbc.com/worklife/article/20200113-the-rise-of-japans-super-solo-culture.

Lynch, William F. *Images of Hope: Imagination as Healer of the Hopeless*. Montreal: Palm Publishers, 1965.

Marks, Isaac M. *Living with Fear: Understanding and Coping with Anxiety*. 2nd ed. Maidenhead: McGraw-Hill, 2005.

Mathewson, Dan. *Death and Survival in the Book of Job: Desymbolization and Traumatic Experience*. LHBOTS 450. New York: T&T Clark, 2006.

May, Katherine. *Wintering: The Power of Rest and Retreat in Difficult Times*. London: Rider, 2020.

Mays, James L. *The Lord Reigns: A Theological Handbook to the Psalms*. Louisville, KY: Westminster John Knox Press, 1994.

McConville, J. Gordon. *Being Human in God's World. An Old Testament Theology of Humanity*. Grand Rapids, MI: Baker Academic, 2016.

McCraw, John G. "God and the Problem of Loneliness." *RelStud* 28 (1992): 319–346.

McKane, William. *Proverbs: A New Approach*. OTL. Philadelphia, PA: Westminster Press, 1970.

McMahon, Darrin M. *Happiness: A History*. New York: Grove Press, 2006.

Middleton, J. Richard. *Abraham's Silence: The Binding of Isaac, the Suffering of Job, and How to Talk Back to God*. Grand Rapids, MI: Baker Academics, 2021.

Milgrom, Jacob. *Leviticus 1–16*. AB 3. New York: Doubleday, 1991.

Miller, Charles W. "Reading Voices: Personification, Dialogism, and the Reader of Lamentations 1." *BibInt* 9 (2004): 393–408.

Miller II, Robert D. "Dragon Myths and Biblical Theology." *TS* 80 (2019): 37–56.

———. "The Zion Hymns as Instruments of Power." *ANES* 47 (2010): 218–240.

Miller, Patrick D. "The Theological Significance of Biblical Poetry." Pages 213–230 in *Language, Theology, and the Bible: Essays in Honour of James Barr*. Edited by Samuel E. Balentine and John Barton. Oxford: Clarendon, 1994.

Mioni, Giovanna, et al. "Time Perception in Anxious and Depressed Patients: A Comparison Between Time Reproduction and Time Production Tasks." *J. Affect. Disord.* 196 (2016): 154–163.

Mirguet, Françoise. "What Is an 'Emotion' in the Hebrew Bible? An Experience That Exceeds Most Contemporary Concepts." *BibInt* 24 (2016): 442–465.

Moberly, R. W. L. *The Bible in a Disenchanted Age: The Enduring Possibility of Christian Faith.* Grand Rapids, MI: Baker Academic, 2018.

Moore, Rick D. "A Home for the Alien: Worldly Wisdom and Covenantal Confession in Proverbs 30:1–9." *ZAW* 106 (1994): 96–107.

———. "The Integrity of Job." *CBQ* 45 (1983): 17–31.

Morales, L. Michael. *Who Shall Ascend the Mountain of the Lord? A Biblical Theology of the Book of Leviticus.* NSBT 37. Downers Grove, IL: InterVarsity Press, 2015.

Morrow, William. "Consolation, Rejection, and Repentance in Job 42:6." *JBL* 105 (1986): 211–225.

Moschella, Mary Clark. "Positive Psychology as a Resource for Pastoral Theology and Care: A Preliminary Assessment." *J Pastor Theol* 21 (2011): 1–16.

Moughtin-Mumby, Sharon. *Sexual and Marital Metaphors in Hosea, Jeremiah, Isaiah, and Ezekiel.* OTM. Oxford: Oxford University Press, 2008.

Murphy, Roland E. *The Tree of Life: An Exploration of Biblical Wisdom Literature.* 2nd ed. New York: Doubleday, 1996.

Nelson, Alissa Jones. "Psychology, Physiology, Society, and Spirituality: Interpreting Job with Insight from Psychological and HIV-Positive Perspectives." Pages 166–201 in *Power and Responsibility in Biblical Interpretation: Reading the Book of Job with Edward Said.* Sheffield: Equinox, 2012.

Newsom, Carol A. "Positive Psychology and Ancient Israelite Wisdom." Pages in 117–135 in *The Bible and the Pursuit of Happiness: What the Old and New Testaments Teach Us about the Good Life.* Edited by Brent A. Strawn. Oxford: Oxford University Press, 2012.

Nielsen, Kirsten. "Post-Traumatic Stress Disorder and the Book of Job." Pages 62–70 in *Trauma and Traumatization in Individual and Collective Dimensions: Insights from Biblical Studies and Beyond.* Edited by Eve-Marie Becker, Jan Dochhorn, and Else K. Holt. SANT 2. Göttingen: Vandenhoeck & Ruprecht, 2014.

Noth, Martin. *Leviticus.* Translated by J. E. Anderson. Revised. OTL. Philadelphia, PA: Westminster Press, 1977.

Nouwen, Henri J. M. *The Wounded Healer*. London: Darton, Longman and Todd, 1979.

O'Connor, Kathleen M. *Lamentations and the Tears of the World*. Maryknoll, NY: Orbis Books, 2002.

———. *Jeremiah: Pain and Promise*. Minneapolis, MN: Fortress Press, 2011.

Oeming, Manfred, and Konrad Schmid. *Job's Journey: Stations of Suffering*. CrStHB 7. Winona Lake, IN: Eisenbrauns, 2015.

O'Keefe, Theresa. "Growing Up Alone: The New Normal of Isolation in Adolescence." *JYM* 13 (2014): 63–84.

Ortlund, Eric N. "Exegetical Difficulty and the Question of Theodicy in the Book of Job." *JESOT* 7 (2021): 90–112.

———. *Piercing Leviathan: God's Defeat of Evil in the Book of Job*. NSBT 56. Downers Grove, IL: IVP Academic, 2021.

Pascal, Blaise. *Pensées*. Revised. Translated by A. J. Krailsheimer. London: Penguin Books, 1995.

Popcak, Gregory. "Anxious Hearts: A Faithful Look at a Frightening Emotion." *America* (Jan. 2017): 19–23.

Pasternak, Ariel-Ram, and Shamir Yona. "Numerical Sayings in the Literatures of the Ancient Near East, in the Bible, in the Book of Ben-Sira and in Rabbinic Literature." *RRJ* 19 (2016): 202–244.

Perdue, Leo G. *Proverbs*. IBC. Louisville, KY: John Knox Press, 2000.

Peters, Kurtis. "Jonah 1 and the Battle with the Sea: Myth and Irony." *SJOT* 32 (2018): 157–165.

Peterson, Christopher. *A Primer in Positive Psychology*. Oxford: Oxford University Press, 2006.

Rachmann, Stanley. *Anxiety*. 4th ed. London: Psychology Press, 2019.

Reimer, David J. "Good Grief? A Psychological Reading of Lamentations." *ZAW* 114 (2002): 542–559.

———. "The 'Foe' and the 'North' in Jeremiah." *ZAW* 101 (1989): 223–232.

Reinhartz, Adele. "The Destruction of the Jerusalem Temple as a Trauma for Nascent Christianity." Pages 275–288 in *Trauma and Traumatization in Individual and Collective Dimensions: Insights from Biblical Studies and Beyond*. Edited by Eve-Marie Becker, Jan Dochhorn, and Else K. Holt. SANT 2. Göttingen: Vandenhoeck & Ruprecht, 2014.

Reno, R. R. *Genesis*. BTCB. Grand Rapids, MI: Baker Academic, 2017.

Richter, Hans-Friedemann. "Hielt Agur sich für den Dümmsten aller Menschen?" *ZAW* 113 (2001): 419–421.

Riesman, David, with Nathan Glazer and Reuel Denney. *The Lonely Crowd: A Study of the Changing American Character*. Abridged and revised. New Haven, CT: Yale University Press, 2020.

Roberts, J. J. M. "The Motif of the Weeping God in Jeremiah and Its Background in the Lament Tradition of the Ancient Near East." *OTE* 5 (1992): 361–374.

Robinson, Marilynne. *When I Was a Child I Read Books*. London: Virago, 2012.

Rokach, Ami. "Loneliness and Life: From Beginning to End." Pages 69–89 in *Psychology of Loneliness*. Edited by Sarah J. Bevinn. New York: Nove Science, 2011.

Roth, W. M. W. *Numerical Sayings in the Old Testament: A Form-Critical Study*. VTSup 13. Leiden: Brill, 1965.

Samet, Nili. "How Deterministic is Qohelet? A New Reading of the Appendix the Catalogue of Times." *ZAW* 131 (2019): 577–591.

———. "Qohelet 1,4 and the Structure of the Book's Prologue." *ZAW* 126 (2014): 92–100.

Sargiannidis, Ioannis et al. "Anxiety Makes Time Pass Quicker while Fear Has No Effect." *Cognition & Emotion* 197 (2020): 1–12.

Saur, Markus. "Prophetie, Weisheit Und Gebet. Überlegungen Zu Den Worten Agurs in Prov 30, 1–9." *ZAW* 126 (2014): 570–583.

Savarikannu, Balu. "A Polyphonic Reading of Lamentations 3." *JAET* 20 (2016): 25–43.

Scalise, Pamela J. "Baruch as First Reader: Baruch's Lament in the Structure of the Book of Jeremiah." Pages 291–307 in *Uprooting and Planting: Essays on Jeremiah for Leslie Allen*. Edited by John Goldingay. LHBOTS 459. New York: T&T Clark, 2007.

Schaefer, Arthur Gross, and Steve Jacobsen. "Surviving Clergy Burnout." *Encounter* 70 (2009): 36–66.

Schart, Aaron. "Deathly Silence and Apocalyptic Noise: Observations on the Soundscape of the Book of the Twelve." *Verbum et Ecclesia* 31, Art. #383 (2010): 1–5.

Scott, Greg, and Rachel Lovell. "The Rural Pastor Initiative: Addressing Isolation and Burnout in Rural Ministry." *Pastoral Psychol* 64 (2015): 71–97.

Seligman, Martin, and Chrisopher Peterson. *Character Strengths and Virtues: A Handbook and Classification*. Oxford: Oxford University Press, 2004.

Seligman, Martin. *Authentic Happiness: Using the New Positive Psychology to Realize Your Potential for Lasting Fulfillment*. New York: The Free Press, 2002.

Seow, C. L. "Qohelet's Eschatological Poem." *JBL* 118 (1999): 209–234.

Seybold, Klaus. "Zu den Zeitvorstellungen in Psalm 90." *TZ* 53 (1997): 97–108.

Shanahan, Lilly. "Does Despair Really Kill? A Roadmap for an Evidence-Based Answer." *AJPH* 109 (2019): 854–858.

Sharot, Tali. *The Optimism Bias: Why We're Wired to Look at the Bright Side*. London: Constable & Robinson, 2012.

Shemesh, Yael. "Suicide in the Bible." *JBQ* 37 (2009): 157–168.

Simundson, Daniel J. "Mental Health in the Bible." *Word & World* 9 (1989): 140–146.

Smith, James K. A. *How to Inhabit Time: Understanding the Past, Facing the Future, Living Faithfully Now*. Grand Rapids, MI: Brazos Press, 2022.

Smith Jr., Archie. "Rock: An Unlikely Metaphor for Spirituality, Family Therapy, Mental Health and Illness." *Pastoral Psychol* 66 (2017): 743–756.

Smith, Mark S. *The Priestly Vision of Genesis 1*. Minneapolis, MN: Fortress Press, 2010.

Specter, Francesca. *Alonement: How to Be Alone and Absolutely Own It*. London: Quercus, 2021.

Spencer, F. Scott, ed. *Mixed Feelings and Vexed Passions: Exploring Emotions in Biblical Literature*. RBS 90. Atlanta, GA: SBL Press, 2017.

Spittler, Rudolf P. "Testament of Job." *Old Testament Pseudepigrapha*. Vol. 1. Edited by J. H. Charlesworth. Garden City, NY: Doubleday, 1983.

Steck, Odil H. "Zu Eigenart und Herkunft von Ps 102." *ZAW* 102 (1990): 357–372.

Steimer, Thierry. "The Biology of Fear- and Anxiety-Related Behaviors." *D Clin Neurosc* 4 (2002): 231–249.

Steinbock, Anthony J. "The Phenomenology of Despair." *Int J Philos Stud* 15 (2007): 435–451.

Steinmann, Andrew E. "Three Things. Four Things. Seven Things: The Coherence of Proverbs 30:11–33 and the Unity of Proverbs 30." *HS* 42 (2001): 59–66.

Sterba, Editha, and Sterba, Richard. *Beethoven and His Nephew: A Psychoanalytic Study of Their Relationship*. Translated by William R. Trask. London: Dobson Books, 1957.

Sternberg, Meir. *The Poetics of Biblical Narrative: Ideological Literature and the Drama of Reading.* Bloomington, IN: Indiana University Press, 1987.

Stewart, Anne W. "The Poetry of Wisdom and Imagination: Intellectual Contributions of *Wisdom in Israel.*" Pages 185–210 in *Gerhard von Rad and the Study of Wisdom Literature.* Edited by Timothy J. Sandoval and Bernd U. Schipper. AIL 4. Atlanta, GA: SBL Press, 2022.

Stossel, Scott. *My Age of Anxiety: Fear, Hope, Dread and the Search for Peace of Mind.* London: Windmill Books, 2014.

Strawn, Brent D. ed., *The Bible and the Pursuit of Happiness: What the Old and New Testaments Teach Us about the Good Life.* Oxford: Oxford University Press, 2006.

———. *The Old Testament Is Dying: A Diagnosis and Recommended Treatment.* Theological Explorations of the Church Catholic. Grand Rapids, MI: BakerAcademic, 2017.

Srokosz, Meric, and Rebecca S. Watson. *Blue Planet, Blue God: The Bible and the Sea.* London: SCM Press, 2017.

Stulman, Louis. "Reading the Bible as Trauma Literature: The Legacy of the Losers." *CBW* 34 (2014): 1–13.

Swenson, Kristin M. *Living through Pain: Psalms and the Search for Wholeness.* Waco, TX: Baylor University Press, 2005.

Swinton, John. *Finding Jesus in the Storm: The Spiritual Lives of Christians with Mental Health Challenges.* Grand Rapids, MI: Eerdmans, 2020.

Thomas, Philip S. *In a Vision of the Night: Job, Cormac McCarthy, and the Challenge of Chaos.* Waco, TX: Baylor University Press, 2021.

Tilford, Nicole L. *Sensing World, Sensing Wisdom: The Cognitive Foundation of Biblical Metaphors.* AIL 31. Atlanta, GA: SBL Press, 2017.

Tillich, Paul. *The Courage to Be.* The Fontana Library: Theology and Philosophy. Glasgow: Fountain Books, 1977.

Tworuschka, Udo. "Einsamkeit—Ein Religionswissenschaftlich Vernachlässigtes Phänomen." *ZMR* 59 (1975): 30–43.

Ulrich, Eugene. "From Literature to Scripture: Reflections on the Growth of a Text's Authoritativeness." *DSD* 10 (2003): 3–25.

van Bruggen V. et al. "Structural Validity of the World Assumption Scale." *J Trauma Stress* 31 (2018): 816–825.

Vanhoozer, Kevin, and Martin Warner, eds. *Transcending Boundaries in Philosophy and Theology: Reason, Meaning, and Experience.* Hampshire: Ashgate, 2007.

van Leeuwen, Raymond C. "Proverbs 30:21–23 and the Biblical World Upside Down." *JBL* 105 (1986): 599–610.

Vogels, Walter. "The Spiritual Growth of Job: A Psychological Approach to the Book of Job." *BTB* 11 (1987): 77–80.

Volf, Miroslav. *Exclusion and Embrace: A Theological Exploration of Identity, Otherness, and Reconciliation.* Nashville, TN: Abingdon, 1996.

von Rad, Gerhard. *Wisdom in Israel.* Translated by James D. Martin. London: SCM Press, 1972.

Waltke, Bruce K. *The Book of Proverbs. Chapters 1–15.* NICOT. Grand Rapids, MI: Eerdmans, 2004.

Watson, W. G. E. *Classical Hebrew Poetry: A Guide to Its Techniques.* Sheffield: Sheffield Academic Press, 2001.

Weber, Beat. "Toward a Theory of the Poetry of the Hebrew Bible: The Poetry of the Psalms as a Test Case." *BBR* 22 (2012): 157–188.

Weems, Renita J. "Gomer: Victim of Violence or Victim of Metaphor?" *Semeia* 47 (1989): 87–104.

Welch, Edward T. "Bible Basics for the Fearful and Anxious." *JBC* 34 (2020): 69–79.

Wenham, Gordon J. *Genesis 1–15.* WBC 1. Nashville, TN: Thomas Nelson, 1987.

———. *The Book of Leviticus.* NICOT 3. Grand Rapids, MI: Eerdmans, 1979.

Westermeyer, Paul. "'A Mighty Fortress' and Psalm 46 in Context." *Word & World* 34 (2014): 398–407.

West, Gerald. "The Poetry of Job as a Resource for the Articulation of Embodied Lament in the Context of HIV and AIDS in South Africa." Pages 195–214 in *Lamentations in Ancient and Contemporary Contexts.* Edited by N. C. Lee and C. Mandolfo. Atlanta, GA: SBL, 2008.

White, B. G. "Fighting Anxiety with the Old Testament." *CT* (2020): 57–60.

Whitehouse, Dick, and Gwynn Devey. *Understanding Anxiety: Identifying the Causes and Discovering Freedom from Anxiety.* Aylesbury: Alpha, 1996.

Witherington, Ben. *Jesus the Sage: The Pilgrimage of Wisdom.* Minneapolis, MN: Augsburg Fortress, 1994.

White, Shawn P. "'Why Were the Former Days Better Than These?' An Examination of Temporal Horizons in Ecclesiastes." PhD diss., University of Edinburgh, 2013.

Whitters, Mark F. "Jesus in the Footsteps of Jeremiah." *CBQ* 68 (2006): 229–247.

Whybray, R. N. *Wealth and Poverty in the Book of Proverbs*. JSOTSup 99. Sheffield: JSOT Press, 1990.

Wiersbe, Warren W. *Be Patient: Waiting on God in Difficult Times*. Colorado Springs, CO: David C. Cook, 1991.

Williams, J. G. "The Power of Form: A Study of Biblical Proverbs." *Semeia* 17 (1980): 35–58.

Winterton, Adriano et al. "Associations of Loneliness and Social Isolation with Cardiovascular and Metabolic Health: A Systematic Review and Meta-Analysis Protocol." *SysRev* 9 (2020): 1–7.

Wolff, Hans Walter. *Anthropology of the Old Testament*. Translated by Margaret Kohl. London: SCM Press, 1974.

Wyatt, Nick. *Myths of Power: A Study of Royal Myth and Ideology in Ugaritic and Biblical Tradition*. UBL. Münster: Ugarit-Verlag, 1996.

———. "The Mythic Mind." Pages 151–188 in *The Mythic Mind: Essays on Cosmology and Religion in Ugaritic and Old Testament Literature*. Bibleworld; London: Equinox, 2005.

———. "The Mythic Mind Revisited: Myth and History, or Myth versus History, a Continuing Problem in Biblical Studies." *SJOT* 22 (2008): 161–175.

Yoder, Christine Roy. "On the Threshold of Kingship: A Study of Agur (Proverbs 30)." *Int* 63 (2009): 254–263.

"YouVersion 2021 Downloadable Stats." https://docs.google.com/spreadsheets/d/1G0NLDOyN5PHNCmKhlPzjBc_BvGha5qd1v0AS16yfMjM/edit#gid=0.

Zuckermann, Bruce. *Job the Silent: A Study in Historical Counterpoint*. Oxford: Oxford University Press, 1991.

Author Index

Scripture Index